S0-BBO-325

Trends in Collective Bargaining

A SUMMARY OF RECENT EXPERIENCE

331.116
w-67

31429

HD
6483
T9.4

A TWENTIETH CENTURY FUND REPORT

THE TRUSTEES of the Fund choose subjects for Fund investigations, underwrite the expenses of each project and appoint special committees which formulate programs for action based on the findings. The Trustees, however, assume no responsibility for the findings or the recommendations for action that result.

TRUSTEES

A. A. BERLE, JR.	MORRIS E. LEEDS
FRANCIS BIDDLE	ROBERT S. LYND
BRUCE BLIVEN	JAMES G. MCDONALD
PERCY S. BROWN	WILLIAM I. MYERS
HENRY S. DENNISON	CHARLES P. TAFT
JOHN H. FAHEY	HARRISON TWEED
OSWALD W. KNAUTH	W. W. WAYMACK

OFFICERS

JOHN H. FAHEY, *President*

HENRY S. DENNISON, *Chairman, Executive Committee*

MORRIS E. LEEDS, *Treasurer*

EVANS CLARK, *Executive Director*

J. FREDERIC DEWHURST, *Economist*

LABOR COMMITTEE OF
THE TWENTIETH CENTURY FUND

THE COMMITTEE, whose members are listed below, formulated the program for action, to meet the problems of collective bargaining, which is contained in Chapter 15. The Committee is wholly responsible for that chapter. The authors, Messrs. Williamson and Harris, are responsible for Chapters 1 to 14 inclusive.

WILLIAM H. DAVIS, *Chairman*
Director, United States Office of Economic Stabilization;
formerly Chairman, National War Labor Board

WILLIAM L. CHENERY
Publisher, *Collier's Weekly*

HOWARD COONLEY
Chairman of the Board, Walworth Company, Inc.;
formerly President, National Association of Manufacturers

CLINTON S. GOLDEN
Assistant to the President, United Steelworkers of America,
affiliated with the Congress of Industrial Organizations

FRAZIER MACIVER
Vice President, Phoenix Hosiery Company

SUMNER H. SLICHTER
Lamont University Professor, Harvard University

ROBERT J. WATT
International Representative, American Federation of Labor

EDWIN E. WITTE
Professor of Economics, University of Wisconsin

Trends in Collective Bargaining

A SUMMARY OF RECENT EXPERIENCE

By

S. T. WILLIAMSON

HERBERT HARRIS

Report and Recommendations by the

LABOR COMMITTEE

New York

THE TWENTIETH CENTURY FUND

1945

COPYRIGHT 1945 BY THE TWENTIETH CENTURY FUND, INC.

MANUFACTURED IN THE UNITED STATES OF AMERICA
BY THE ACADEMY PRESS, NEW YORK

181

33<del>1.116</del>   HD
<del>W67</del>   6483
31429   T9.4

FOREWORD

WAR'S END is a natural time to take account of stock in every department of our economic life: to review the past, to analyze the present, to project the future. This book is an attempt to make an accounting of this kind in the field of labor-management relations.

World War II had a tremendous impact on the processes of collective bargaining. A growth that would have taken many years in peacetime was induced, by the artificial climate of war, in less than four. Much of this forced growth will probably survive in the more natural atmosphere of peace.

But, to realize the significance of what happened during the war and to lay down constructive policies for the peace, the essential elements of collective bargaining, and their prewar developments, should be kept very much in mind. It is our hope that this book will help to create this sort of understanding for the public and will stimulate wise action by management and labor to improve collective bargaining practices in the years to come.

This volume is focused on what might be called the *internal* processes, problems and issues of collective bargaining. Outside of its focus are many other subjects external to collective bargaining but closely related to it—such as the relation of government to labor. A previous Fund survey dealt with that particular field. The volume, *Labor and the Government,* published in 1935, contains the findings.

This present book is the outgrowth of a survey of collective bargaining in the United States which the Fund began, under the directorship of Dr. H. A. Millis, back in 1939. The authors have drawn largely for their source material from the first report of this survey, *How Collective Bargaining Works*—a series of intensive case studies of collective bargaining growth and practices in sixteen leading United States industries with brief accounts covering thirteen more. The entire project has been carried on with the advice and counsel of the Fund's Labor Committee, under the Chairmanship of William H. Davis, one of the best informed and most distinguished authorities on labor relations in the United States. Other members of the Committee have ably represented the viewpoints of labor, business and the public.

The Committee's program for action report (Chapter 15) was unanimous—with reservations only on particular points. That all the members of so diverse a group should have agreed on a broad plan of action in so controversial a field is remarkable—a heartening demonstration of the value of the democratic process.

Mr. Golden has joined the Committee in its unanimous endorsement of the report so far as its conclusions were, in his opinion, based on factual investigations into the relations between unions and management. But he has objected to the proposals about the internal affairs of labor unions on the ground that the staff of the original survey had not made any substantial study of these problems. While he has signed the report as a whole, his specific objections on these points are set forth as footnotes to the text. Other Committee members also have recorded their reservations or disagreements on minor points in similar footnotes.

To the members of the Committee who gave unsparingly of their time in attending meetings and reviewing manuscripts goes the deep appreciation of the Fund. They have performed a genuine public service. The Fund is also indebted to the authors of the main body of the volume for their able and lucid analysis of matters often far from simple. Mr. Williamson is responsible for Chapters 1 to 11 inclusive; Mr. Harris, for Chapters 12 to 14 inclusive. Mr. Harris also assisted the Committee in drafting its report and recommendations for action contained in Chapter 15.

EVANS CLARK, *Executive Director*
The Twentieth Century Fund

330 WEST 42D STREET
NEW YORK 18, NEW YORK
AUGUST 30, 1945

CONTENTS

Chapter   *Page*

1. WHAT IS COLLECTIVE BARGAINING?   1
2. BARGAINING AGENCIES FOR THE WORKERS   10
3. EMPLOYER BARGAINING AGENCIES   22
4. UNION RECOGNITION   34
5. COLLECTIVE AGREEMENTS   49
6. WAGES   61
7. HOURS OF WORK   79
8. JOB SECURITY   92
9. WORK RULES AND TECHNOLOGICAL CHANGE   104
10. THE ADMINISTRATION OF AGREEMENTS   116
11. UNION-MANAGEMENT COOPERATION   130
12. GOVERNMENT COLLECTIVE BARGAINING   142
13. IMPACT OF WAR   162
14. THE HUMAN SIDE   188
15. REPORT AND RECOMMENDATIONS OF THE LABOR COMMITTEE   215
    The Role of Collective Bargaining   215
    The Economics of Collective Bargaining   225
    The Politics of Collective Bargaining   236

INDEX   251

Contents

1. ...
2. ...
3. ...

Chapter 1

WHAT IS COLLECTIVE BARGAINING?

A BARGAIN IS AN AGREEMENT, and it takes at least two to make a bargain. A collective bargain is an agreement made by or in behalf of a group, and collective bargaining is therefore the method by which a group agreement is reached. Under such an all-inclusive definition, diplomats negotiating treaties, or trustees of a church discussing a mortgage with directors of a savings bank might be said to be bargaining collectively. But, as words have come to be used, the term "collective bargaining" now applies almost exclusively to relations between working people and those who employ them. Workingmen bargain collectively when they or their representatives negotiate and adjust conditions of their employment with one or more employers.

Working people are protected under federal law in the right to organize for collective bargaining; and employers are required to bargain collectively with representatives chosen by a majority of their employees. Even so, there is no hard-and-fast definition of collective bargaining. One may search court decisions, reports of government commissions, the writings of social scientists and still not find a definition which has the finality and precision of a mathematical formula. But as the term is employed in everyday usage, as well as in the interpretation of law, collective bargaining requires labor unions.

Although it is not a commodity like a pound of butter or a ton of coal, labor is bought and sold like a commodity. A price is offered for it, another may be asked for it, and somewhere between the two figures a price may be set upon it. Acting alone, one person sells his labor to an employer who buys the work of many hands. If he won't accept the employer's terms, another workman may do so; he has little influence upon the terms of his employment because he is bargaining individually. But many workingmen acting together in a trade union attain bargaining power. If they refuse an employer's terms, it may be difficult to replace them; and if the union includes all who work at the same occupation, it is impossible for an employer to hire others.

At its beginning, collective bargaining is therefore a process of give and take—or else. The union has something to offer which the employer needs—labor. The employer has something which workingmen need—jobs. If union men do not get what they want, they may quit work—or not work quite so well. The employer may decide that union demands involve too great a sacrifice, because they may place him in an inferior competitive position and might force him out of business. Under such circumstances, collective bargaining is a substitute for industrial conflict. Although it is an alternative for force, it is also recognition that force is frequently too high a price to pay. For force can be too great a gamble to undertake; always there is a risk of losing—and even victory may bring mortal wounds.

But force is not the only underlying element in collective bargaining. One side needs the other. A depressed working class means less demand for products and services which the employer has made it his business to provide. A depressed industry means fewer jobs. The well-being of both employer and workingmen depends upon the other's well-being.

Wherefore, if collective bargaining is regarded merely as a substitute for force, whatever agreement an employer and a workingmen's union negotiate is simply a truce. But when it is an around-the-table process which reconciles the conflicting interests of two sides which cannot get along without each other, the resulting agreement is a treaty and even an alliance.

Many persons, including employers, fail to realize that the conclusion of an agreement about wages and working conditions is merely the beginning. For the practice of collective bargaining goes far beyond the initial stages of haggle, give and take. It covers not only small groups but the big plants, huge areas and even whole industries. It has become a way through which management and organized labor learn to live together. It applies principles of representative democracy to industry, and it has worked out a sort of industrial common law for the conduct of union-management relations. It is thus a continuous, adaptable, evolving, many-sided, process in which a negotiated agreement is only the introduction; and its success or failure largely depends upon the spirit and attitude of those who practice it or are covered by it.

Workers' Aims

Whether they bargain collectively or individually, working people have the same fundamental objectives. Two questions uppermost in the mind of a job hunter approaching a prospective employer are: "How much is the pay? What are the working hours?" Those questions are also basic when unions bargain with employers. The individual job hunter also might like to know, although he rarely asks, answers to these questions: "How hard shall I be worked and under what conditions? How secure is the job? What are the chances of advancement? Is length of service a feature in my continued employment? What protection have I against unjust discharge? What attention will be paid to complaints I might have of unfair treatment? Or of other injustices connected with my employment?"

The individual job hunter has little chance to make answers to these questions part of the conditions of his going to work. But, when associated with others and represented by spokesmen —that is, through collective bargaining—such questions do figure in his employment. They may not be phrased as simply, but they are behind such words as trade agreements, wage scales, piece-work rates, craft differentials, overtime, seniority, grievances, union recognition, closed shop, bargaining units, shop stewards, impartial chairmen, arbitrators and other terms, far more technical, for the various parts of collective bargaining machinery.

With the failures of this machinery the average citizen is more familiar than with its day-in and day-out operation. He knows more about the breakdowns of collective bargaining machinery than he does of the machinery itself. He reads or hears more about its disorders than its orderly working. He might see wrecked automobiles or stalled cars along the highways without concluding that automobiles are useless. And whatever his opinion of hit-and-run drivers he does not conclude that all motorists are irresponsible. But when strikes occur, or are threatened, or when management and labor spokesmen cannot agree, the unusual may seem to be general. The chances are that there was more public knowledge about the 2,500 strikes during 1940 than about the 50,000 and more collective bargaining agreements in force during the same year—or how they developed.

Beginnings of Collective Bargaining

Before 1820, when the first mechanical production of goods worthy of note appeared, strikes and lockouts were the only methods of settling disputes between employers and those who worked for them. Printers, carpenters and others who labored at trades or crafts occasionally laid down their tools and struck for higher wages or shorter working days. Except for such sporadic and rarely united actions, they knew no other means of seeking their ends.

By the middle 1820's there were a few local unions. Some were of men who worked with tools and others included the ever increasing number of workers at machines. These unions were organized by trade, and each was independent of the other. Within a decade many large city employers had dealings with these locals. Employers agreed to pay certain wages, in return for which the unions agreed not to strike; and this was the beginning of collective bargaining in the United States.

Such bargaining was desultory, however, partially because labor unions were occupied with many matters besides better wages and hours. They entered politics to stop imprisonment for debt and to end other laws which burdened the lowly and unfortunate. Politically the unionists were whipped, but many of the laws they fought were erased or modified; which enabled unions to concentrate more upon wringing concessions from employers and upon extending their organizations. Having negotiated favorable local and regional agreements, a few trades formed national unions which sought to include all workers in their field in the country and thus protect local standards from outside competition. But collective bargaining remained only one activity of these unions, which were still many purposed with interests in cooperative movements, fraternal affairs and land and currency panaceas. And thus matters stood at the beginning of the Civil War and the end of the first half-century of American industrialism.

Between the Civil and Spanish-American wars, American industrialism became of age. Meanwhile, labor unionism passed from childhood to adolescence. Some trades and crafts were quite thoroughly organized and exerted considerable power in collective bargaining. But the labor movement as a whole was attempting the impossible feat of riding two tracks in opposite directions at the same time. One track was toward more benefits under the current economic system for one's own trade. The other headed toward "one big union," "labor solidarity," and inclusion of unskilled labor, farmers, foremen, and even small businessmen who favored changes in the economic system. The latter was the Knights of Labor which inspired little solidarity but much turbulence both within and without its ranks.

By the 1890's the Knights of Labor had little power left, and the labor movement was headed by the newly organized American Federation of Labor, which, as its name indicates, was the opposite of the "one big union" idea. The AF of L stressed the autonomy of national organized trade and labor unions. It sought the extension of unionism, collective bargaining, and social legislation. It abandoned all other goals but these and concentrated upon "business" unionism.

Thus, the nineteenth century saw three stages of the labor movement: first stage, weak and confused; second stage, militant and visionary; third stage, concentration upon collective bargaining.

Collective Bargaining Established

The twentieth century ushered in a new phase of the industrial age: mass production, which requires a standardized product, much automatic machinery, and great division of labor into separate, simplified tasks. Its gigantic new industries, comprising many crafts, were difficult for unions to organize without jurisdictional disputes with other trades; and even had employers been favorably disposed toward dealing with unions (which they weren't) an agreement with one union threatened trouble with another. The rise of mass production, therefore, impeded spread of union-employer relations.

World War I, however, marked a turning point in collective bargaining. Before this country entered the war, government had taken no part in union organization and negotiation of trade agreements except to mediate in disputes. But with a war's outcome depending heavily upon uninterrupted production, the federal government established a War Labor Board to intervene in disputes which might lead to strikes and other work stoppages; and, to ease the strain upon its mediation machinery, the Board laid down a labor policy which "recognized and affirmed" trade unions and collective bargaining.[1] Employers were warned against preventing their employees from joining unions, or discriminating against union members. Employees were warned against coercing fellow workers into joining unions, or coercing employers into dealing with unions. This was a balanced policy which recognized no privilege to one side which it would not grant to the other.

Although this was not law but a set of principles, it constituted the first governmental blanket endorsement of collective bargaining. Union membership nearly doubled: from 3 to 5 million. Company unions, also upheld under these principles, rose to 40 per cent of trade-union membership.

After the war, unionism tried to preserve its gains, hostile employers sought to return to former nonunion conditions. Although organized labor regards the 1920's as a period of setbacks, nevertheless, the decade yielded governmental support of collective bargaining far beyond official endorsements of World War I days. In 1926 came the Railway Labor Act, the first federal law to recognize the right of labor to organize without interference, although applied to only one industry. Six years later came the

1. U. S. Bureau of Labor Statistics, "National War Labor Board," *Bulletin No. 287*, 1922, p. 32.

Norris-LaGuardia Anti-Injunction Act which retained some of the even-handedness of World War policy by upholding the right to organize and bargain collectively and also recognizing the right of a worker to "decline to associate with his fellows." The Act recognized the existence of company unions by declaring that no worker should be compelled to join one, or be forbidden to join a trade union. But it had no teeth for enforcement.

Collective Bargaining Guaranteed by Law

Next came the banking crisis of 1933, a new Administration and, temporarily, a spirit of united effort similar to that of the World War. In such an atmosphere the National Industrial Recovery Act was passed. Labor's landmark was the Act's famous Section 7(a) which wrote into law policies laid down in 1917 and applied, to a limited extent, in the Railway Labor and Norris-LaGuardia Acts. Section 7(a) granted the right, free from interference, to organize for collective bargaining. It also outlawed attempts to force job seekers to join company unions or to refrain from joining trade unions.

For a while, results were the same as in 1917. Union membership soared. So did new unions. And so did company unions. Then administration of the codes became inextricably snarled; and, two years later, the Supreme Court of the United States unanimously pronounced NIRA unconstitutional. While NRA slowly expired, its labor features, considerably strengthened and with a whole row of administrative teeth added, were written into the Wagner National Labor Relations Act. Collective bargaining now became compulsory when requested by a labor organization which, free from employer domination, represents a majority of employees. Enforcement of the Act was vested in a National Labor Relations Board with powers to hold plant elections for determination of employees' choice of a labor organization, to compel employers to meet for collective bargaining, and to protect employees against employer discrimination for union activities. This act also meant the end of the company-dominated union.

In 1937, the Supreme Court upheld the basic features of the National Labor Relations Act, and collective bargaining through unionism became the order of the day. By federal statute, by various state laws, and by court decisions, the right to bargain collectively is now more protected in the United States than in any other country in the world.

The Issues

Few issues have so bitterly divided the people of the United States as those arising out of labor relations. Small wars have been fought over them, and the toll of dead and wounded, though uncounted, must lie in the thousands. No one side has had a monopoly of virtue or of violence.

Scarcely any other domestic question arouses such heated partisanship, such firmly held opinion, or such sweeping, dogmatic assertion. One can find partial evidence to support almost any view of collective bargaining, and unbiased examiners have extraordinary difficulty in making broad generalizations upon the subject because virtually every conclusion is in need of qualification. On the other hand, this very necessity for approximation and qualification indicates collective bargaining's vitality and flexibility.

World War I saw a wide spread of union-management relations. Experience in World War II was the same in even greater proportion, though with some limitations. Hours and overtime pay already were adjusted to a great extent in conformance with government directive. Wage rates were limited by Presidential orders rather than by free play of collective bargaining. Government trends may be to further regulation. But signs multiply of increasing cooperation between union and management to quicken production; and this too must have considerable effect upon collective bargaining of the future. What pattern that will be is hazardous prophecy, but it seems reasonable to expect that past experience will determine the basic design.

Consequently, World War II is a good bench mark from which to begin a general survey of collective bargaining. What was its machinery? How did that machinery work? Where and why did it succeed? Where and how did it fail? Why were labor relations smooth in some industries and, under apparently similar conditions, turbulent in others? In what industries are labor relations backward? Where have union-management agreements brought unsettled conditions? In what industries has collective bargaining been practiced with high sense of economic and public responsibility? By what yardsticks shall collective bargaining be measured? And what effects have public opinion and industrial leadership upon union-management relationships?

This examination does not propose to take sides or determine whether collective bargaining is the best means of maintaining industrial relations, or whether some other method is better. Collective bargaining is a fact, but the record is still incomplete. Collective bargaining has followed many roads. Some led up blind alleys. Others led through rough country to fields and industrial peace—though not, as yet, to industrial Utopia. But along the way are signposts.

Chapter 2

BARGAINING AGENCIES FOR THE WORKERS

BEFORE PEARL HARBOR, more than 11 million, or between one third and one quarter of all full-time wage and salary workers of the United States, were covered by collective bargaining agreements with employers.[1] Several factors, however, stand in the way of this being any but a rough yet serviceable estimate.

The chief factor is the absence of completely comparable figures. Reports of union membership, of the number of persons employed in any given industry, and of union and nonunion workers in various manufacturing establishments are not "as of" the same date; they may be as wide apart as a year, or even two or more years. Another factor is the virtual impossibility of a uniform measurement of union membership. Some unions report as members only those who have paid their dues, whereas other union membership figures include not only those who paid dues but employees who join, work with the union, and support its policies without paying dues regularly. A third factor is the great rise in employment and the large, but as yet incompletely recorded, shift in occupations since the United States was brought actively into war production.

Estimates of the coverage of collective bargaining agreements are based upon general union membership. Some establishments are wholly unionized, with union membership a required condition for continued employment. This accounts for about 40 per cent of all workers under labor agreements.[2] Other establishments operate under labor agreements with unions, but not all employees

1. U. S. Bureau of Labor Statistics, *Extent of Collective Bargaining at Beginning of 1942*, Serial No. R. 1457, p. 1; *How Collective Bargaining Works*, The Twentieth Century Fund, New York, 1942, p. 19.
2. U. S. Bureau of Labor Statistics, *op. cit.*, p. 1.

are union members. Still others may be untouched by collective bargaining, although some employees are members of unions. The number of unorganized employees whose wage scales and working conditions are directly determined by union-management negotiations is probably sufficient to rank union bargaining power with union membership.[3] Consequently, the number of working people under collective bargaining agreements may approximate the 12 million union members reported at the end of 1944.[4]

Whether union membership is accepted at one third or one quarter of all American wage earners, neither proportion gives quite the proper perspective of the coverage of collective bargaining. Unions have made little attempt to organize domestic service, white-collar workers, or 3 million agricultural workers. Real effort and considerable progress have been made in organizing the 4 or 5 million federal, state and local government employees, but bargaining in these fields is strictly limited. Less than 10 per cent of the 10.5 million engaged in wholesale and retail trades, personal service, clerical, technical and professional occupations is unionized.[5] Furthermore, only a small number of unions have many Negro members although most are open to Negroes, who comprise one tenth of our population. And while few unions specifically ban women, some are none too friendly to admitting them.

Since whole segments of our working population are virtually unorganized, it follows that collective bargaining must be heavily concentrated in other occupations. It holds a dominant place in manufacturing, coal mining, building and transportation. At the end of 1941, about 55 per cent of all workers in these industries were employed under union conditions, and scarcely any branch of manufacturing industries is entirely without written labor agreements.[6] In recent months collective bargaining has spread. Early in 1941 only two giant industries—railroads and coal mining—were almost completely covered by agreements. They were joined within the year by the automobile industry. At the begin-

3. *How Collective Bargaining Works*, p. 17.
4. Labor Research Association, *Labor Fact Book*, International Publishers, New York, 1945.
5. U. S. Bureau of Labor Statistics, *op. cit.*, p. 1.   6. *Ibid.*

ning of 1941 the rapidly expanding aircraft industry was only partially organized; by the end of the year, union agreements governed working conditions of a majority of employees in this industry. The second World War, like the first one, was ideal "growing weather" for union membership.

Union Structure

The organization which is the bargaining agent for a working-man with his employer may be a craft union, most of whose members belong to the same trade or skilled occupation. Or it may be an industrial union, consisting of members of different occupations who work in the same industry, or in related industries. The union may be affiliated with the older American Federation of Labor, in which various forms of craft unionism have been strong, or with the newer Congress of Industrial Organizations, which tended to industrial unionism.[7] Or it may be an unaffiliated union like one of the railroad brotherhoods, most of which are basically craft unions,[8] or like the United Mine Workers of America, which is an industrial union that was expelled from the AF of L, later seceded from the CIO, and recently applied for reaffiliation with the AF of L.[9] Or it may be an independent union, that is, a group of employees in the same establishment or working for the same company who have their own union. Such an organization may have stemmed from one of the pre-Wagner Act company-dominated unions, or may have grown subsequently, but it no longer can be tied up with management.

In their essential forms, most unions are alike. The basic unit is the local union or lodge. Its jurisdiction may embrace a certain

7. There are few purely craft or purely industrial unions in either organization. What is loosely called a craft union may be actually a federation of crafts. The Newspaper Guild (CIO) is as much a federation of crafts as the AF of L pressmen's union. The United Steelworkers of America, frequently described as an industrial union, cuts across many industries.

8. Sticklers for detail, which if given frequently confuses a picture, will point out that the engineers' brotherhood includes some firemen, the firemen's brotherhood has a few engineers, that the conductors' union has some brakemen, and that some conductors are members of the trainmen's union, which is the largest brotherhood and includes many miscellaneous employees.

9. United Mine Workers, District 50, includes rayon workers, electrical power employees, dairy farmers, button makers organized by the UMW.

city, or may cover one establishment, or even a subdivision of a large plant. Its activities include election of its officers, membership drives, dues collection and handling of individual grievances. Depending upon its size, strength and coverage, it may or may not negotiate labor agreements with employers.

Most locals are part of a national or international union. It may call itself a brotherhood, league, association, an order, or an alliance, but it is still a union. If it has no locals or no membership outside the United States, it is known as a "national union." If it has locals or members in Canada, it is an "international union." The union's title generally indicates its coverage. The International Union of United Automobile, Aircraft and Agricultural Implement Workers of America is an organization with local unions in the United States and Canada of working people who make automobiles, airplanes and farm machinery; whereas the National Maritime Union of America has no locals outside the United States—actually none are away from the East Coast.

Whether affiliated or not, whether craft or industrial, whether semi-industrial like the International Association of Machinists which was long in the AF of L, or whether semi-craft like the CIO Textile Workers Union, a national or international has virtually complete autonomy over its own affairs. It may leave collective bargaining to the local union, or it may engage in it directly. Control of policies is generally invested in an executive committee and direction of union affairs usually rests with the organization's president. Usually the final authority is the convention which elects the top officers and which is composed of delegates representing union locals. Some conventions are annual, others are at longer intervals, and a few like the hod carriers', have not been held for long periods—even a dozen years or more.

Inasmuch as they grant and suspend local union charters, nationals and internationals have considerable control and disciplinary power over locals. Although that control varies among different internationals, it raises some common problems.

The varying relations between the international body and local unions are shown in the following outline of practices in some of the nation's leading bargaining agencies for employees.

The Printing Trades Unions

The printing trades unions comprise some of the oldest as well as the strongest unions in the American labor movement. Their internationals retain a rather tight control over the locals. Between conventions the executive council, which includes international officers, is the final authority upon union affairs, and it may issue union "laws" which relate to working rules and conditions and which are observed by locals and publishers alike in collective bargaining agreements. Locals may bargain with employers but all agreements must be approved and guaranteed by the international.

No strike may be called without authorization of the international, and a local which violates international laws or the orders of international officers may be disciplined by fine or suspension or even by revocation of its charter. Upon many occasions controls such as these have restrained local unions from militant action which their membership was ready to take. They also serve to compel locals to live up to their agreements; but especially among the larger locals there is considerable feeling that greater local autonomy would be desirable.[10]

Construction and Clothing

The building and construction trades unions have greater local autonomy than do locals in the printing trades. Painters and carpenters are required to submit their local agreements to their national organizations for examination and advice, but usually local committees have full power to negotiate and settle with contractors and employers' associations. Such committees are often local building trades councils which cover all building and construction union locals in a certain locality. They frequently underwrite trade agreements and supervise strikes, but they have been less successful in ironing out jurisdictional disputes between different craft locals.

A national counterpart of local building councils is the Building Trades Department of the American Federation of Labor. The department sets up building councils, but its principal aim is the

10. *How Collective Bargaining Works,* p. 138.

settlement of jurisdictional disputes. In this vexing field it has not had monumental success. As a result of its awards, the carpenters' union—the largest in the department—has been outside the department, through suspension or secession, nineteen out of thirty-two years.[11]

Capably led local building trades councils have brought stability and order to local building and labor conditions.[12] Ruthlessly led councils, however, have occasionally resulted in racketeering and chaotic economic and labor conditions in local building industries.[13]

The Amalgamated Clothing Workers of America, which represents men's clothing workers is among the strongest and most progressive of American labor organizations. It is also one in which authority over policy and actions is concentrated largely in the hands of the international officers. The general convention, which constitutionally is the union's supreme authority, has little control in practice. It has met but thirteen times in twenty-six years. The general executive board, which consists of the president, secretary-treasurer and fifteen other members, not only determines national policies and approves admission of locals, but supervises local activities and controls national and local industrial relations.[14]

Steel and Rubber Unions

The United Steelworkers of America, with a membership of about one million, is a product of one of the most remarkable organizing campaigns in labor history—a campaign neither led nor controlled by steelworkers. It was a campaign which did not begin with an autonomous national union but with a temporary administrative organization staffed and supported by the United Mine Workers of America, whose expressed purpose in organizing steelworkers was to unionize an industry owning captive coal mines which had resisted unionism. The chairman and secretary-treasurer of the Steel Workers Organizing Committee were United Mine Workers officials. A staff of about 250 SWOC employees organized steelworkers' lodges, supervised their affairs and in many cases

11. *Ibid.*, p. 202. 12. *Ibid.*, p. 200.
13. *Ibid.*, pp. 881-83. 14. *Ibid.*, p. 397.

even selected the local officers. Lodges signed up new members, collected dues, handled grievances and occasionally negotiated supplementary agreements with employers, but the SWOC did the real collective bargaining. In 1937, a year after organization began, the SWOC had signed up 300,000 steelworkers. Five years later, with double the number of members, the SWOC became the United Steelworkers of America, an autonomous CIO union.[15]

The United Rubber Workers of America, likewise a CIO affiliate and also built up by the 1937 organizing campaigns, is in striking contrast to the SWOC. A strong spirit of local autonomy prevails among the rubber workers. Their organizing campaigns and strikes were directed largely by their local officials with infinitely less financial and personal assistance from the CIO than was given the steelworkers.

In attempting to organize their own industry, the rubber locals ran head on to a number of problems familiar to the labor movement. Frequently unwise attempts to force nonunion workers into the organization made more difficult the rubber workers' task of selling their union.[16] The rubber workers' experience showed that it is difficult to persuade members to pay dues in bad times as in good, to take an active part in union affairs and to remain loyal to the union even though gains are slow in coming—problems of breaking down the natural inertia of workers which have been characteristic of the history of most American labor unions.[17]

Variations in Control

Here have been sketched varying extents of international union control in unions of five diverse industries—printing, building, steel, men's clothing, rubber manufacture. All told, they comprise some 3 million members or, roughly, one quarter of total union membership in the United States. Some are craft unions; others are industrial; but their structure does not appear to determine the strictness of control by the international union.

In both printing crafts and in the men's clothing industry, the international holds tight reins over the locals. In building trades and the rubber industry, locals have more autonomy, with pos-

15. *Ibid.,* pp. 534-38.   16. *Ibid.,* p. 678.   17. *Ibid.*

sibly greater tendency to irresponsibility. There have been innumerable instances in which local unions going out on strike in violation of written agreements have been disciplined by the internationals. On the other hand, union employees negotiating an agreement with an employer are unable to make their own terms but are bound by "laws" and policies laid down by the international officials—a condition which has been attacked as "undemocratic" and counter to "free collective bargaining." The moot point is whether international union control is "undemocratic" or whether it upholds "responsible" unionism and orderly collective bargaining.

Another point is the size of locals. A local union which may have between 50 and 400 members is far more likely to show individual independence than one of the new industrial locals which may have as many as 10,000 members. A workingman who belongs to a local in which there are thousands of members has little more chance for expression of his individuality than in the shop organization of a great manufacturing establishment.

Union Dissension

One serious problem confronting orderly collective bargaining grows out of dissension in the organized labor movement—out of jurisdictional disputes, of rival unions in the same field and of personal animosities which are either causes or results of the foregoing. Although students of collective bargaining make finer distinctions, the term "jurisdictional dispute" is now popularly accepted as a disagreement between unions over the right of one or the other to represent a particular group of employees, or over which union is to control certain work.

Such disputes have long plagued organized labor. They are more frequent among craft than industrial unions because changes in occupations, new materials and new production methods which may require retraining or regrouping of skills, and new industries create situations where craft jurisdictions conflict. Sometimes also industrial unions compete for members. And finally, jurisdictional warfare reacts upon employers; they may have concluded a labor agreement with a union in the expectation of gaining labor peace, only to find that they have secured nothing of the sort—merely more union trouble—which doesn't make them like unionism any the more.

Rival unionism arises out of a number of causes. Two causes, however, are at the bottom of most rival unions: ambition and dissatisfaction. When either a left wing or a conservative group gains control of a union—local or international—the group on the outside sometimes secedes to form a new union. Again, personal ambitions and jealousies among leaders may split a union wide open. Or corrupt leadership may compel honest union members to revolt and form a new organization. Outstanding rival unionism is the gulf between the American Federation of Labor and the Congress of Industrial Organizations; all other examples are pale in comparison.

The AF of L

Slightly more than 100 national or international unions are affiliated with the American Federation of Labor. In addition, there is a fluctuating number in independent and federal locals.[18] These unions reported, as of August 31, 1944, a dues-paying membership of more than 6,800,000 and an estimated 500,000 additional on a nondues-paying basis.[19]

The AF of L is not a union. It is a confederation of autonomous national and international unions. An individual workingman is not a member of the AF of L; he takes out a card in a local trade union whose national or international is an AF of L affiliate. The Federation has no jurisdiction over him—unless he is one of the 300,000 in one of the independent or federal locals which are directly under AF of L headquarters. The big majority of AF of L affiliates are unions along craft lines, organized according to special skill or occupation. Some local unions may be more of the industrial type. And a few are outright industrial unions, outstanding of which is the International Ladies' Garment Workers'

18. A federal union is one under direct control of AF of L national headquarters and one which has not attained strength or coverage to become an autonomous national or international. It serves as a recruiting station for existing or for new national unions. CIO counterpart is the "organizing committee."

19. U. S. Bureau of Labor Statistics, *op. cit.,* p. 1; see also *Labor Fact Book,* p. 53.

Union (membership 237,000) which includes many occupations —cutters, stitchers, finishers—and which left the Federation and then reaffiliated.

The chances are, therefore, that a business concern whose employees are organized by AF of L affiliates, and which requires many skills in its operations, has dealings not with one but a number of AF of L unions. Also one craft union probably deals with employers in many industries. A contractor engaged on a housing project may have labor agreements with unions of carpenters, painters, bricklayers, plumbers, hod carriers, electricians. On the other hand, the International Association of Machinists has some 4,000 agreements in such industries as railroads, machine tools, iron and steel fabrication, and dozens of others.

Under its constitution, the AF of L has little control over its affiliated unions. It may admit or expel them, but it has no other powers of discipline over them. One of its functions is to define, the jurisdiction of affiliated unions on the principle that only one union may have jurisdiction over any particular line of work. Many times its jurisdictional awards have been flouted because the recalcitrant union well knows that the AF of L will not go to the extreme of invoking its drastic power of expulsion. Late in May of 1943, the International Association of Machinists, one of the oldest and largest affiliates, broke with the Federation over a jurisdictional dispute with the carpenters' union as to which union should represent workers in plants making wooden airplanes.

In a sense control in the AF of L is the other way around. Affiliates have more power over the AF of L than the Federation has over them. This is through the Federation's annual convention, in which delegates from national and international unions cast one ballot for each 100 members in their union. Delegates from state federations and city centrals have but one vote. Thus, control of the convention is in the hands of the autonomous unions. Delegates are usually the presidents and executive officers of these unions, with the result that the convention may be likened to a congress of ambassadors from sovereign unions.[20]

20. *Encyclopaedia of the Social Sciences*, Macmillan, New York, 1930, Vol. 2, p. 25.

Psychologically, if not structurally, AF of L unions were not suited for the organization of new mass production industries for collective bargaining. As we have seen, a few industrial unions were affiliated with the Federation, but the bulk of mass production workers were not receptive to collective bargaining along the lines of AF of L—favored craft unions.

The go-ahead signal which the National Industrial Recovery Act gave to the extension of collective bargaining opened new frontiers which the AF of L could not cultivate without being torn by conflicting claims of its affiliated craft-type unions. Craft and semi-industrial unions were unwilling to yield jurisdictional rights. Since it was merely a central body of autonomous unions, the Federation was neither equipped, nor was it intended to assume, general responsibility for organizing efforts; and leaders of international unions were reluctant to risk the funds of their unions to organize groups which previously had been lethargic to the labor movement.[21]

The CIO

The 1934 AF of L convention authorized industrial charters and formed federal unions in a number of mass production industries—at the same time reiterating its traditional policy to "fully protect the jurisdictional rights of all trade unions organized upon craft lines."[22] The next year's convention voted down a proposal to organize mass production workers into industrial unions. A month later, officers of eight unions formed the Committee for Industrial Organization to promote unionization, ostensibly within the AF of L framework, of unorganized workers in mass production industries.[23] When this committee refused to disband, the AF of L Executive Committee expelled all unions participating in the CIO, and this action was upheld at the Federation's next convention.

Within a short time the labor movement was split into two rival groups, one mainly craft and the other chiefly industrial. By

21. *How Collective Bargaining Works,* p. 10.
22. AF of L, *Proceedings,* 1934, p. 41.
23. Committee for Industrial Organization, *Industrial Unionism,* p. 13.

the time the Committee for Industrial Organization became the Congress of Industrial Organizations and an independent federation of some three score unions, the CIO had extended collective bargaining, through strikes and less violent persuasion, on a wide industrial front.[24] Among other industries, were steel, automobiles, rubber products, electrical manufacturing, shipbuilding, and textiles. Its reported membership at the end of 1944 was 6 million. The United Mine Workers, numbering around 600,000 were part of the CIO until they seceded after the 1940 Presidential elections. This union now seeks affiliation with the AF of L.

Two of the most important among many results of AF of L and CIO rivalry have been: a wide split in the American labor movement, accompanied by an extension of collective bargaining. Despite the loss of a number of powerful unions to CIO, AF of L membership has increased. And original CIO unions not only added to their membership, but their new industrial unions organized hitherto unorganized mass production industries and brought under collective bargaining more than 2 million more workers.

Hitherto, labor dissension and rival unionism have resulted in loss of membership. Thus far, history had failed to repeat itself.

24. Unlike the AF of L, the CIO has not operated on the principle that one union alone has a right to organize in a given line of work. It has so far not settled this matter at all, granting jurisdiction on a broad basis to its affiliated union. In this respect, the CIO resembles British trade unions.

Chapter 3

EMPLOYER BARGAINING AGENCIES

BROADLY SPEAKING, labor is better organized for collective bargaining than are the employers. It is true that the American labor movement is plagued by jurisdictional disputes, that it is split by rival unionism; yet these divisions are not so much over collective bargaining's objectives as over methods of achieving them. Division among employers is greater. Not only are they divided over collective bargaining itself; those who oppose it disagree over how it shall be fought, and those who are reconciled to it differ over the extent of its acceptance.

Some employers are dead set against unionism; they would smash it. This group is now smaller than it was before passage of the National Labor Relations Act which limits an employer's antiunion activity. A larger group accepts collective bargaining as an inescapable fact, but won't engage in it any more than it has to. A steadily increasing group is of the opinion that legally protected unionism is here to stay—and is trying to get along with it. Still another group of employers accepts unionism as an ally—after, that is, their establishments are unionized.

Regardless of whether they are forward-looking or believe in things-as-they-are, few employers welcome union organization of their working forces. If they prefer one or two unions, their preference is, to them, the lesser evil. One widely held employer theory is that if a work force receives good wages, works reasonable hours and is given just, considerate treatment, there is no need for unionism and collective bargaining. When such conditions exist in a plant, the task of union organization is sometimes difficult. An employer of his own free will may have granted what unions forced from other employers. Although wages and working conditions may be higher than union standards, he finds that he receives no credit from unionists for correcting evils which the labor movement proposes to wipe out; instead he is charged with obstructing the progress of unionism. Likewise "paternalistic" employers, who provided homes, hospitals, insurance and commissaries for their employees, have often discovered that their benefactions did not forestall union organization. For, in a sense, employees are as individualistic as employers.

Even the employer who upholds "in principle" the right of workers to organize often looks with uneasiness on actual unionization of his own work force. Union negotiators have had experience in collective bargaining; he has had none and therefore may be at a disadvantage when dealing with a union for the first time. After years of playing his cards close to his chest to keep information from his competitors, it is difficult for him to lay them on the table with the union and play them from there. When his shop is unionized, the employer passes from a situation with which he is familiar into a period of uncertainty and readjustment. These are among many reasons why the transformation of a nonunion into a union employer is generally a more bitter experience than the conversion of a nonunion worker into a union member.

American employers are products and beneficiaries of a system of individual enterprise and competition. Temperamentally, they are accustomed to individual action. They are seldom unanimous when they organize for some purpose, they fear loss of personal prerogatives when they organize, and they generally unite in a less binding manner than do working people in unions. Employers are not so well united *in* as *against* collective bargaining. No group of employers defends the right of labor to organize with quite the vigor and ingenuity of the hostile employer groups which oppose unions. While this may be understandable, it is sometimes overlooked when unionism is charged with trying to destroy employers. Collective bargaining becomes adulterated with other ingredients when one or both sides are bent upon exterminating or crippling the other.

Between collective bargaining in the United States and in Great

Britain and Sweden, where it is highly developed, are two principal differences. One is that employer-union negotiations in this
country are still largely upon a plant and company basis,[1] whereas
British and Swedish labor agreements are national in scope.
Another difference is that British and Swedish bargaining is collective on the part of both sides; working people are represented
by unions and management by employer associations.

The extension of collective bargaining frontiers in this country, however, has brought three important changes in employer
activities. The employer association is increasing in importance.
Labor relations assume a greater place in managerial technique.
And the employer-dominated "company" union is an outlaw.

Associations of Employers

Among American employers there is no single counterpart to
the National Confederation of Employers' Associations—which
is British employers' central authority on labor questions. Com-
mercial and economic matters are left to the Association of British
Chambers of Commerce and the National Union of Manufacturers. In this country, the Chamber of Commerce of the United
States and the National Association of Manufacturers share some
functions similar to those of the two British bodies. They include
employers in many fields, but they are not all-inclusive—the NAM
comprising some 9,000 industrialists. Nor are they primarily employer organizations. Although these bodies publicize employers'
points of view and take official stands upon labor questions and
government administration of labor laws, questions relating to
labor are merely segments of their spheres of interest.

American employers are without the national leadership which
unionists have in AF of L and CIO; they are more thoroughly
organized nationally in trade associations than in employer organizations. The typical trade association is a sort of clearing
house for management in the same industry. It watches legislation, competition with other industries and chances for increased
business for its own industry. Labor matters are frequently a side
line. The American Newspaper Publishers Association, for in-

1. Exceptions: glass industry and occasional soft coal agreements are national.

stance, is a national trade body. It has had for forty years a special standing committee for a "better understanding between union members and their employers," and to compile data and assist individual publishers or local associations of publishers in negotiations with printing trades unions. Until recently, the ANPA had an open-shop department for nonunion publishers;[2] while at the same time the organization as a whole was fighting collective bargaining.

Somewhat along the lines of a national trade group is the Association of Railway Executives. It, however, goes further than other management organizations in labor relations in that its parleys with the Railway Labor Executives' Association amount to direct negotiations. This is the only notable example of collective bargaining on a national scale by a management body which is not strictly an employers' association.

Associations of employers developed locally in this country after the appearance of labor unions.[3] Such groups have been of two types: combatant and negotiatory.

"Combatant" Organizations

Outstanding example of the combatant employers' organization was the National Erectors' Association, comprising employers in iron and steel construction, which was organized to fight the closed shop.[4] Employer groups of this type were the first answer to the spread of unionism. They were not all-inclusive affairs. The unity of the organization did not depend upon enrollment of competitors. And in many instances, an employer might have had contractural relations with unions—and yet belong to an association dedicated to wipe them out.

So far as collective bargaining is concerned, the important point about combatant employer groups is that some of them developed into the negotiatory type—associations which are bargaining agents

2. *How Collective Bargaining Works*, pp. 44-46.
3. Employers' associations are of ancient origin. Tablets excavated in Hittite ruins in Asia Minor reveal an appeal by a building trades employers' group for government restraint against certain workmen's practices. *Encyclopaedia of the Social Sciences*, Vol. 5, p. 509.
4. *How Collective Bargaining Works*, p. 898.

for employers on local, regional and national scales. In 1886, employers in one industry banded together as the Stove Founders' National Defense Association "for resistance against unjust demands of workmen." Five years later, this association of aggressive origin was negotiating national agreements with the iron molders' union and continued this practice until well after the first World War.[5] Most of the early employer associations in the clothing industry were formed to fight unions and now they are manufacturers' bargaining agents for regional or "market" agreements.[6] On the other hand, the National Metal Trades Association was founded in the hope of equaling the success of the stove makers in peaceful negotiations of national agreements. Within three years, after anything but peaceful negotiations, the association became rabidly antiunion.[7]

"Negotiatory" Agencies

A negotiatory association is to the employer the nearest counterpart of what a union is to an employee. In most cases, however, the union is the stronger cohesive force. Few employers' associations, past or present, have sought to impose such discipline as fines upon recalcitrant members. Nor does it appear that threats and expulsions have been particularly effective. A more powerful deterrent to backsliding and offending members of employers' associations has been the presence of a strong union. Some local associations of employers in the building trades which have difficulty in organizing a working majority of contractors in their territories welcome union cooperation. They look to union locals to act as economic policemen—to regulate and equalize competition by enforcing uniform labor and wage standards upon nonassociation employers.[8]

Clothing workers have gone further in this direction than other large unions. Some, like the International Ladies' Garment Workers' Union, have even organized employer associations. Under some ILGWU agreements, employer associations and even former members of such organizations may be required to post bonds

<hr/>

5. *Ibid.*, pp. 891-93.
7. *Ibid.*, pp. 897-98.

6. *Ibid.*, pp. 403-05.
8. *Ibid.*, p. 206.

guaranteeing performance of their labor contract obligations.[9] Nonunion members who are beneficiaries of agreements secured by manufacturers' associations may be directed to pay their share of administrative expenses;[10] and some agreements contain clauses under which union approval must be secured for new members of an employers' association, or which would bar from membership applicants who have disputes pending with the union.[11]

Agreements with employers' associations are more prevalent among craft than industrial unions—although clothing and coal mining are exceptions. They are almost universal in the building trades, and employer associations in printing trades have local and frequently regional union agreements.

By and large, however, labor unions seek the practice of collective bargaining upon a national scale. In the first stages of organization they may gain footholds in plants of employers less able to resist, but once collective bargaining is established in an industry, they prefer to negotiate with strongly organized employers. In highly competitive industries a high state of employer organization is difficult, but since unions generally press for uniformity in working conditions and in rates of pay, they frequently urge employers to organize associations for collective bargaining covering competitive areas. Employer and manufacturer associations assemble labor facts for their members and educate new members in the technique of negotiating with unions; consequently, they can play an important and constructive role in collective bargaining and are desirable from both management and union point of view.[12] Thus, the apparent anomaly of a strong union welcoming the prospect of negotiating with representatives of a strongly welded employers' association.

San Francisco Employers' Council

The most all-inclusive employers' association so far developed in this country is the San Francisco Employers' Council, of which

9. Bureau of National Affairs, *Collective Bargaining Contracts*, Washington, 1941, pp. 240, 430.
10. *Ibid.*, p. 385.
11. *Ibid.*, pp. 428 ff.
12. *How Collective Bargaining Works*, p. 652.

the moving spirit has been Almon E. Roth.[13] This is a federation of city-wide employer associations in some two dozen industries, and it resembles in structure San Francisco's Central Labor Union. Each group is autonomous within the employers' council and each employer association deals separately with the unions, substituting a master or industry-wide labor contract for individual and single plant agreements.

The council offers its affiliated employer associations the services of its negotiatory staff and fact-finding organization. The employer associations are thus able to match union bargaining power. One result of master contracts has been to remove questions of wages, hours and working conditions from competition within the same industrial group. Another has been to reduce potential hazards of labor strife from many to one in each industry.

The San Francisco Employers' Council was formed early in 1939. For years the city had been plagued by violent labor disputes and between forty and sixty serious strikes annually. In the council's first eighteen months, it settled 217 controversies and negotiated 154 agreements. In the first seven months of 1941 there were only nine minor strikes—five of them jurisdictional— all of which were settled through the council's intervention. The council was formed not to smash unionism but to get along with it and strengthen employer bargaining power. On occasions it will be tough. When a series of unauthorized "quickie" strikes broke out in one industry and union leaders reported they could not control their stewards, the organized employers shut down operation until assured by union leadership that it had the situation in hand.[14]

Labor Relations Executives

The general spread of collective bargaining to big industry has been either accompanied, or followed, by a change in managerial practice. Although a sense of concern and responsibility for employee welfare and working conditions is not an exclusive attribute

13. Formerly president of Rotary International and comptroller and treasurer of Stanford University; now president of National Federation of American Shipping.

14. For accounts of the San Francisco Employers' Council, see *Reader's Digest*, October 1940; *Business Week*, February 17, 1940.

of union or nonunion employers, the advent of unionism in a large industrial plant usually results in greater executive control of labor policies and in foremen being entrusted with less arbitrary authority. The determination of industrial relations policies has become an important function of top management and is often vested in an executive committee, consisting of the president and other high officers, which lays down all major policies. Most corporations whose employees number in the thousands have a director of industrial relations who occupies an important place in the managerial hierarchy. This official is either directly under the vice president in charge of operations or else is a vice president himself and functions under the president or top executive officer.

Such a director has both advisory and executive duties. He is consulting expert when an executive committee formulates labor policy, and a clearing house of information on interpretation and administration of that policy. As an executive he supervises training programs, employment and welfare plans, insurance and annuities—matters which were in the province of the "personnel director," who flourished in the 1920's. He also represents his corporation in negotiations with international union officers of unsolved grievances, and in such a capacity he is a bargaining agent.

When one corporation has a number of plants, a somewhat similar managerial structure prevails in each plant. At the head is a works manager who reports to the corporation's vice president in charge of operations. Consulting with the works manager, and advising department superintendents and foremen in matters within the labor field, is the plant industrial relations officer. Responsibility for the administration of labor relations policies rests with the company and plant operating officials. The industrial relations officer's activity is largely advisory.

Labor agreements generally are negotiated by top executives, and, except for taking part in grievance settlements, an industrial relations director is not an employer's bargaining agent in the strictest sense of the term. However, because of his detailed knowledge of labor problems and week-in and week-out relations with union officials, a director of industrial relations plays a large part in the collective bargaining process.

This is the industrial relations structure prevailing in the gigantic steel industry[15] and many others. Top executives negotiate agreements made by the large rubber companies. At Firestone, a company vice president is joined by a superintendent of the labor department in union discussions and among some smaller companies, plant managers and labor relations men represent the companies.[16] Throughout the industrial field are countless shadings of the foregoing, most of which are indicative of the major importance which labor relations assume in big corporation policies.

In smaller plants, the tendency is to vest labor matters in the chief production executive, making him responsible for the negotiation and interpretation of labor contracts and for the training of foremen and superintendents. In both large and small plants in newly organized industries there have been heavy job casualties among old-time technical men and foremen who were unable to adjust themselves to union conditions.

"Company Unions"

Although the employer-dominated union, outlawed by statute, no longer has a place in the American industrial scene, it is not yet merely a historical incident.[17] Since the company union was a creation of management and has been abandoned by compulsion only recently, its principles are therefore representative of the labor attitude of a large group of employers. There appear to have been two strong incentives for the establishment of such bodies. One was to stave off trade unionism by a controlled substitute. The other was a desire to correct conditions which encouraged the rise of trade unions.

15. *How Collective Bargaining Works*, pp. 542-44.   16. *Ibid.*, p. 673.
17. Collective bargaining is beset with a verbal jungle of conflicting definitions. Typical of confused terminology are the "company union" and the "independent union." The National Labor Relations Board defines a company union as one which is organized, financed or dominated by the employer, whether it operates in a single plant or company or upon a broader basis. The implication is that this is a "fake" union because the employer merely pretends to engage in collective bargaining and is, in effect, bargaining with himself. An independent union likewise may cover a single plant or company; but even though it has no affiliation with unions operating over a larger area, it is a bona fide union of employees independent of employers and free from domination by them. The discussion in this and the following section does not relate to independent unions but to company-dominated unions.

Company unions were better suited to mass production industries and large plants than to small establishments. They varied in detail and were known by a wide range of titles—employees' committees, works' councils, industrial assemblies, employee representation plans. In fundamentals, most of them were alike: employees elected committeemen who met with management to exchange views, to make suggestions or to press recommendations. Final decision rested with management.

Such shop organizations enabled employees to learn the whys and wherefores of certain management policies; they enabled employers to learn firsthand some things which were on employees' minds. Some company unions handled grievances and might even examine wage schedules and company working rules. In general, however, meetings between management and employee committees merely discussed; they did not determine or negotiate. This in the steel industry was termed "collective cooperation," and hopes were aroused in many front offices that the common interest displayed between management and employee-elected committees would make outside unionism unnecessary.[18] A better term for them would have been "collective consultation."

Company unions came to the fore during World War I, when their formation was encouraged by the War Labor Board. Employee representation plans by 1919 covered workers amounting to 9.8 per cent of trade-union membership; and by 1932 the proportion was 40.1 per cent.[19] Although the decline in union membership during the 1920's may make this comparative coverage out of true proportion, it does indicate company unionism's rapid spread as an employer substitute for trade unionism.

Contributions of Company Unions

When employee representation plans first appeared, the AF of L welcomed them as entering wedges for trade unionism and as training grounds for future local union leadership. That welcome sign was soon removed for it was discovered that this employer-fostered move was becoming a serious obstacle to the extension

18. *How Collective Bargaining Works*, pp. 543, 545.
19. *Ibid.*, p. 906.

of craft unionism. By covering all workers in a plant regardless of occupation, a company union's structure more closely resembled an industrial union.

Some leaders of the Committee for Industrial Organization, however, saw considerable organizing effort saved if they succeeded in capturing company unions. This philosophy was expressed by Philip Murray, then chairman of the Steel Workers Organizing Committee: "Our job was to show what real unionism meant. To denounce them all as company agents or stooges would be both untruthful and poor strategy. Therefore we set out to win these employee representatives to the cause of the SWOC and industrial unionism."[20]

CIO organizing campaigns emphasized one contribution and one disadvantage of company-dominated unions. The contribution was that employees not only chose representatives but that these representatives became accustomed to dealing with management. Many officers of steelworkers' local lodges were company-union committeemen—a fact which sometimes smoothed first negotiations with management and sometimes didn't. The disadvantage was that the presence of a company union in a plant divided employees over unionism.

Another disadvantage was the effect that the accomplished fact of a trade union in his plant had upon an employer who previously had prided himself upon having evolved a successful plan of harmonious employer-employee relations. Illustrative of this was the Goodyear Industrial Assembly with a senate and house of representatives elected by employees. It had power by a two-thirds vote to override a management veto but the last word rested with the company's board of directors. Despite its achievements, however, Goodyear's once notable management-employee harmony ceased with an extremely bitter strike in the plant. This became the turning point for unionism in the rubber industry.[21]

Thus, the company-dominated union. Under it, employees had but a voice and little more in the conduct of matters relating to

20. SWOC, *Reports of the Officers to the Wage and Policy Convention,* Pittsburgh, December 14, 15, 16, 1937, p. 9.
21. *How Collective Bargaining Works,* pp. 637, 640.

their employment. The company union had the form but not the substance of collective bagaining. It served a purpose in enlisting employee interest in company policies and sometimes in other problems of production, and its principle of collective cooperation and consultation is applied in union-management cooperation plans now operating under collective bargaining.[22]

22. See Chap. 11.

Chapter 4

UNION RECOGNITION

NOW THAT IT IS PROTECTED by law, the right of working people to organize and negotiate the terms of their employment is no longer seriously questioned in the United States. This leaves as the most bitterly contested issue in American labor relations the unsolved problem of whether union membership shall be made a condition of employment.

Shall all employees covered by collective bargaining be compelled to join unions? Shall employers be required to hire only union members? Shall union men refuse to work with nonunion men? Shall a workingman be deprived of a chance to work because he does not, or will not, belong to a labor union? Shall a nonunion member be a "free ride" beneficiary of better working conditions which were won by a union to which he has contributed nothing?

The crux of the matter lies in the distinction between the closed, union, and open shop. Almost inextricable confusion exists over these forms of union status, and such distortions that the partisans who employ them are befogged over definitions—particularly over what they mean by "closed" and "open" shops. Only rarely are these words encountered in collective bargaining agreements. They have not the same meaning for zealous union spokesmen that they have for rabidly hostile critics of unionism. The interpretations of both do not agree with dictionary definitions— and these, in turn, are counter to popularly held understandings.

Varieties of Union Status

One of the main reasons for this confusion is that employer-union negotiations have produced assortments of "closed" and "open" shops. Unions which have demanded either closed or union shops have frequently compromised for less. Employers have usually resisted both, and made partial or gradual concessions rather than full acceptance of either. The result has been all shades of union status and recognition—from tightly closed shops which none but union members may enter, to establishments where the presence of union men is known but unrecognized. In all shops, however, either some form of compulsion exists regarding union membership, or there is none. Consequently, the various shades of union status and recognition may be listed under one of two classifications:

       1. Compulsory shops
         a. Closed shop
         b. Union shop
         c. Maintenance-of-membership shop
       2. Noncompulsory shops
         a. Preferential shop
         b. Exclusive bargaining shop
         c. Bargaining for members only
         d. Open shop

Closed Shop

In the closed shop only union members may be hired and employees must remain members to retain employment. An agreement clause typical of this arrangement reads: "The Employer shall employ and retain in his employ none but members in good standing of the Local Unions above mentioned. . . . A member in good standing is one who is not in arrears for more than two months in the payment of dues and assessments . . . and who carries a union card."[1] Other agreements leave to union determination what constitutes "members in good standing."

The strictly closed shop has two main variants.

The closed shop with the closed union; the rarer and more drastic variety, limits union membership and restricts free entrance to the union. One example is the Chicago local of the motion picture machine operators.[2]

1. Agreement of Boston Coat and Suit Manufacturers' Association with the International Ladies' Garment Workers' Union (AF of L).
2. *How Collective Bargaining Works,* pp. 834-37.

The closed shop with the open union; has no limitation of membership and no barriers against new members. This is typical of many craft unions, particularly in printing and building trades.

Union Shop

Under the union shop nonmembers may be hired but must become members after a certain period to keep their jobs.[3] New employees are seldom required to take out union cards immediately, and specified time limits before joining the union may run from two weeks to three months and longer. An employer has the privilege, under the union shop, which he does not have under the closed shop, of hiring outside of union membership rolls—provided the person hired is willing to join the union. Although it is found in some AF of L agreements, this form of union status has been encouraged by the CIO in newly organized plants. Whether it is of the closed-shop or the union-shop variety, union membership as a condition of employment appears to prevail in industries where unionism has been long recognized.[4] About four million workers were covered in 1941 by closed-shop and union-shop agreements.[5]

One modification of the union shop is the *percentage shop* in which an employer agrees that a certain percentage of his work force shall be union members in good standing.

Maintenance-of-Membership Shop

No employee is required to join a union under the maintenance-of-membership shop, but all present or future union members must remain in good standing as a condition of employment. This is an attempted compromise between the extremes of closed and open shops which some employers pronounce "a camouflaged closed shop."[6] During the first year of World War II, the National War Labor Board employed the maintenance-of-membership

3. Union spokesmen generally avoid mention of the words "closed shop" and describe even an establishment hiring only union members as a "union shop."
4. See below, "Extent of Union Recognition."
5. U. S. Bureau of Labor Statistics, *Extent of Collective Bargaining at Beginning of 1942*, Serial No. R. 1457, p. 4.
6. Many employers make no distinction between union, preferential and maintenance-of-membership shops, terming all three "closed shops."

formula to break a number of employer-union deadlocks over union recognition.

In this form of union status, the only compulsion rests upon union members who cannot withdraw from the union during the life of the agreement without forfeiting their jobs. On the face of it, the maintenance-of-membership formula preserves a *status quo* between unionism and nonunionism, but it places no restriction upon a union's signing up more members and upon progress toward union-shop or closed-shop status. Comparatively overlooked in the controversy over the WLB's maintenance-of-membership policy was the Board's practice of directing incorporation of a fifteen-day "escape" provision into an agreement so as to enable an employee to quit the union if he chooses before the clause goes into effect. Late in 1942, the WLB announced that, regardless of union constitution and rules, any employee may drop his union membership during the fifteen-day period without losing his job; and employers were warned against inducing employees to quit the union during this escape period.[7] Under this ruling, only those who choose to remain in the union when the maintenance-of-membership agreement goes into effect are covered by the Board's directive.

Preferential Shop

Under the preferential shop union members are given preference in hiring, layoff, or both. The employer is not required to discharge workers who refuse to join a union and he may agree to urge employees to become union members. This formula was devised in 1910 by Louis D. Brandeis in settlement of a prolonged strike in New York City's cloak and suit trade. An employer giving preference in his shop to a minority union would be violating the National Labor Relations Act.

Exclusive Bargaining Shop

Recognition of a union as exclusive bargaining agent for all employees whether union members or not is the basis of the exclusive bargaining shop. This form fulfills the minimum require-

7. *New York Herald Tribune*, November 28, 1942.

ments of the National Labor Relations Act, which deems an employer guilty of unfair labor practice if he fails to bargain collectively and "exclusively" with representatives chosen by a majority
of his employees.[8] It is virtually the same status as when the National Labor Relations Board certifies as sole bargaining agent
the union which wins a plant election.

Bargaining for Members Only

Under the bargaining-for-members-only status a union is recognized as bargaining agent for its own members. For example,
one important union-management agreement section reads: "The
Company recognizes the Union as the collective bargaining agency
for those employees of the Company who are members of the
Union. The Company recognizes and will not interfere with the
right of its employees to become members of the Union. There
shall be no discrimination, interference, restraint or coercion by
the Company or any of its agents against any members because of
membership in the Union. The Union agrees not to intimidate
or coerce employees into membership and also not to solicit membership on Company time or plant property."[9]

Although this status does not equal the protection which federal
law gives collective bargaining, a union has been occasionally—
and temporarily—willing to accept it. Having gained partial
recognition, the union now has a foothold in the plant. It has not
exclusive bargaining rights, but it has achieved much the same
result, because whatever wage increases an employer has granted
the union are generally applied throughout the plant regardless
of union membership. If the grievance procedure set forth in a
bargaining-for-members-only contract is not enjoyed by unorganized workers, nonunionists have an added incentive for taking out
union cards. And, if the agreement improves working conditions
of all plant employees, the union has won a strong advantage: it
has shown nonunionists that in union there is strength and that
by joining up they may enable the union to win further concessions.

8. National Labor Relations Act, Secs. 8(5) and 9(a).

9. Agreement of April 1, 1941 of Carnegie-Illinois Steel Corporation with Steel
Workers Organizing Committee (CIO).

In recognizing the union a little bit, the employer may have hoped to get rid of the union in time. But under the bargaining-for-members status, the advantage is with the union, and about all that the employer has won is a short postponement of the time when he recognizes a union as bargaining agent for all his employees.

Open Shop

The open shop means no union recognition; a nonunion shop. This is the status of about 70 per cent of all wage earners.[10] Formerly an open shop might have been closed to union members and a seeming contradiction in terms, but such employer practice is now outlawed by the National Labor Relations Act. Since the open shop is an establishment where collective bargaining is not yet practiced, further details do not belong in this discussion.

Extent of Union Recognition

By the end of 1942, approximately six million workers were employed under closed-shop and union-shop conditions.[11] These comprised about 45 per cent of all wage earners covered by collective bargaining agreements. No industry is a completely closed shop, but this status affects more than 90 per cent of those under union agreements in the baking, brewing, women's clothing, building construction, hosiery, trucking, and printing and publishing industries. The union shop prevails in the coal mining industry, in which virtually all who work are members of the United Mine Workers.

By December 1942, maintenance-of-membership clauses applied to 15 per cent of all workers under union contract, particularly in electrical and farm equipment, nonferrous mining and basic iron and steel. The checkoff of union dues by employers affected 2.5 million, or about one fifth of all workers under agreement. The preferential shop covered less than 5 per cent and the exclusive bargaining shop covered about 35 per cent of all workers

10. U. S. Bureau of Labor Statistics, *op. cit.*, p. 1.

11. Data for this paragraph from U. S. Bureau of Labor Statistics, *Types of Union Recognition in Effect December 1942*, Memorandum No. 5; *Industrial Relations Problems Arising Under War Production*, Memorandum No. 2, April 1942.

under agreements. Exclusive bargaining rights cover a majority of unionized workers in aircraft, chemicals, iron and steel products, machine tools, and cotton and woolen textiles. Bargaining for members only affects less than one per cent of those under union contract.

Completeness of union recognition appears to vary largely according to the length of time collective bargaining has been practiced in each industry. Closed and union shops prevail where unionism has long been recognized, and exclusive bargaining rights are encountered in more recently organized industries. The notable exception is railroads, a veteran and almost totally unionized industry in which the closed and union shops are prohibited by law and in which brotherhoods and unions have exclusive bargaining rights.

Development of the Closed-Shop Issue

The closed-shop principle is older than trade unionism. Born of the desire to work with others of one's kind, it was present in the guilds of the Middle Ages. After the formation and spread of unions in the early 1800's, it was manifested in the refusal of craftsmen to work alongside of nonunionists. By 1840, closed-shop rules were enforced by American printers, and when the Civil War came, virtually all trade unions favored excluding nonunion members from employment.[12] National unions and federations of unions carried on the principle, and in 1890 the recently established American Federation of Labor officially embraced the doctrine. On the other hand, one large industry in which unionism did not press strongly for the closed shop was the railroads, principally because of union structure and seniority rules, bargaining customs, and accelerating governmental supervision.

A clear-cut exception was the stove industry, which offers evidence that the closed-shop controversy lessens in intensity when there is close union-employer understanding. Between 1850 and 1890, strife was almost continuous between stove manufacturers and the molders' union. Then they "arbitrated" an agreement

12. F. T. Stockton, *The Closed Shop in American Trade Unions*, The Johns Hopkins Press, Baltimore, 1911, p. 24.

which, with minor revisions, has continued for fifty years. As soon as the manufacturers accepted collective bargaining and dropped hostility to unionism, the molders' union lost interest in the closed shop which had previously been one of its most insistent demands. For more than twenty years the union has had but one closed-shop agreement with a stove manufacturer, and that because of reputed discrimination against union men.[13]

The beginning of the twentieth century saw the closed shop so firmly entrenched in union bargaining that it had become difficult for nonunion men to find employment in some trades.[14] But this condition did not last long. Employer interests, mobilizing against the labor movement, centered their attack upon the closed shop, and spearheads of the assault were the National Erectors' Association, the National Metal Trades Association, the United States Steel Corporation, and the National Association of Manufacturers. The latter organization inaugurated a belligerent open-shop drive in 1904, declaring its "unalterable antagonism to the closed shop," an affirmation which has been echoed at a majority of its annual conventions ever since. Both before and after the first World War, unionism sustained heavy losses from organized employer assault, and particularly in the 1920's, closed shops collapsed in a number of industries.

These are highlights of an oblique campaign that probably gained more allies than if it had been directed openly at unionism itself. Behind the drive for the open shop and the "American Plan," its successor in the 1920's—and in the absence of any concerted employer movement to support collective bargaining— organized labor saw a threat to its existence. With renewed intensity, labor leaders demanded closed and union shops on the ground that greater union security was essential. They were inflexible in the contention that the union shop is an integral part of collective bargaining, a stand which they might have been willing to modify under other circumstances. What departures they made from this policy were ones of temporary expediency rather than of modified objective; and if the trend in recent years has been

13. *How Collective Bargaining Works*, p. 893.
14. F. T. Stockton, *op. cit.*, p. 43.

to accept exclusive bargaining rights, or even initial agreements calling for bargaining for members only, the next step has been to press for the union shop.[15]

The Closed-Shop Issue Abroad

European quarrels in the late nineteenth century over closed-shop questions were as bitter as those which still rage in the United States. In Great Britain and Sweden they were settled voluntarily—either informally or by agreement; in Germany they were ended by law.

The subject was long an active issue in Britain. One factor in its virtual disappearance was British industry's eventual and almost complete acceptance of collective bargaining. Another factor was the attitude of nonunion labor which rarely supported management in industrial disputes; when a union called a strike in a plant, nonunionists also laid down their tools and walked out. Few British collective agreements now specify union membership as a condition of employment, and the union shop prevails not by agreement but by custom.[16]

The closed shop was a turbulent question in Sweden until 1906, when it was settled by the Employers' Federation and the Confederation of Trade Unions. These two powerful and almost inclusive central organizations agreed upon a formula whereby employers undertook to recognize workers' rights to organize, and unions recognized employers' rights to engage and dismiss employees without regard to whether or not they were union members. The substance of this understanding was then written into virtually all collective bargaining agreements. The closed-shop versus the open-shop issue evaporated "because of the very large

15. *How Collective Bargaining Works,* p. 24.

16. "Except among the seamen and firemen in the shipping industry closed-shop agreements are exceptional, and do not appear to be seriously sought for. Nevertheless, we were told by both union and employer representatives that in some industries there is virtually a closed shop in practice, as distinguished from one by contract, the employers preferring to engage union men and in some instances, at the request of the union, suggesting to particular individuals that they should join. The checkoff is very exceptional and several union representatives stated their opposition to it." *Report of the Commission on Industrial Relations in Great Britain,* Government Printing Office, Washington, 1938.

proportion of workers who are union members and because the
employers no longer try to break down union organization, preferring to deal with their workers through strong trade unions."[17]
Few charges of antiunion discrimination arise. If not settled by
conciliators within the industry, they go to a labor court which
has power to order reinstatement with back pay.

Pre-Nazi Germany settled the closed-shop question not by evolution as in Britain, nor by employer-union agreement as in
Sweden, but by law. Before World War I, big industrial groups
fought unionism and set up company unions. After the Republic
was established late in 1918, discrimination against unionism was
prohibited by law. This was followed by rapid spread of collective
bargaining. Collective agreements had government backing, their
terms covered union and nonunion employees alike, and under
some conditions they were imposed upon local, regional, and
national competitors of firms with union contracts.[18]

Union and Employer Points of View

In the United States, union and employer attitudes in general
are still so far apart that there are few signs of the noncompulsory-
shop status being accepted in return for union recognition, as happened in Britain and Sweden.

Most unions seek closed or union shops chiefly to strengthen
their organization, prevent discrimination, aid in enforcement of
standards and gain greater control over their membership. Such a
status means to them "union security"—security from employer
hostility and security from dwindling membership and dues. They
hold that all who share in the benefits of collective bargaining
should also share in the responsibilities of union membership.
They liken the union shop to the "integrated bar" in states which
require lawyers admitted to practice to be members of bar associations.[19] And they maintain that under closed or union shops,

17. *Report of the Commission on Industrial Relations in Sweden*, Government
Printing Office, Washington, 1938.

18. H. A. Millis, "German Trade Unions and Collective Bargaining," *American
Federationist*, February 1928, pp. 153-57; Hans Lehman, "Collective Labor Law
Under the German Republic," *Wisconsin Law Review*, April 1935, pp. 324-39.

19. Any lawyer who qualifies may belong to a bar association, and there are no
restrictions against numbers.

unions are more responsible bargaining agents, and that both employers and recognized unions are protected against rival unions.

Some employers find their labor relations improved when operating under closed and union shops. They discover that instead of having less discretion, management is freer to act, because it is easier to get along with a strong labor organization than with a weak, suspicious union which questions almost every managerial rule. Another union-shop advantage frequently cited is a harmonious work force unvexed by feeling between union and nonunion employees; also considerable freedom from jurisdictional disputes. And in industries where competition has been particularly keen, a regional or nation-wide closed or union shop has helped to stabilize wages and remove labor costs as competitive factors.

Employers opposed to closed and union shops maintain that their choice of employees is limited and that they are required to discharge those who have resigned or have been expelled from unions, yet whose work may have been satisfactory. They further claim that some of their workers do not wish to join unions; and that since employers are forbidden by law to prevent their workers from joining unions, they should not compel their workers to do so. Some employers declare it illogical to permit closed shops, in effect monopolies, whereas they themselves are forbidden by antitrust laws to engage in monopolistic practices. Opposition to closed and union shops makes much of the possibility of employees being thrown out of jobs because of arbitrary union actions; but there has been little employer insistence upon agreement clauses requiring union guarantees against unjust expulsion of workers whose employment is contingent upon their remaining union members.[20]

20. A few agreements contain such provisions. In one of the first maintenance-of-membership clauses to be included in an agreement, a compact between the Crown Zellerbach Corporation and the paper mill brotherhoods stipulates that an employee who claims unjust expulsion from a union shall remain at work until his appeal has been decided by the brotherhood's international president. An agreement between the Boston Consolidated Gas Company and the United Mine Workers, District 50, authorizes an arbitration board of three to review an employee's appeal against union suspension, expulsion or exclusion. The board consists of one arbiter chosen by the

Many students who are in neither camp hold a viewpoint between extreme positions of employers and organized labor. They question the desirability of industry-wide closed or union shops. They believe that union shops were needed for security of unions which were not firmly established; but now that the right to organize is guaranteed by law, the strongest threat to unionism is removed.

Another leading issue raised is whether a union with complete control over the labor supply in a trade or an industry should be regulated, just as are single bodies which control transportation and communication facilities. In the absence of collective bargaining, the individual worker has small protection against arbitrary acts of an employer. Under a closed or a union shop, the individual worker has no safeguards against arbitrary exercise of union power except what the union chooses to give him.

Acceptance of the closed or union shop raises a host of questions. What about the open door to unionism, regardless of sex or color? Or the right of men to move from one industry to another regardless of union affiliation? And the right of union members to protection from loss of their jobs because of the action of political enemies within the union? Or the right of employers to pick the best possible men for the jobs? Finally, has the time come for public policy to regard unions as quasi-public and not private organizations?

At present, it rests with a union whether there shall be reasonable membership requirements, protection against unjust expulsion, guarantees to minorities and barriers to seizure of power and self-perpetuation in office. The fact that comparatively little is known about union admission requirements and initiation fees gives further point to proposals for public supervision of unions.[21] Guarantees may exist in most union rules and constitutions, they may be included in some collective agreements, but still the moot point remains: what shall be done in their absence.

---

union, one by the aggrieved employee and the third selected by the other two arbiters. Pending arbitration decision, the employee remains at work.

21. Information is scanty. "Studies of these matters are needed." Sumner H. Slichter, *Union Policies and Industrial Management*, The Brookings Institution, Washington, 1941, p. 96.

Attitude of Government

Government has handled the union-shop question gingerly. Its basic policy is that the issue should be decided voluntarily by those involved and not by Washington. "The Government of the United States will not order, nor will Congress pass legislation ordering, a so-called closed shop," President Roosevelt announced in November 1941.[22] Under the National Labor Relations Act, a union-shop agreement is not deemed unfair labor practice if it is the result of legitimate collective bargaining.[23] The Railway Labor Act outlaws the union shop in the railroad industry, making it a criminal offense, punishable by fine or imprisonment, for a carrier to compel employees to join labor organizations.[24] Although it is a seeming contradiction that federal statutes both allow and prohibit union shops, the railroad situation is different; railways are a closely government-regulated industry in which the union shop could not exist without involving government.

It may be inferred from this that government rejects labor's contention that the closed shop is an integral part of collective bargaining. The National Labor Relations Board has power to certify a union as exclusive bargaining agent in an establishment where employee elections have been held, but it has no legal authority to require employees to join the union which bargains for them. The federal law which protects collective bargaining as a right, permits but does not compel union shops.

Since government regards the union shop in private industry as a matter which management and labor should decide, may unions exert economic pressure to force employers to grant union shops? The courts are scarcely consistent on this point. Some state courts have outlawed strikes for union shops, others have upheld them, still others have wavered.[25]

22. *Labor Relations Reporter,* November 17, 1941.
23. National Labor Relations Act, Sec. 8(3).
24. 44 U. S. Stat. 577 (1926) ; 48 U. S. Stat. 926 (1934).
25. Strikes over union shops have been customarily upheld by California, Illinois, Minnesota, and New York courts. Similar trends are found in court decisions in Arkansas, Connecticut, New Hampshire, Florida, Nebraska, and Oklahoma. Strikes for union shops were long illegal in Massachusetts, New Jersey, and Pennsylvania courts—with like trends in Missouri, Georgia, Washington, Kentucky, and North Carolina. In recent years Pennsylvania and Maryland have moved to the permissive

During the first World War, the War Labor Board declined to decide labor disputes which involved a change of union status. In the defense emergency of World War II, the National Defense Mediation Board took a hand in such matters to assure uninterrupted production. It recommended a union shop in a Bethlehem Steel shipyard dispute on the ground that the adamantine position of one out of 39 shipbuilders should not hold up production; and it rejected United Mine Workers' demand for a union shop in "captive" soft coal mines, holding that since 95 per cent of the industry was already union shop, the mine workers did not need the remaining 5 per cent for "union security."[26] In the captive mine case, the National Defense Mediation Board majority opinion voiced "the principle that the emergency should not be used either to tear down or to artificially stimulate the normal growth of unionism." When the country went on a war footing, the National Defense Mediation Board was succeeded by the National War Labor Board, which continued both this principle and the general practice of applying the maintenance-of-membership formula.

The Outlook

Experience, both in this country and abroad, shows that unions do not press for the closed shop as determinedly when all or most employers in an industry accept unionism. If management showed heartier acceptance of labor's right to organize and exhibited greater willingness to engage in collective bargaining, organized labor would have less provocation to demand "union security." But a vicious circle is created by management's opposition to the spread of unionism because of union insistence upon the closed or union shop as security against employer opposition to unionism. That circle cannot be broken except by both management and organized labor—by management ceasing to oppose extension of unionism and by organized labor ceasing to maintain that the union shop is an essential in collective bargaining.

If the impasse continues, the prospect is that public opinion

---

side, and conflicting decisions have come from Massachusetts and New Jersey. A Wisconsin statute invalidates closed-shop contracts unless approved by a two-thirds vote.
   26. Subsequent arbitration upheld the mine workers.

will call upon government to end it. As we have seen, government favors the growth and spread of unionism; it encourages a situation in which organized labor might no longer feel in need of the union shop for its security. Yet government policy rejects the labor thesis that union shop and collective bargaining are inseparable. Legislation, therefore, would follow one of these courses:

1. Outright prohibition of closed and union shops
2. Imposition of closed and union shops under governmental regulation
3. Government regulation of unions having closed or union shops

In any case, unionism and free collective bargaining would stand to lose.

Chapter 5

COLLECTIVE AGREEMENTS

AN AGREEMENT ARRIVED AT through collective bargaining may be a treaty, a code, and, in some respects, a contract. As a treaty, it aims at the reduction of disputes. It states conditions under which work is offered and accepted, and it is buttressed by detailed codes for performance of that work.

The agreement has more flexibility than a lawyer-drawn contract. It imposes no obligation upon an employer to offer work or upon a workingman to accept it. In Germany and elsewhere upon the European continent, a collective agreement was a legally binding contract. In Britain it is usually a statement of intention, and its observance rests upon the good faith of its makers. In the United States, the courts now generally regard an agreement as a contract but, as will be seen later, considerably different from the usual business contract.

No one knows how many collective agreements are in force in the United States. The largest single collection of such documents is the 12,000 on file in the Division of Industrial Relations of the United States Bureau of Labor Statistics, but this number is far from complete. Probably 50,000 employer-union agreements are in existence.[1] The largest known number of agreements in any one industry is on the railroads—some 4,000 filed with the National Mediation Board set up under the Railway Labor Act. And the largest number of agreements negotiated by any one union is the more than 4,000 held in a score of industries by the International Association of Machinists, which for more than half a century, and until 1943, was an AF of L affiliate.

1. Estimate from Florence Peterson, Chief of Industrial Relations Division, U. S. Bureau of Labor Statistics.

The Purpose and Forms of Agreements

An agreement may cover a single shop and a handful of employees in it; or it may take in entire industries and apply directly to scores of thousands of working people. But whatever form it takes, and no matter what its length, or completeness of coverage, the purpose of a collective bargaining agreement essentially is the same as this preamble to a New York City carpenter-contractor agreement: "To establish and maintain wages, hours, and working conditions for the work covered by this agreement; . . . to prevent strikes and lockouts; to ensure the peaceable adjustment and settlement of any and all grievances, disputes or differences that may arise."

The usual agreement specifies the extent of recognition which an employer accords to a union. It establishes wage rates, hours of labor, working conditions, and seniority. It lays down the grievance procedure and whether disputes arising out of it may be submitted to arbitration. It specifies its own duration and the ways and means of renegotiation. Some agreements are standardized documents prepared by the international union which establishes more or less uniform conditions throughout an industry. But most agreements are as individual as fingerprints; almost every item is a product of give-and-take negotiation, reflective of union pressure and of employer resistance. Some 2,000 different clauses relating to almost every conceivable subject have been classified from American labor agreements.[2]

Collective bargaining agreements may take many forms. Almost always the agreement is written, though it need not be. For many years there were no written agreements in the unionized men's clothing industry in Philadelphia, and verbal understandings about some matters not formally covered by written agreement have been known to have been made in the steel and automobile parts industries.[3] Sometimes working conditions have been codified in a unilateral declaration signed and perhaps posted on bulletin boards by an employer who "bargained collectively" but remained

2. Bureau of National Affairs, *Collective Bargaining Contracts*, Washington, 1941, p. 87.
3. *How Collective Bargaining Works*, pp. 556, 596.

intransigent about recognition of a union. The courts, however, have ruled that if the other side demands it an employer must sign an agreement covering whatever terms have been jointly determined. On the other hand, unions may issue unilateral declarations of working conditions without consulting employers. Typical are the "rules" laid down by the printers' union.

In general the agreement is a joint document, signed by both negotiating parties. It may be a page long, as were some early understandings on the railroads, or it may cover one hundred printed pages, as do a few current railway brotherhood agreements with the carriers. And sometimes its working rules may be fifty pages or more, like some codes in pressed ware departments of the glass industry.[4] If the document is brief and general, it is known as an "administrative agreement." It leaves much to the good sense and good will of management and the local union and allows for mutually considered adjustments of situations as they arise. If it contains detailed codes which leave little to the discretion of the parties involved, it is known as a "legislative agreement." The administrative variety is more sought for than obtained. The legislative agreement reflects either painstaking cooperation or mutual distrust.

Coverage and Term

Whether agreements are national, regional or local generally depends upon the scope and membership of the bargaining units. If unionized employers in an industry are country-wide, and comprise a closely knit group, a trade agreement on a national basis may result—as in railroads, men's clothing, stoves, glass bottles, and, sometimes, soft coal. If costs and competitive conditions are the same in certain parts of the country, an agreement may be regional, as in Pacific Coast shipbuilding. Local agreements are more frequently encountered among craft unions which bargain with all unionized employers in a local or metropolitan area. Chief examples of these are the building trades, printers and pressmen.

Agreements with great mass production corporations—steel, rubber, autos, aluminum and airplanes—have a somewhat com-

4. *Ibid.*, p. 698.

parable framework. These concerns may have branches or other plants in many sections of the country. Sometimes an agreement may apply merely to one plant, or in rare cases a craft union may have coverage of a small department within a plant. Other union-management agreements may be multiple plant, or they may be company-wide. Sometimes the same terms are negotiated with more than one company. For example, instead of dealing jointly with the glass workers' unions, Pittsburgh Plate Glass and Libbey-Owens-Ford each have separate but virtually identical agreements.

The trend of agreements is toward wider coverage. Most industrial unions prefer national agreements because differentials are wiped out[5] and all employers in an industry have virtually the same labor costs.

The more flexible the agreement and the easier it is to modify, the better are its chances of survival. Short-term collective bargains which are renewable fare better than rigid, long-term ones, and opportunities for annual agreements are favored by most governmental agencies. The National Labor Relations Board, and labor boards in New York and other states which have "little Wagner Acts"[6] and certify unions as exclusive bargaining agents, won't uphold new employee elections until an agreement has run for one year. Most current union-employer agreements are for a year, and a big proportion of them contain clauses which automatically renew the agreement from year to year if neither party gives termination notice—usually thirty days before expiration date. The simplest amending procedure of all is change of the agreement, at any time, by written consent of both parties. Some contracts which run for three years are renewable thereafter for one year if no formal notice otherwise comes from either side.

How Agreements Are Made

Few useful generalizations can be made about the negotiation of labor agreements. Proposals may be discussed, terms arrived at, and a document drawn up and signed with the greatest of

5. Differentials are discussed in Chap. 6.
6. Other states are Massachusetts, Rhode Island, Pennsylvania, Wisconsin, Michigan, Minnesota and Utah. Only in the first two states are labor's rights protected to the same extent as in federal statutes.

casualness and informality. Or a trade agreement may be negotiated by "joint conferences" with much of the formality and protracted sessions of a diplomatic conference drafting an international treaty. A corporation may entrust negotiations to its industrial relations manager because of his experience in dealing with union officials. Or other executives of the company may handle the matter while the labor relations expert remains on the side lines lest too active a part in drawing up the bargain would jeopardize his usefulness as conciliator during the administration of the agreement. For the union, a workers' committee may be present, but usually a union official more experienced in negotiation is chief spokesman.

Sometimes the management asks that a group of employees be present so that it may have firsthand knowledge of the dealings. Some union officials have plenary powers to negotiate contracts, but most labor organizations require ratification by their locals. Bituminous coal agreements must be approved by the rank and file. The same applies to some collective bargains in the electrical manufacturing industry. Locals of the Federation of Flat Glass Workers of the CIO pass upon the wage scales set up in their trade agreements.

According to experienced negotiators, agreements are more easily reached when talk is frank and no stenographer is present to take down what is said. Sometimes collective bargaining has collapsed because one side insisted upon a stenographic record of all discussions.[7] Frequently the more off-the-record the negotiations are, the more may be found on the record in the agreement. In industries where large annual management-union conferences take place, agreements that might be impossible of attainment at full plenary sessions sometimes come out of subcommittees and caucuses. An outstanding exception to the unwieldy, many-representatives conference method is the Atlantic City joint conference of the glass container and flint glass industries, usually attended by some twenty-five from each side. Meetings alternate between manufacturers' and union leaders' hotels, and first one group and

7. Immediate cause of breakdown of negotiations between Air Associates, Inc. and United Automobile Workers (CIO), July-August 1941.

then the other provides the meetings' chairman. For several decades, harmonious results have been almost a tradition at these
meetings.

Test of Provisions

During the negotiation of a labor agreement, both sides are
concerned with the settlement of immediate issues, but a great
many administrative difficulties could be avoided if the document
is carefully checked to assure that it provides a satisfactory basis
for day-in, day-out relations between union and management. One
student of collective bargaining[8] proposes the following tests of
clauses of a union-management agreement. Does the agreement:

1. Indicate clearly what workers are included and what workers are
excluded?
2. Provide for machinery for settling disputes about its interpretation?
3. Provide machinery for the peaceful settlement of charges that one
side or the other has violated its terms?
4. Clearly provide how management may operate under disputed conditions?
5. Bind the union not to pass working rules which either conflict with
terms of the agreement or encroach upon the freedom of management?
6. Define adequately some orderly procedure for its renewal?

The Place of Arbitration

One great mystery about collective bargaining to many laymen
is why labor and management reject arbitration when they are
deadlocked over terms of an agreement. They do not see why
the negotiators shouldn't be willing to entrust their differences to
decisons by neutral outsiders. They see, in fact, arbitration employed successfully in some labor disputes and do not understand
why it cannot be applied successfully to all disputes.

The layman, however, is apt not to see the difference in employer-union relationships when an agreement is being negotiated
and when an agreement has been signed and goes into effect. Were
arbitration invoked to decide the terms to be written into a labor
compact, the result would not be an agreement but a decree.
Union and employer would begin their relationship under con-

8. Sumner H. Slichter.

ditions imposed by an outside party rather than under an agreement freely negotiated. It is the almost unanimous opinion of unionists, government mediation officials and employers experienced in dealing with unions that, except in wartime, arbitration has no place in the writing of a labor agreement. The acceptable place for arbitration normally is when employer and union are deadlocked over disputes arising out of their agreement.[9]

The rejection of arbitration when negotiating agreements does not imply that union or management discourages outside intervention when they cannot agree over contract clauses. Government conciliation has saved many a dispute from the industrial warfare stage and has encouraged many an employer and union to keep at their negotiations until an agreement is reached. The United States Department of Labor has stationed 120 commissioners of conciliation throughout the country in or near important production and distribution centers. These commissioners may enter a situation where a strike is threatened at the request of the disputants or of public officials—or they may enter the picture of their own accord in a controversy vitally affecting the public interest. A commissioner offers guidance and advice in drawing up an agreement. He may suggest and urge a certain solution, but he cannot prescribe, for the agreement must be the voluntary decision of the two contracting parties.

In the peacetime participation of third parties in labor relations conciliation is employed to break deadlocks over drawing up agreements; whereas arbitration is invoked to settle disputes arising out of agreements. In wartime unions and management formally renounced the right to strike and lockout for the duration, and the settlement of disputes they cannot resolve were handed down by the National War Labor Board.[10]

When Violations Occur

Because they rest upon good faith rather than upon legal force for their observance, most employer-union agreements in the United States are very much like treaties between nations. For al-

9. For discussion of arbitration of these disputes, see Chap. 10.
10. For discussion of government arbitration in wartime, see Chap. 12.

though the observance of treaties is upheld by international law, their enforcement is chiefly in the hands of the signatory countries. Violation of the pact by one nation gives ground for the other nation to abrogate the treaty. In labor relations, if one side fails to carry out its undertaking, a clause in an agreement may release the other side from its obligations after formal notice. And just as nations may resort to force against treaty breakers, so are parties to a labor agreement likely to take forceful measures against violators of their codes. That force is stoppage of work. An employer's weapon is discharge or a lockout. Union labor's weapon is the strike.

Sometimes an agreement specifically authorizes an employer to punish violations by individual employees or groups. A labor agreement in an aircraft plant gives management the right to lay off or discharge the offenders.[11] This unusual procedure is virtual transfer to the employer of disciplinary powers which unions generally prefer to keep in their own hands. Other discharge authorizations are not so sweeping—for example, a women's clothing agreement stipulates discharge only after union consent.

A union's strongest retaliation against employer violation of agreements is a strike. An agreement may stipulate that no strikes shall be called for any cause; if so, unions regard themselves free of obligations after employers repudiate them—just as there is legal justification for one side to tear up a contract when the other has violated its terms. Some agreements authorize strikes when employers violate contracts.

When groups or associations of employers make collective labor agreements, unions may have a leverage against a single employer-violator by forcing other employers to withdraw all support. That force may be through strike or by agreement clauses pledging united employer action against an offending employer.

Garment unions frequently exact further assurance of management's good faith by requiring employers to post bonds or cash as security "for the faithful performance of this agreement."[12] And

11. Agreement between Bell Aircraft Corporation and United Automobile Workers (CIO).

12. Agreements with employers held by International Fur and Leather Workers Union (CIO) and International Ladies' Garment Workers' Union (AF of L).

from these deposits fines may be assessed against violators by the industry's impartial chairmen or other arbitrators. In rare cases, an agreement's preamble may contain the familiar legal contract phrases, "Therefore, in consideration of the sum of one dollar by each to the other in hand paid . . . the parties hereto agree as follows—"[13]

Strikes and Lockouts

Most agreements ban strikes and lockouts for the duration of the compact. Between the AF of L metal trades and Pacific Coast shipbuilders there is an absolute prohibition against stoppage of work and a guarantee for arbitration of all disputes. In addition to outlawry of strikes and lockouts, some garment trade agreements forbid even threats of them. Most compacts which mention the subject are not so drastic in their proscriptions—the unions merely promise that they will not "sanction" or "tolerate" interruption of work.

Among other varieties of no-strike clauses are:[14] no strike permissible unless or until all efforts fail to adjust the dispute; no strike unless with union sanction; no strike unless approved by majority of employees eligible for union membership. Virtually all agreements with clauses like these require advance strike notices of from twenty-four hours to seven days. Some agreements which ban strikes within a plant authorize union walkouts for outside causes—sympathetic strikes or refusal to handle "hot goods" from strike-bound plants. A few agreements proscribe sympathetic strikes for any purpose, and others contain such clauses as "neither the union nor any of its members shall participate in or encourage any sit-down or slow-down strikes."[15] Other strike prohibitions are against walkouts to secure changes in an existing contract or while negotiating a new agreement. In some cases picketing is specifically banned. The usual penalties which

13. Agreement between Boston Coat and Suit Manufacturers' Association and International Ladies' Garment Workers' Union (AF of L).

14. For more than two score diverse clauses relating to strikes and lockouts see Bureau of National Affairs, *Collective Bargaining Contracts*, Washington, 1941, pp. 515-27.

15. Agreement between Lockheed Aircraft Corporation and International Association of Machinists.

labor agreements lay down for unauthorized strikes are: discipline of the outlaw strikers by the union, discharge of the strikers by the employer, or release of the employer from his contract.

Among penalties for lockouts in violation of agreement are union cancellation of contract or reinstatement with back pay if the lockout should be arbitrated with findings against the employer. Contrasted with strikes, however, lockouts are rare. Employers can gain the same end by other means—for instance by imposing conditions which would provoke a strike.

Labor Agreements and the Law[16]

An employer and a new executive sign a contract. The executive agrees to work for the employer at a certain salary and for a certain length of time. For the duration of the contract, the employer agrees to pay a stated salary. If one party to that contract violates its provisions, the other can go to court about it, and the law give him redress.

An employer and a union of workingmen conclude a collective bargaining agreement. One agrees to pay certain wages for certain tasks, the other that its members will remain at work during the life of the agreement. Should one side not live up to the agreement, may the other obtain legal redress?

Although most collective bargain agreements state that they are "contracts" between employers or employer associations and trade unions, they differ from ordinary business contracts. Under an individual contract between employer and executive, one is obligated to hire and the other is obligated to render his services. Under a collective bargain agreement, there is no guarantee of employment to union workingmen or of a labor force to an em-

16. This section was prepared with the assistance of Edwin E. Witte, Chairman of the Department of Economics, University of Wisconsin, and Chairman of Regional War Labor Board, Region 11. Acknowledgment is also made of an unpublished memorandum upon labor law prepared for Carlos Israels, Esq. of New York City, by Shirley Adelson and Boris I. Bittker of Yale Law School.

For discussions of legal aspects of collective bargaining, see W. G. Rice, Jr., "Collective Labor Agreements in American Law," *Harvard Law Review*, 1931, pp. 572-608; T. R. Witmer, "Collective Labor Agreements in the Courts," *Yale Law Journal*, 1938, pp. 198-240; "The Present Status of Collective Labor Agreements," *Harvard Law Review*, 1938, pp. 520-33.

ployer. One is not obligated to work, the other is not required to offer work.

But other undertakings in a trade agreement are now legally binding in virtually every state. When employers and unions pledge to refrain from certain acts, the courts may enjoin them against breaking those pledges. Employers have been denied the right to make individual contracts with employees counter to terms of union agreements. They have been enjoined from paying wages under the agreed-upon scale and from moving their factories to other localities in violation of "runaway shop" clauses in their union agreements. Regardless of whether or not a union is incorporated, it has legal liabilities.

There is no comprehensive "law" of collective bargaining agreements. Although unions have been negotiating with employers for more than a century, the trade agreement is basically new to the law. There has been no clarifying legislation reflective of public sentiment that employers and unions who make labor agreements should keep them; the only principles the courts could apply are those of common law and of precedent as new cases came up haphazardly for determination. Moreover, both parties to trade agreements generally preferred to rely upon their economic strength rather than upon uncertain legal remedies to compel observance.

The result has been probably more learned legal comment upon collective bargaining agreements under the law than there have been cases involving them. Although the law of trade agreements has not stabilized, it is apparent that the old concepts of union-employer agreements as mere statements of intent have been abandoned; and that there is developing a general law of labor contracts which differs in many respects from the law of business contracts, yet is linked to them in terminology and to some extent in principle. The courts now generally uphold these agreements as "contracts." They have rejected the argument that an agreement obtained after a strike is invalid because it was obtained under "duress." This was on the ground that a legally called and conducted strike does not constitute duress. Also rejected, both by common and statute law, are contentions that union-employer agreements violate antitrust laws.

Although they uphold labor agreements as contracts, the courts are not yet entirely sure what sort of contracts they are—whether between an employer and his employees, or between an employer and a union with employees as third party beneficiaries, or whether, as they purport to be, contracts between a union and an employer or an association of employers. Also in the legal jungle are many other matters which lead out of the collective bargain. How responsible, for instance, are union members and officers for acts of their colleagues? What is the dividing line between discipline and democracy in determining the liability of unions for acts of their members and officers? What legal remedies are there for unjust expulsion from a union; and what are the rights of workers barred from unions and employment?

Chapter 6

WAGES

WHEN A WORKINGMAN first said to an employer, "I won't work for less," then and there began bargaining over wages. This was not collective bargaining. Having solely his own labor to offer, the workingman bargained only for himself. He was a retailer of labor, whereas the employer hired many workers on a wholesale basis.

Under such conditions the individual bargainer of his own labor is at a disadvantage. If he won't work for the wage offered him, the employer finds others who will. But when a number of workers agree among themselves not to work for less than a certain sum, the employer's search is harder, even fruitless, and he may come to terms through a collective bargain.

Just as "how much is the pay?" is uppermost in the mind of a man who takes a job, so wages and rates of pay are and have been major concerns of labor unions. Of all union objectives, they have been pressed with the greatest force and determination. Comprehensive, nation-wide figures for strikes have been compiled for well over sixty years. During that time, wages have been the cause of more labor disputes than any other issue.[1] Management and unions have little or no disagreement over methods of payment, but other wage questions provoke fundamental conflict between employer and organized labor. In a sense, then, the wage schedules of a trade agreement are a truce in that conflict.

Wage Results

The results of collective bargaining over wages must not be

1. Florence Peterson, "Strikes in the United States," *Bulletin No. 651*, U. S. Bureau of Labor Statistics, 1938.

judged in too-sweeping terms. It cannot be said that they are wholly "good" or completely "evil." It is almost beyond question, however, that collective bargaining has:

1. Promoted wage increases and retarded wage cuts
2. Brought more standardized pay rates
3. Obtained higher wages for union members than are paid for the same tasks in nonunion shops
4. Forced many a nonunion employer to raise his workers' pay
5. Helped to raise the pay of unskilled union workers
6. Forced the cutting of other production costs to allow for increased wages, thereby promoting further managerial efficiency and technological improvement

Unquestionably also, collective bargaining over wages as practiced in some cases and in some instances—an important distinction from the above—has:

1. Increased prices for the consumer—as in the building trades
2. Added to burdens of depressed industries—as failure to make adjustments during lean days in coal and railroads
3. Discouraged exceptional individual performance—as in some union establishments paying time wages

There appears to be no evidence that collective bargaining has raised labor's share in the national income. Hard times and "prosperity eras" have come and gone. National income has climbed peaks and tobogganed into valleys on the statisticians' charts. Prices have risen and fallen. Living costs have fluctuated. Wage rates have risen at times steadily, at others microscopically. Union organization has had periods of great activity and of severe loss of membership. Union bargaining power has waned and waxed again. Union agreements upon wages cover between one quarter and one third of all wage earners. Despite all these changes, which include many unpredictables, the proportion between labor's income and the national income has remained virtually the same.

In 1920, private pay rolls were 59.4 per cent of national income. In 1938, after great spread of union organization and more collective bargaining than ever before, they were 61.9 per cent. Between 1929 and 1939, hourly earnings in manufacturing rose from 59 cents to 71.6 cents an hour. The cost of living dropped about

15 per cent. Nevertheless, the share of private pay rolls in national income rose only from 59.7 per cent to 61.9 per cent.[2]

It appears, then, that collective bargaining cannot be charged with raising the standard of living by raising wages—and cannot be expected to. It likewise appears that what a union can do for a small group, unions of the country cannot necessarily do for labor as a whole.

Wage Desires

When union and management negotiate a wage schedule, what does each side want? The employer wants his labor costs within the limit of what his business can bear. He does not want wages to be so high as to be out of line with his producing and selling costs, or out of line with labor costs of his competitors. For an employer hires both men and money. An increase of five cents an hour means $102 more to a workingman during the year, but to an employer it also represents the price (interest) of a year's hiring of $2,000.

Labor wants equalized pay and more money. "A fair day's pay for a fair day's work" is nice-sounding rhetoric, but about as unserviceable a guide as the measurement, "as long as a piece of string." A more revealing terse expression of labor's wants is the saying attributed to Samuel Gompers, "The object of the trade union is to bring to the workers more and ever more of the product of their toil." Put in other words, "A prime objective of collective bargaining is the redistribution of the proceeds of production."[3]

"More and ever more" epitomizes organized labor's wage aims. Early in the century, coal and the garment trades were low-wage industries. Their unions demanded "a living wage." That claim for all occupations received public approval, support of arbitrators, and, ultimately, legal sanction in state minimum wage laws and in the nation-wide minimum of the federal Fair Labor Standards Act.

The next union wage goals were "a decent standard of living,"

2. Data from Sumner H. Slichter.
3. Clinton S. Golden and Harold J. Ruttenberg, *The Dynamics of Industrial Democracy,* Harper, New York, 1942, p. 151.

then "an American standard of living," and, finally, "a saving wage." All these progressive objectives likewise received general support—so much so that when opportunity arises, particularly around election time, almost every political and economic group claims credit for achievement of "the American way" and "the highest wages and living standards anywhere in the world."

But all wage goals are not simple. Does a union seek high wages or high rate of employment? The wage policy of many a union depends upon the size of its membership, or must be reconciled with its employment policy. That is, will it seek to maintain high wage levels even though that means fewer members employed, or will it endeavor to keep all its members employed and sacrifice wage standards? Is it concerned with hourly rates or with annual income?

Wage and Living Standards

Unions strive for uniform or standard rates of pay for the same work performed by the same skill in the same trade. Examination of hourly pay in various industries shows that averages in plants covered by union agreements are higher than in unorganized shops;[4] and under most circumstances the union scale is higher than wages paid by nonunion establishments. Many wage scales in union agreements show departures, or "differentials," from standard rates. Such departures might seem inconsistent with union preference for uniformity unless a wage standard is likened to a military trench—a defensive position against attack and a point of departure from which to gain more ground.

That comparison applies particularly to union wage attitudes upon the arrival either of prosperous or hard times. Organized labor has held, without much contradiction, that living standards and wages in peacetime should not go down while production, employment, profits and national income expand. In a small number of agreements an attempt has been made to link wages to that expansion. One provided that wages shall rise and fall with the price of the product. Another called for revision of pay rates

4. See studies of earnings and hours in various industries, which are published in separate bulletins from time to time by the U. S. Bureau of Labor Statistics.

when there were changes in the margin between cost of materials and the product's selling price.[5] A larger number provided for upward wage revision should living costs rise. But these were notable exceptions. In most agreements, wage rates were more or less frozen for the duration of the compact.

Living standards rose so steadily throughout the years in this country that increases in wages were regarded as normal. Under conditions of expansion, no change in wage rates would be equivalent to a wage cut; but when hard times come, a decline in living costs is not so noticeable at first as an advance. Consequently, employers who propose wage reductions are almost certain to meet with determined union opposition—despite the fact that some arguments the union once put forward for increasing wages have now boomeranged. A few unions like the Amalgamated Clothing Workers and those in container and flint glass did not oppose wage cuts when business fell off,[6] but most unions resisted reductions until jobs were at stake. It thus appears far easier through the collective bargaining process to increase wages in time of prosperity than to lower them during depression.

The Problem of Differentials

Although union bargaining practice tends toward uniform wage rates for the same jobs, it makes exceptions. Living standards vary in different parts of the country and so do living costs. An allied complication is the migration of nonunion or antiunion firms to take advantage of the lower wages in localities of low living costs and standards. Furthermore, most trade agreements are negotiated locally, with the result that members of the same trade in neighboring cities may have different rates of pay. Finally, separate crafts in some industries negotiate their own agreements and thus make possible wide differences between wages of comparable occupations.

In cases like these, it is almost impossible to apply uniform wage standards, because, paradoxically, they would create more

5. Bureau of National Affairs, *Collective Bargaining Contracts,* Washington, 1941, pp. 603-04.
6. *How Collective Bargaining Works,* pp. 422-30, 713-15.

inequalities. Hence, collective bargainers set up "differentials," or allowances designed to even out inequalities arising from local standards or from competitors' lower wages. Negotiators of wage schedules in a labor agreement may have to consider geographical differentials, competitive differentials, craft differentials—and, conceivably, all three.

Geographical Differentials

A carpenter's hourly pay is higher in Boston than in Bangor. A cutter of men's suits is paid more in Chicago than in Rochester. A steelworker is paid less in Birmingham than one performing the same work in Pittsburgh. Yet the wages of all of these workers have been determined by collective bargaining—the carpenters by local agreements, the clothing workers by market or regional agreements, and the steelworkers possibly by an agreement of national coverage with one corporation having plants in the North and South.

These are three examples of geographical wage differentials which allow for disparities in living costs and are designed to equalize rather than favor the workers in any locality. Although recognizing the need for these differentials, unions do not particularly like them, and the tendency is to decrease rather than to add to their number. Craft unions have had more to do with geographical differentials than have industrial unions. Hourly wage rates variations in the building trades depend upon whether the agreement covers urban or rural areas, large cities or small ones—and likewise upon how far the trade is unionized in a locality.[7]

The printing trades make much of geographical differentials. Wages paid in a comparable locality are important considerations in agreement negotiations covering mechanical departments of newspapers. If Chattanooga typesetters win a higher scale, the same raise is demanded by Knoxville printers, and if Knoxville gets it, the Chattanooga printers try to maintain their differential.[8] By and large, such flanking movements by local unions in the same craft are rare because union internationals must approve local agreements. And even though the typographical union does

7. *Ibid.*, pp. 208-10.   8. *Ibid.*, p. 77.

not favor a national wage, pay rates have been pulled up in low-wage centers and differentials have been narrowed. In 1939 there were 14 geographical differentials, contrasted with 23 ten years before.[9]

Industrial unions sometimes seek geographical differentials for regional areas but seldom for cities. A garment union like the one in men's clothing used to negotiate different pay scales for various regions or "markets."[10] Collective bargaining in steel has brought elimination of differentials in the North but separate pay schedules are retained for the North and for the South.[11]

The extension of collective bargaining to the automobile and rubber products industries brought curious anomalies in geographical wage differentials. The auto workers' union opposes them, and most differentials in the motor vehicle branch were wiped out because agreements negotiated with big companies having plants in many parts of the country were on a virtual national basis. On the other hand, agreements covering auto parts manufacture tended to be local, and the first result of collective bargaining in this branch of the industry was an increase of geographical wage differentials.[12]

In the rubber products industry the average hourly wage of workers was 20 per cent higher in Akron than elsewhere with the exception of Detroit. Apparently this high differential had two main causes: first, Akron is a center for skilled rubber workers, and, second, the wage increases which were made in Akron in pre-union days. One result has been attempts by some Akron companies to move elsewhere to escape the high wage rates they themselves established to forestall union organization of their plants. The other result was union insistence upon the high Akron wage differential which encouraged migration to nonunion areas.[13]

Causes of geographic differences are fairly clear-cut: inequalities between big cities and small towns in labor productivity and between different sections of the country, such as the North and the South, in supplies of labor and capital for investment. Collective bargaining's approach to these inequalities is likely to be hit-

9. *Ibid.*, pp. 157-59.   10. *Ibid.*, p. 429.   11. *Ibid.*, p. 551.
12. *Ibid.*, p. 615.   13. *Ibid.*, p. 663.

or-miss and spotty. The wage adjustments tend to equalize the results rather than to diminish the causes. Rarely are long-range policies followed which might encourage a better distribution of labor or attract a flow of investment capital to sections of the country now long on labor and short on capital.

Competitive Differentials

Other wage scale differentials have been set up to equalize competition between both union and nonunion establishments. Some of these are so closely allied to geographical differentials that there is little difference between the two varieties. The question of whether a certain wage rate may be applied to one establishment —even to one locality—frequently depends upon whether it will hold in the face of competition elsewhere. It may also depend upon a union's ability to organize nonunion employers in other localities and bring their wage scales into line with those of unionized plants.

This is both a regional and a competitive problem. The cotton textile industry saw a migration from unionized New England mills to the Carolinas where labor costs were low, labor was plentiful, and unions were unknown. Other Southern states saw migration of other nonunion manufacturing establishments—accompanied by losing union fights to organize the new territories.

In 1938 came the federal Fair Labor Standards Act which set a minimum hourly wage for all work in interstate commerce. Although it necessitated little or no upward revision on wage schedules in collective bargaining agreements, the new law did serve as a sort of floor for the nation's wage structure and narrowed the difference between "sweated" wages and union standards.

The purpose of most competitive differentials is to establish uniform labor costs among employers operating in the same regional markets. Wage schedules in regional agreements of the men's clothing industry—an industry in which labor relations have been extremely sensitive to changed economic conditions— took into account not only actual but potential nonunion competition.[14] It used to be the practice of soft coal miners to negotiate

14. *Ibid.*, p. 423.

agreements covering an entire competitive field. In an industry in which labor is from 65 to 70 per cent of total costs, wages paid by nonunion competitors were an important factor in preparing union scales; but by 1941 all remaining nonunion fields in the South were organized and under collective bargaining and regional differentials were abandoned.[15]

Twelve years of collective bargaining since 1929 in full-fashioned hosiery has shown a swing-around-the-circle in meeting competition-caused wage problems. From the "Army Game" policy of playing on variations between plants to get raises or reductions, it was decided to "eliminate labor as a competitive factor," apply uniform wages for identical work and "compete solely on efficiency of management." That put union mills uniformly at a disadvantage with nonunion competitors, whereupon unions adopted the practice of securing from each plant the highest wages compatible with continued operation.[16]

Collective bargainers have had choices of several methods of wiping out competitive differentials in wage schedules. An employer may agree to pay wages equivalent to those of his competitor, or a union may undertake not to accept lower rates from an employer's competitor.[17] Finally, an employer may agree to match the wages paid by his highest-paying competitor. The first Ford-United Automobile Workers' agreement contained this clause:

"The Company will pay rates in the several classifications at least as high as those paid by the major competitor, named below in its respective industry:

"(a) in the auto industry
"(b) in the cement industry
"(c) in the glass industry
"(d) in the steel industry
"(e) in the tire industry

"The Union agrees to name the competitor within ten days."

As in geographic differentials, union policies upon competitive differentials are frequently hit-or-miss. As we have seen, the general run of wages is higher in union than in nonunion establish-

15. *Ibid.,* p. 241.   16. *Ibid.,* p. 455.
17. Bureau of National Affairs, *op. cit.*

ments. If he is able to cut other costs, a union employer is enabled to compete on an equal basis with a nonunion shop; but the record of collective bargaining is cluttered with instances in which unions had sufficient bargaining power to make it virtually impossible for union employers to keep their accounts in the black instead of the red ink column. Not only were union wages more than in nonunion shops, but union work rules hamstrung employers' efforts to cut costs so as to carry the burden of higher wage rates.

The ultimate result, of course, strengthened the position of nonunion employers and finally weakened the union; but frequently the union rank and file did not realize the consequences of their make-work rules. Higher union leadership may have seen the danger and sought to avert it, but its hands were tied by the fact that the agreements it negotiated must be ratified by a membership more interested in immediate gains than in long-range effects. Thus one of the perils of competitive differentials is when they impose make-work rules rendering it impossible for an employer to carry out production economies sufficient to pay for increased union labor costs.[18]

Systems of Wage Payment

Such matters as wage standards and differentials, influence of competition upon pay schedules, adjustments for changed living costs are basic factors common to any system of wage payment. Separate and equally important issues arise over the wage structure—whether pay shall be according to the time worked (time wages) or according to the amount of work performed (incentive wages). There is no pronounced employer-versus-union united front over timework as against piecework, which is the simplest form of incentive wages. The nature of the work usually determines which shall be adopted. But in fixing standards for either time or incentive wages, union and management attitudes come into conflict.

18. For detailed coverage of problems of competitive differentials, see Sumner H. Slichter, *op. cit.*, Chapters 12 and 13, "Results of Competition Between Union and Non-Union Plants" and "Control of Cost Differentials Between Union and Non-Union Plants," respectively.

Time Wages

A standard time wage is the minimum sum per hour, day, week or month for a specified group or classification of employees. This standard varies according to skill and sometimes according to service. For instance, there may be a minimum in a certain trade, for full-fledged journeymen, possibly two or more rates for different lengths of service, another for handymen and helpers, another for common labor, and special rates for apprentices.[19]

Virtually all of the building trades, the bulk of the service trades, a large majority of public utility and transportation industries, and about one half of manufacturing are on time wages.[20] This means that the majority of employees covered by union agreements are paid according to time wage standards.

Union pressure raised the number of auto workers on time wages to 80 per cent of total.[21] Aside from this, however, there is little evidence that collective bargaining is responsible for the big proportion of time wage earners in this country, for it would be virtually impossible to pay many occupations in any other manner. Operations such as newspaper presses and blast furnaces depend, not upon individuals, but "crews" and teams paid on time-worked basis. Where power-driven machines and not human speed and skill determine the output and where individual output cannot be measured, any form of base pay other than of the straight wage is not possible.

Too rigid an application of time wage scales tends to protect mediocrity and to hold down the ambitious. Employers complain that time wage standards are not adjusted to efficiency; that some

19. Example of minimum rate schedule from 1940 agreement between Beech Aircraft and International Association of Machinists:

Special rating	87.5 cents an hour		
Tool and die makers	82.5 "	"	"
Journeymen	72.5 "	"	"
Class A production workers	62.5 "	"	"
Class B production workers	55.0 "	"	"
Helpers	50.0 "	"	"
Laborers	47.5 "	"	"

20. Sumner H. Slichter, *Union Policies and Industrial Management*, The Brookings Institution, Washington, 1941, p. 282.

21. U. S. Bureau of Labor Statistics, *Industrial Relations Problems Arising Under War Production*, Memorandum No. 2, April 1942, p. 3.

workers are paid more and others are paid less than they are worth, and that there is no rewarding incentive for individual performance. Although nothing in a time wage scale may prevent an employer from giving higher pay to his best workers, other agreement clauses regulate hiring, lay-offs, and seniority, and thus limit adjustment of a work force upon an efficiency basis. Moreover, union rules which limit output and speed of production are definite barriers against exceptional performance.[22] Where printers are forbidden to set more than a certain measure of type or painters may not cover more than a limited area a day, employers have no cause to offer better pay for better work.

Union policy as to time wages tends toward uniformity. There is also a general sentiment against a few men receiving more than others on a job simply on account of greater speed. Nonunion establishments may have more pay grades for specified occupations than under union agreements. This variation is small, and the fact that a large proportion of nonunion shops do not adjust time wages to performance is a commentary upon the eagerness of employers to reward zeal.

Where departures from uniformity have been made in union-management negotiated time wage scales, the measurement has been more frequently length of service than appraisal of performance. Standard Newspaper Guild agreements set forth progressively increasing pay over a five- or six-year period.[23] Some building trade unions used to grade their members on the basis of competency, but the practice gradually was abandoned, principally because of dissension among union members when first-grade men were driven in times of depression to accept lower ratings.

In the field of time wages, then, collective bargaining appears to have accomplished more on the side of uniformity than of grading workers according to their effort.

Incentive Pay: Piecework

Employers in many industries prefer piecework, or "payment by result" to time work because it gives them precise knowledge

22. Make-work rules are discussed in Chap. 9.
23. *How Collective Bargaining Works*, p. 115.

of labor costs. Thus equipped, they may reach closer estimates of their total costs and selling prices. Also the incentive of piecework is largely responsible for a 15 to 30 per cent better output than if the same work were performed under regular time wages.[24]

But even in some individual output operations, piecework is unsatisfactory. The process may be one in which spoilage mounts with increased output. Cost of materials wasted may exceed savings made by accelerated production. Or quality may have been sacrificed. Sometimes machines cannot stand excessive speed and break down under the strain of burdens they were not designed to carry. Sometimes, also, the piecework system shoots factory morale to bits by provoking quarrels among the working force and arousing envy and discontent among the less proficient. All of which usually means a large labor turnover—and added costs.

If four deft pieceworkers can produce, say, as much as five average and six mediocre workers, it follows that their output might defy union share-the-work philosophy and result in a smaller work force. But it does not follow that unions in general oppose piecework and favor the more uniform earning level of day wages. Actually unions are divided over this issue. Union agreements in coal mining, hosiery, cigar making, flint glass, and textiles carry detailed price lists for piecework. Such trades as printing and building are firmly against piecework; and some building trades go so far as to ban it in their constitutions.

Straight Pay versus Piecework

Of all industries, however, the issue of straight pay versus piecework probably has vexed most of the garment trades. Fur and hat and cap workers are paid under both systems. Women's clothing workers officially have opposed piecework since 1916, but most local union agreements specify it. Cloth hat and cap workers opposed piecework in 1919 and favored its return five years later. The same year the hat makers sought to give up piecework, the men's clothing workers' union declared for it and have tried ever since to extend it throughout the industry.

24. H. A. Millis and Royal Montgomery, *The Economics of Labor,* McGraw-Hill, New York, 1945, Vol. 3, pp. 396-97.

Many unions have good reason to favor piecework when they have a hand in its application and when they are satisfied that it is precisely measured, uniformly applied, and not "loaded" against the employee. It enables individual workers to increase their earnings without raising employers' labor costs; the man whose work improves doesn't have to ask for a raise; he gets it automatically by his increased output. It is easier for unions to secure regional and national wage agreements in industries where piecework operates satisfactorily because labor costs are more uniform than under time payments. One of the sharpest spurs to cutthroat competition is absent if all competitors have the same piece rates.

Even if industry-wide or regional agreements are not obtained, a union shop operating under the piece system is better able to meet nonunion competition, for time-paid union workers frequently do not produce as much as nonunionist pieceworkers. Besides a chance for higher earnings, there are other individual advantages. A pieceworker is not under the close supervision necessary to keep production at efficient levels under time payment. He is more on his own. Moreover the age of workers is not such an acute problem under piecework. Employers have less provocation to weed out older men because piecework operators are paid only for what they turn out.

Union Participation in Fixing Rates

True collective bargaining of terms of employment implies that a union should have freedom to participate, if it chooses, in the determination of piece rates. In some newly organized industries, management may insist upon continuing to set these rates; and if for some reason a union wishes no part in fixing rates, it can protect its members by an agreement clause providing for settlement of a piecework dispute through the grievance procedure laid down for handling any other dispute.[25] The rates may be jointly worked out and incorporated in the agreement. This is the custom in coal mining. Or a separate schedule may be attached to an agreement, a procedure of some aircraft labor relations.

25. See Chap. 10 for grievance procedure.

Or the agreement itself may specify one of the many ways in which piecework rates are to be worked out—whether by foremen and shop stewards, or by joint conferences of union and employer representatives.

In the garment trades, unions have almost complete participation with management in setting wage rates and job standards. Most of the piece rates in the men's clothing industry are established under the Amalgamated Clothing Workers' stabilization program.[26] They are made jointly by a representative of management and a union deputy who is responsible to the union's price maker. Both rate setters are so thoroughly familiar with rates and operations that time studies are rarely necessary, and they try to set a price upon a new or changed operation that shall not lower the worker's usual hourly earnings. If his earnings are reduced, the rate is readjusted, but if they are more favorable the rates are seldom reduced. And if rate setters disagree, which is infrequent, appeal is made to the impartial chairman of the region.[27]

Collective bargaining of piecework pay can be an irritating matter in establishments which manufacture specialty products or goods dependent upon changing fashions and consumer tastes. Each change in the product may call for many changes in manufacturing processes and almost continual readjustment of piece rates. If rates are determined by management alone—and under these circumstances generally by foremen—they come under constant questioning from the unions. If they are jointly determined, fewer suspicions may be aroused but friction can develop. And further friction is certain when management cuts piece rates and establishes not the average as a gauge but the output of the most proficient. Even when piece rates are mutually acceptable, disputes may arise from irregular flow of work or from inefficient placement or breakdowns of machinery.

In expanding industries and labor forces, union leadership must iron out ill feeling over piecework among its members. Slower, newer workers are plagued by a system which favors faster more

---

26. An example of union-management cooperation outlined in Chap. 11 and discussed in *How Collective Bargaining Works*, pp. 436-43.
27. *How Collective Bargaining Works*, p. 425.

competent ones. In an industry undergoing technological transformation in which craftsmen are displaced by specialized operators, piecework is likely to cause turmoil. Under such circumstances the old-line craft unions fight the system bitterly. And in newly organized industries, piecework comes under the displeasure of militant new unions whose slogan is "solidarity" of the workers. They oppose piecework because it may provoke rivalry and enmity and endanger intra-union harmony.

The Incentive Bonus

Few employer-union differences result over the choice of either timework or piecework. Strong disagreement arises over employment of a third system which combines features of the first two. This is the incentive bonus, or gain-sharing system. In some forms it is known as "scientific management"; in others, it approaches profit sharing.

As we have seen, pay under the "straight wage" is according to time spent rather than measurement of output; under the piece wage, the measurement is output, without regard to time. An incentive bonus plan calls for measuring both time and output; and organized labor has looked upon it with a suspicious, even jaundiced eye. The system's object is greater output at reduced cost through encouraging a labor force to make more money. First is determined a basic cost of average production. If labor can produce more in the same or less time it may get all of the gain realized—or it may share the gain with the investors, or with management.

Probably nearly 25 per cent of manufacturing industry operates under some form of incentive bonus.[28] These systems have increased in mass production industries since 1930, notably in steel, electrical goods, rubber products and automobiles, and particularly in large plants.[29] Rarely has an incentive bonus been intro-

28. *Encyclopaedia of the Social Sciences,* Vol. 8, p. 678.
29. In 1930 a National Industrial Conference Board survey of 1214 manufacturing plants found 367 using time wages only, 599 on piece rates, 146 were using piece rates combined with other incentives, and 102 on incentive system other than piece rates. The place occupied by incentive systems is more important than these figures indicate, for the proportion was greater in large plants. Of 57 plants employing between 1500 and 3500, twelve used piece rates combined with other incentives. Of

duced in an establishment already unionized, for these plans are holdovers from nonunion-shop days.

First to appear nearly a generation ago was the Halsey premium plan, and soon after came Frederick Taylor's scientific management and differential piece plan. Later came the Rowan modification of the Halsey plan, the Merrick modification of the Taylor plan, the Gannt task and bonus system, the Emerson efficiency bonus system, the Bedaux point system, the Haynes-Manit system, the Parkhurst differential bonus system—and a cloud of further modifications.[30]

Most of the plans call for careful determination, first, of standard rate of production, and second, unit cost of production. They usually require intensive job analyses and time studies and standardization or rearrangement of production operations. Then the amount of an individual worker's incentive bonus is determined from records of time or output saved, or under the Bedaux, Manit and Parkhurst systems, from calculations of "points," "Manits," or "units."

Obviously, such calculations, however scientific, are not readily understood, and their very complication and mystery arouse workingmen's suspicion. And when time studies are performed by outside staffs, the fact that these measurements are made without firsthand familiarity with the jobs or workers under survey creates further distrust and anxiety. Labor has been in determined opposition against management-controlled and imposed incentive bonus plans and organized job studies. For more than a quarter of a century its influence has been behind legislation which forbids adoption of these systems in government plants.[31]

---

36 plants employing more than 3500, piece rates with other incentives prevailed in 14 and 4 have incentive systems without piece rates. National Industrial Conference Board, *Systems of Wage Payment,* New York, 1930, p. 5.

30. Incentive systems are described and analyzed by the following: C. Canby Balderston, *Profit Sharing for Wage Earners,* Industrial Relations Counselors, New York, 1919; *idem, Group Incentives,* University of Pennsylvania Press, Philadelphia, 1930; Geoffrey C. Brown, "The Bedaux System," *American Federationist,* September 1938; Charles W. Lytle, *Wage Incentive Methods,* Ronald Press, New York, 1938; National Industrial Conference Board, *ibid.,* and Studies in Personnel Policy, No. 19, *Some Problems in Wage Incentive Administration,* New York, 1940.

31. Beginning with 1914-1915 riders have been attached to Army, Navy and Post Office appropriation bills, specifying that no part of the appropriation "shall be

For many a nonunion employer, an incentive bonus plan offered a chance to offset union inroads without some of the handicaps which newly unionized establishments encountered. It met labor's demands for higher earnings without sacrifice of efficiency and without increasing production costs. Under certain conditions, which are now recognized and observed by enlightened management, there might be a likelihood that such plans would survive in unionized industries and become acceptable devices in collective bargaining.

Those conditions are virtually the same for union acceptance of rate setting under the piecework system. The first condition is that an incentive plan shall be a joint endeavor of management and union. One of the fundamentals for success of any production effort is employee interest and cooperation; and that cooperation becomes more complete by enlisting union support.

"Give workers as a formally organized group a say-so in setting wage rates, work standards, job evaluations, and in making time and motion studies, and they will produce all they can within the limitations of physical endurance, health, and fatigue; deny workers such a say-so and they will engage in restrictive practices out of self-protection."[32] Behind that statement is the philosophy that if individual cooperation is stimulated, group cooperation will yield greater earnings and output. Application of union management cooperation comes up later,[33] but a fundamental of it is the incentive for increased earnings.

---

available for the salary or pay of any officer, manager, superintendent, foreman or other person or persons having charge of the work of any employee of the U. S. Government while making or causing to be made with a stop watch or other time-measuring device a time study of any job of such employee between the starting and completion thereof, or of the movements of any such employee while engaged upon such work; nor shall any part of the appropriations made in this act be available to pay any premiums or bonus or cash reward to any employee in addition to his regular wages, except for suggestions resulting from improvements or economy in the operation of any government plant." . . . *Public Law 441*, 77th Congress.

32. Golden and Ruttenberg, *op. cit.*, p. 183.   33. See. Chap. 11.

Chapter 7

HOURS OF WORK

FOREMOST IN THE MIND of one who takes a job is: "How much do I get?" Probably next in importance is: "How long do I work?" The answer was simple at the beginning of the industrial age. Hours of labor were alike for craftsmen and farmers: from sunrise to sunset.

Demands for shorter hours inspired some of the earliest recorded strikes. Philadelphia carpenters, who worked from six a.m. to six p.m. laid away their hammers and saws in 1791 and struck for an hour off for breakfast and another hour off for dinner. They didn't get their ten-hour day, nor did the next generation of carpenters, but the longing for less working time, such as they manifested, was a strong impetus to the American organized labor movement. And since this manifestation was a strong impetus, the story of how working hours became shorter is one of the best combined illustrations of how organized labor gains long-range objectives, how it adjusts short-range strategy and tactics, and how government aid is invoked in the winning of what hitherto had not been won through collective bargaining.

Not until the Civil War was the ten-hour-day goal in sight. It and other shorter working-hour goals were reached somewhat according to this schedule:

1. More than three generations passed before the ten-hour day and sixty-hour week became general; whereupon organized labor declared for an eight-hour day.[1]

2. One generation passed before the eight-hour day, forty-eight-hour week arrived; whereupon organized labor declared for a five-day week.

1. Allowing 33 years to a generation.

79

3. One-half generation passed before the five-day, forty-hour week became a national standard. Before this was achieved, came union labor declarations for a thirty-hour week.

This rough, but accurate-enough tally reveals some of the restless, fluid spirit of collective bargaining; after one target falls, the sights are raised at another. It also raises the question: Why did labor gain subsequent leisure time so much quicker than it won the ten-hour day?

Although technological advance is largely responsible, a partial explanation is that shorter hours were not pressed vigorously in collective bargaining negotiations until fairly recently. Otherwise, a different story would be told by the recorded causes of a half century of strikes and lockouts. In the years between 1886 and 1892, the fight for the ten-hour day was virtually won and the American Federation of Labor came out for the eight-hour day; working hours during that period were the sole or an important cause of 10 per cent of labor disputes. Between 1889 and 1903 the percentage was 13. Between 1916 and 1922, at the peak and over the crest of the eight-hour-day movement, the percentage was about 24.

Between 1933 and 1939, the NRA and its codes of shorter hours came and went, and there had been one year of the Fair Labor Standards (Wages and Hours) Act. Disputes over hours were less—some 17 per cent. But in 1937, the year before the Fair Labor Standards Act was passed and the Supreme Court upheld the Wagner Act, hours of work were a major factor in 32.2 per cent of industrial disputes, an all-time high.[2]

Shorter Hours Issues

Clearly, shorter hours became more of a fighting issue in the last quarter century. Progress was slow during most of the long battle for the ten-hour day because the issue raised was very

2. Percentages for strikes involving hours in the years between 1886 and 1937 are from H. A. Millis and Royal Montgomery, *The Economics of Labor,* McGraw-Hill, New York, 1945, Vol. 3, pp. 700-01. The percentages are medians of the percentages for each year within the five year-groups, and they are computed from tables in "Strikes in the United States, 1880-1936" and "Analysis of Strikes in 1937," *Bulletin No. 651* and the May issues of the *Monthly Labor Review,* respectively, published by the Bureau of Labor Statistics of the U. S. Department of Labor.

largely a "moral" one. One side contended that the laboring man could not become an intelligent citizen if he had no time for family life, or for leisure, recreation, and self-improvement. Others resisted on the ground that "idleness"—their word, in this instance, for "leisure"—brings improvidence and "temptation." As long as the "moral issue" was not accompanied by other reasons and factors, cleavage was sharp and resistance was tenacious. But when the economic argument was raised and it was shown that more efficient work was done under shorter hours, a dent was made in the previously solid resistance by appeal to enlightened self-interest.

Gradually labor leaders discovered what they had not realized before: a shorter workday under most circumstances would necessitate more hands to do the same work, which, in turn, would mean more union members and stronger unions. If hours of work could be reduced without sacrifice of pay, support would be certain from the rank and file. Consequently, union leadership is on a solid basis with its membership, when it contends that work, being limited, should therefore be divided through shorter hours.

Proposals to spread work by means of shorter hours found support from sympathetic employers during times of depression, but the union position that work is limited, that there is just so much work to go around, ran counter to the long-range views of many economists. Failing to receive economist support on the "lump of labor" argument for shorter hours, union leadership stressed after World War I a theory more acceptable to economists. This is the "rolling snowball doctrine": that higher hourly wages and wider employment through shorter hours increase buying activity, and that greater buying stimulates industrial production and in turn creates more employment. By a different argument, therefore, some economist sanction was won for the same but previously disputed purpose: fewer hours, more workers, greater union and bargaining strength.

Other union arguments aimed at employers also took a persuasive turn. Health advantages were stressed. Tired employees meant sluggish and interrupted production. Shorter hours meant higher production per hour than long hours. And upholding this were studies showing that reduction of hours from ten to eight a day often brought greater output and lowered unit costs.

It would be an extravagant claim that collective bargaining alone brought about shorter working hours. Certainly, if one single factor in recent years had to be named, it would be technological advance. Nevertheless, there is evidence that by the early 1930's organized working people worked fewer hours than the unorganized. In 1931 the American Federation of Labor reported that approximately one seventh of the nation's union workers had attained the five-day week. Contrasted with this, a 1930 survey of the United States Bureau of Labor Statistics reported that the five-day week was enjoyed by only 5.2 per cent of factory workers, who were then largely unorganized.

Yet many factory employees on the five-day week were unorganized. In 1926, the same year the American Federation of Labor officially set its five-day-week goal, the nonunion Ford Motor Company went on a Monday-through-Friday basis. This move not only gave further impetus to the AF of L move, but it was followed by many sparsely and spottily unionized concerns. The nonunion five-day-week move appears to have been only partially influenced by what was accomplished by collective bargaining. Many industries during the early 1920's closed down Saturday afternoons until it was discovered more economical to work five than five and a half days. Keeping a plant open merely for a half day did not justify the expense.

Reducing Hours by Law

Before this, another event had momentous effect. In 1916, negotiations between the railway brotherhoods and the carriers collapsed over demands for a basic eight-hour day. As is customary in such affairs, the next move was a strike call and an attempted settlement of the issue through economic pressure. In this case the economic pressure went far beyond application upon recalcitrant carriers. With our entry into World War I imminent, a threatened tie-up of the nation's transportation system was vastly more serious even than in normal times. What the brotherhoods failed to get written into a collective bargaining agreement, they now sought by applying pressure upon government to write into law. The result was the Adamson Act, the first federal law which standardized working hours throughout an industry, and the first notable success of organized labor to gain its ends through national legislation rather than through continued negotiation with employers. (Already most states had laws restricting working hours of women and minors and in some occupations.)

Seventeen years elapsed before the federal government again took a hand in setting labor standards. Under the National Industrial Recovery Act of 1933, the President would approve or pass upon maximum hours of labor, minimum rates of pay and other conditions of employment as written into NRA codes; where no agreements were reached, he could prescribe such labor standards. In 85.5 per cent of the codes, the forty-hour week was set up; of the remainder, half established higher and half laid down lower standards.[3] Although NIRA was declared unconstitutional three years later, and although NRA codes were frequently defied, the Blue Eagle had nevertheless given great impetus to the forty-hour week.

As union organization and recognition accelerated, the problem of longer hours in unorganized shops and industries became acute. Again, unions turned to government and sought through legislation the universal application of standards they had partly won through union recognition and bargaining. First, came the Walsh-Healey Act which requires the eight-hour day and forty-hour week of all companies holding government contracts. Next, came the Fair Labor Standards Act establishing a basic forty-hour week in all industries engaged in interstate commerce.

Standards for Working Hours

It is a widely held misconception that the federal Fair Labor Standards Act makes the forty-hour week compulsory in American industry. This law places no ceiling on working hours. It merely sets a standard and, with few exceptions, requires time-and-a-half payment for all hours worked beyond forty in one week. During depressions, production is so anemic that most in-

3. Millis and Montgomery, *op. cit.*, Vol. 1, p. 482.

dustrial work weeks are less than the law's standard. In more active times this standard encourages spreading of work, but when there is more work than there are workers to perform it within the standard week, whether in peace or the urgency of war, the forty-hour work week is knocked galley-west. The result is equivalent, for the time being, to a general wage increase.

Since time-and-a-half payment for more than forty hours' weekly work generally prevailed in collective agreements made before the Act was passed, the immediate effect of the Fair Labor Standards Act was to bring the same benefits to unorganized employees. Its far-reaching effect, however, is that while it protects what organized labor has already won in this field, it also limits the control of collective bargaining over standard hours and overtime payment.

One section of the collective bargaining agreement usually specifies the standard working day, number of hours in a work week, and rates of overtime pay. Obviously, that section depends upon the nature of the work and whether the industry involved engages in interstate commerce and consequently is under the federal Fair Labor Standards Act. Essentially the section is a reconciliation, free or reluctant, of the union aim for the most equitable division of available work and for more leisure among the most employees, with management's aim for hours and work weeks yielding the greatest output at lowest unit cost.

With few exceptions, a labor agreement's standard work week is not the maximum number of hours an employee shall work a week. A standard work week need not be the actual work week; and neither management nor union expects it to be. It is merely an anchoring device—with considerable rope. Workday standards vary from five hours or less for some railroad men (they may be on duty longer) to twelve hours and more for hotel workers, barbers and store delivery drivers (they may not be actually at work all that time) whose locally performed labors do not entitle them to the protection of federal laws on hours. The prevailing standard workday is eight hours.

About the most complicated of all daily standards is the railroad "run"—a sort of double standard of hours and mileage. To snatch a few examples from through-service schedules: a full day's pay for freight conductors is for a run of 100 miles or less completed in eight hours or less; for passenger engineers and firemen, a run of 100 miles or less in five hours or less; for passenger conductors and trainmen, 150 miles in seven and one half hours or less. Overtime is figured when either runs or hours are exceeded. Because some railroad speeds from which standard runs were figured were slower than they are now, it is possible for a railroad man to be paid for hours he did not work. Examination of annual earnings, however, shows no exorbitant pay from this feature; and if it should, the chances are that the loudest protests would come from the high-bracket man's fellow employees.[4]

Aside from some continuous-operation industries, the usual prewar collective bargaining standard was the forty-hour week. There were numbers of exceptions, as there are to almost any generalization about labor agreements. A thirty-hour week was standard for Pacific Coast longshoremen and a few construction workers. A thirty-five-hour week prevailed in coal mining and in women's clothing. A thirty-six-hour week applied to plate glass makers, movie theater projection machine operators, and most Akron rubber workers. Some printing trades had a thirty-seven-and-a-half-hour week and some unions opposed further reductions. Standard work weeks of more than forty hours have been almost universal in trucking and in retail and service trades. And after a year of war, government decrees raised the work week in some war industries to forty-eight hours.

Ever since the basic forty-hour week became federal law, the thirty-hour week was not strongly pressed outside of formal union pronouncements, and this only as an emergency depression measure.

Work Sharing and Seniority Problems

When hard times or slack seasons come to an industry, either the number of workers must be reduced (which means layoffs and unemployment) or the work available must be shared (which means reduced hours and less pay for all). This dilemma falls

4. How Collective Bargaining Works, pp. 346-51.

more heavily upon unions than upon employers, for usually the rank and file has conflicting ideas about which choice to make. If the attempted solution is layoffs and the customary principle prevails that the last to be hired shall be the first to go, the older men are protected and the first casualties are younger workers from whose ranks come unionism's most aggressive members.[5] If there are no layoffs and work is shared, the burden falls heaviest upon older men with more mouths to feed.

Considerable bitterness over this issue between older and younger men is reported in the railroad brotherhoods.[6] In printing trades, where unionism is of even longer standing than on the railroads, various arrangements for sharing the work during the depression "showed widespread recognition that brotherliness required more than mere protection of seniority rights."[7] In some steel plants, younger men forced work sharing even to the point of one or two days' work a week, rather than permit layoffs. In other steel locals where older men controlled, the pendulum swung the other way.[8] Some other newly organized industries have placed limits below which work cannot be shared. Early agreements in the rubber industry provided for unlimited work sharing. Matters reached such a stage where one could do better on WPA. The plan was derided as "share the misery" and was changed to provide for layoffs when the work to be shared amounted to twenty-four hours a week or less.[9] For five years similar provisions have been written into some electrical manufacturing and glass agreements.[10]

In the garment trades the slack-season custom is equal division of all work among all workers. Particularly in the men's clothing industry, where overtime is forbidden, unlimited work sharing appears to have drawn people from other trades and given the industry more workers than it can support.[11] An even more serious problem was faced in the building construction industry where

5. Chap. 8 discusses layoff and seniority problems.

6. *How Collective Bargaining Works*, pp. 355-56.

7. *Ibid.*, p. 149.   8. *Ibid.*, p. 554.   9. *Ibid.*, p. 659.

10. *Ibid.*, p. 797; Bureau of National Affairs, *Collective Bargaining Contracts*, Washington, 1941, p. 512.

11. *How Collective Bargaining Works*, pp. 420-21.

some share-the-work devices were viewed as adding to the situation they were designed to relieve.[12]

Thus it appears that no hard-and-fast principle of work sharing can be applied in collective bargaining. Work sharing has been a traditional policy of American organized labor, but the experience of some industries has shown that the practice can be carried too far; and that one way of meeting the problem is to resort to layoffs after working hours fall below certain limits.

Vacations With Pay

One of the latest newcomers among clauses in collective bargaining contracts is the annual vacation with pay, which appears to have originated outside organized labor. The paid vacation was a custom of the "front office" later applied to salaried clerical help and occasionally to the work bench. Generally it was a privilege which went with a salary and year-round employment. It was not applied to complicated wage schedules or when layoffs were usual, but during the 1920's it was included in personnel and employee welfare plans of many nonunion employers.

Unions handled the subject cautiously at first, regarding it as outside their objective of negotiated wages, hours and working conditions. Their attitude is typified by the designation "gratuities" long given to vacations by the Typographical Union. But what was once looked upon as a privilege has come to be deemed a right within the last half-dozen years, and paid vacations now figure in union collective bargaining programs.

In 1940 the Bureau of Labor Statistics reported that one quarter of all organized labor was covered by paid vacations.[13] Even more revealing of unionism's adoption of vacations are developments in the automobile industry. In 1938 vacation clauses were written into 19 per cent of the contracts. In 1941, 58 per cent of the contracts covered vacations.[14] This is noteworthy because employ-

12. *Ibid.*, pp. 210-11, 213, 223.
13. "Vacations With Pay in Union Agreements," *Monthly Labor Review*, November 1940. See also National Industrial Conference Board, *Vacations With Pay for Wage Earners*, New York, 1935.
14. *How Collective Bargaining Works*, pp. 624-25.

ment in automobile plants was rarely continuous. The prevailing tendency in auto plants was to grant vacations during the layoff season. In some other industries, notably electrical manufacturing, prewar vacations were taken by the whole force at the same time, thus enabling a plant to shut down and conduct inventories. Generally, however, vacations are staggered.

Three forms of vacation pay are encountered in bargain agreements: full pay for the one- or two-week vacations; a percentage of the employee's annual earnings; or a fixed lump sum. Whether the vacation is one week or a fortnight usually depends upon length of service. One week off may require from two to five years of service. Two weeks off, as in the rubber industry, may begin with five years' service; in some steel contracts a fortnight's vacation is not authorized until after fifteen years. With so many shadings, it is not surprising that the vacation picture is complex. In the automobile parts plant collective agreements there are ninety-eight different vacation plans.[15]

Issues and Problems of Overtime

Standardized work weeks, sharing the work, paid vacations—all these have their problems, but the thorniest subject of all is extra pay for overtime. For ten years after the depression began, overtime was merely one of many topics in industrial relations. Then World War II broke out. War industries mushroomed, need for skilled workers in some trades became acute, and the problem of how to spread enough work for all dissolved into a new one: whether there were enough workers to do the work.

The threat of war drew nearer to a rearming United States, then war came, and overtime became one of the most heatedly discussed—and least understood—topics of the day. First, was a widespread misconception that federal law limited the hours a man might work, or that American labor was not working, and would not work, more than forty hours a week and consequently was delaying war production. Next, when the fact was realized that production workers were on the job regularly for forty-eight, fifty-four and even sixty hours a week, the query arose of why

15. *Ibid.*, p. 624.

there should be overtime pay for regular work. Finally, as war production moved to a three-shift-a-day and six- and seven-days-a-week basis, questions were more insistent. A tank or a gun or an airplane turned out on a Saturday is no different from one turned out on a Tuesday—why should Saturday's work be paid more, at overtime rate?

With infinite variation, questions like these were raised. They came from persons plainly puzzled and seeking information, or from those who feared that war efforts were sagging, or from honest doubters of labor's patriotism, or from calculating anti-unionism, sometimes part of a concerted move to amend or repeal the Fair Labor Standards Act.

Out of the polemics and prejudice, one thing was apparent: that the overtime issue had gone far beyond the field of collective bargaining. But it is doubtful whether many unionists realized that this was a natural outcome when a matter is removed, even partially, from negotiation and written into statute. It is also doubtful whether many employers who sought repeal of the Fair Labor Standards Act reflected whether excess overtime in abnormal times was not preferable to further tinkering with wage scales.

Temporarily disregarded, therefore, was the relationship between overtime and collective bargaining. For instance, although federal law does not limit overtime, a few unions do. Employees in some union printing shops may not work more than their standard hours if competent substitutes are available. Stereotypers and printers make overtime cumulative, to be canceled at some future time by layoff in favor of a substitute. In a number of garment trade agreements overtime is prohibited outright.

Most industries do not have such drastic overtime restrictions. They may have peaks and hollows of productivity, like automobiles and radios, which call for either overtime or for lower hours; and overtime can't be predicted in such occupations as railroading, where locomotives may break down and extra sections must often be run. In most industries, too, neither employers nor employees favor complete prohibition of overtime work. Almost anyone who works doesn't mind picking up extra money, and many a union favors lower work weeks because of the overtime pay they would bring to its members. Most employers agree that overtime should be kept at a minimum and that it warrants extra pay; and they don't like prohibited overtime because they would have to hire and train more help in an emergency. On the other hand, it is sometimes less expensive to hire and teach new employees than to pay overtime. An employer's cost sheets generally can tell him where this point is reached; and there is some evidence that the overtime problem has spurred many an employer to greater efficiency in his plant.[16]

Calculating Overtime

Where does overtime begin? Labor contracts with Akron rubber companies set a six-hour day and a thirty-six-hour week as standards, then "in emergencies" allow forty hours of work within a week at regular overtime rates. Such an arrangement gives management forty-hour weeks for peak production while the union does not have to alter its thirty-six-hour-week standard.[17] But how long does an "emergency" last without becoming a regular practice? How long may peak production continue without becoming normal production? There have been strikes over such questions. Mass production industrial management contends, in effect: "Give us flexible working hours; then we can keep the same force in operation in peak and slack periods." Unions reply: "Flexible working hours undermine our standards. If your production were planned properly, it would not have such peaks and valleys."

Also, when does a shorter working-hour standard become merely a device to secure a general wage increase? What is the meaning of a standard work week which is rarely observed in practice? A situation like Akron in reverse image develops out of

16. A matter closely related to working hours and overtime adjusted through collective bargaining was the haphazard custom of ordering extra people to report for work, then keeping them waiting, idle and without pay, for some emergency. The practice was not universal, but it caused far more employee resentment than was caused by many momentous issues. Thus it is that some labor agreements require a guarantee of two or more hours' pay to compensate those who are not put to work. In some industries, notably railroads and printing, the guarantee is a day's pay. Such provisions appear to have benefited both sides. They removed a just complaint and encouraged more efficiency among departmental supervisors and others who make up daily work schedules.

17. *How Collective Bargaining Works*, p. 646.

the thirty-hour week of Pacific Coast longshoremen. They have a basic six-hour day with fixed starting and closing hours. Long-shore work performed outside these hours is overtime. Their standard hours are rarely their normal working ones, for long-shoremen handle freight at all hours of the day and night; and employers complain that frequently overtime makes up 40 per cent of their weekly pay rolls.

Such an exceptional case illustrates the wide differences in work-ing-hour and overtime standards. Still more variety was found in agreements which laid down two scales of overtime payment. Most pre-World War II agreements in the automobile industry stipulated overtime at the federal standard of time and a half; but for Sunday and holiday work the overtime rate was double pay. In plants where the twenty-four-hour day and the six- or seven-day week prevail, unions have sought to vary the shifts so that all may take advantage of the week-end overtime pay. This raises the question whether, in some cases, overtime is not as much a penalty as a bonus payment. On the other hand, where double time was allowed for Sunday and holiday work (this was before wartime government decree banned double time) have come com-plaints that this device encouraged Monday absenteeism; having received two days' pay for one Sunday's work, the temptation was to take another day off.

Viewing overtime as a whole, experience points to the advan-tage of an hours-per-week standard between depression limits and peak production, with extra overtime payment in place of an im-mediate rise of wage rates. Experience has not wholly resolved these questions: What is a proper balance between production and leisure? How may these balances be adjusted or stabilized for prosperous or hard times, for labor shortage or work shortage, and for peace or war? And how far will government set other labor standards that were laid down and adjusted by collective bargaining?

Chapter 8

JOB SECURITY

ONCE A MAN HAS A JOB, knows how much he will be paid and what his working hours are, his next immediate question is, "How long can I keep the job?" He turns from present to future and to thoughts of security. The longer he holds that job, the stronger those thoughts become. When he grows older, he wants protection against displacement by younger men. If the working force must be reduced, he probably believes that the last to be hired should be first to be laid off. If the working force is increased or if there are vacancies, he wants a chance for promotion. If he belongs to a skilled trade, he doesn't want it "so filled up that there's not enough work to go around." If he has worked many years for the same employer, he believes that he's of more usefulness than some beginner and that his long years of service merit special consideration. And at all times he wants protection against unfair discrimination and unjust discharge.

A union which neglected such questions would not hold its members long and eventually would lose recognition as bargaining agent. An employer who disregards them is almost sure to have a discontented working force, split by personal feuds, and unwilling to work together. Hence the attempt in writing a collective bargaining agreement to lay down rules for hiring, promotion, transfers to different departments, layoffs, discharges, and entrance to the trade.

These rules are sometimes referred to as "job control." The phrase makes many a nonunion employer see red by its implication that the union seeks to dictate these arrangements or to have them under its direction. Few unions have anything approaching complete control, but certain procedures for hiring, firing and layoffs have been worked out by agreement. Under collective bargaining the employer has lost the privilege of being as arbitrary or as ornery as he chooses in such matters. Both agreement and law, federal as well as in many states, prevent him from discharging employees for union activity. Also, depending upon the amount of union recognition he has accorded (see Chapter 4), his choice of workers may be limited to union members—or he may agree either to urge new employees to join unions or to require them to do so.

Only under rare forms of the closed shop is an employer's choice of workers completely limited. However, most maritime jobs are not filled by choice but from hiring halls by strict rotation.[1] The efficiency or teamwork of crews brought together by this method is questionable, but the possibility is removed of favoritism of one man over another either by employers or by union officials. That possibility does exist when vacancies are filled by members chosen by a union local's business agent, as has been the practice of the Chicago local of motion picture machine operators.[2] A ruthless official can take advantage of this system to reward favorites and penalize his annoyers, while a weak official may be intimidated enough to give preference to strong cliques. Even though the opportunity may be more frequent than the practice, such situations do not safeguard working people against unfair discrimination, which is one of the objects of collective bargaining. The power to discriminate has been merely transferred from employer to union official.

Without some form of "control" of the labor supply in its field, unionism has little bargaining power and little to offer in collective bargaining. Usually it seeks that control by organization, by signing up members and by pressing for closed- or union-shop agreements. There is little or no evidence that union-employer bargaining increases the labor supply, but union policies in many cases raise the number of employed—through work sharing and by limitations on hours. Some craft unions go to other extremes. They seek to protect the jobs of their skilled members by "control of entrance to the trade." They may hold down the numbers of

1. *How Collective Bargaining Works*, p. 937.   2. *Ibid.*, p. 834.

union members; they may impose high initiation fees, a practice more notorious than prevalent; and they may limit the number of apprentices in trades where this earn-while-you-learn system continues.

The Decline of Apprenticeship

Apprenticeship is a holdover from old handicraft days in skills which require long training.[3] It does not figure to any extent in mass production, hence industrial unions are little concerned with it. It is, however, a concern of highly skilled crafts, and their unions usually demand a limiting ratio of apprentices to full-fledged craftsmen (journeymen). Because the war found us with a serious shortage of skilled workers, the question naturally arose whether limitation of apprentices by collective bargaining had an important part in creating this shortage.

But such restrictions were not sudden. They had been applied in the printing industry for eighty years,[4] and for the last forty they had been familiar clauses in many agreements. Had these agreements been directly responsible for holding down the number of apprentices, one would have expected to find fewer youngsters learning trades in union than in nonunion shops. Only a few of such disproportions came to light. Most comparative figures showed a situation quite the opposite—union apprentices in proportion to journeymen were more numerous than nonunion ones.[5]

The number of apprentices has declined over the years. Operations in industry after industry became wholly or partially mechanized and displaced highly trained skills. Also, a boy had little incentive during depression years to spend from three to five years learning a trade in which jobs were scarce or which might become virtually obsolete. At present, the apprentice trades which require years to acquire are principally in the handicrafts.[6]

3. "A trade apprentice is a youth or young man who has contracted with the Company to spend a period of years (normally four years) learning a trade under a specific program of instruction." Agreement of Aluminum Company of America with Aluminum Workers of America (CIO).

4. *How Collective Bargaining Works*, p. 68.

5. Sumner H. Slichter, *Union Policies and Industrial Management*, The Brookings Institution, Washington, 1941, pp. 32-34.

6. *Encyclopaedia of the Social Sciences*, Vol. 2, p. 145.

There are many signs that apprenticeship does not meet the future needs of the industries in which it operates. Publishers and building contractors complain that union apprentice ratios, which vary from one apprentice to every four, or even to every fifteen, journeymen, fail to maintain a suitable labor supply. At the same time, few employers in these trades have taken on apprentices in numbers up to union quota limits.[7] They don't want the bother and expense of training when they have no assurance that apprentices will remain in their employ after completing training; and this appears to be the story in other apprentice trades. In some large cities schools for apprentices in building and printing trades are jointly supported by union locals and employers. By and large, these endeavors are the extent of union-management cooperation in training a future labor supply.

With other and more direct causes of the decline of apprenticeship, collective bargaining's part appears to have been not so much union restriction as joint indifference. The mere fact that employer-union bargaining is such a flexible process may be one deterrent to negotiators against taking up long-range problems. Moreover, most agreements with apprentice clauses are in craft industries which usually bargain locally; therefore, unless there is some standardization, a broad over-all program is difficult to chart. Some states have encouraged apprentice training, but not all; and that gap may be filled by the federal Apprenticeship Act of 1937, out of which came standards for apprenticeship agreements. Because some trades train apprentices for as long as five years, it is too early yet for complete information upon the results of this act; but one obvious effect is the general adherence of labor agreements' apprentice clauses to government approved programs.[8]

Restrictions on Membership

Other artificial restrictions upon the number of working members of a trade are high admission fees—some as high as $500. Sometimes they have the effect, and sometimes they are the result,

7. *How Collective Bargaining Works,* pp. 68, 211.
8. Some agreements in recent war production industries liberalized prewar apprentice quotas.

of a "closed" union. A New York City electrical workers' union gave "working permits" to nonmembers at daily or weekly fees; and applicants who were ready to pay the somewhat high initiation fee ($100) were occasionally told that no new members were being admitted.[9] The Chicago motion picture operators' union has been virtually closed to new membership since 1925. When there were more jobs than members could fill, it issued "permits" to nonunion operators for 10 per cent of their earnings.[10] Flagrant inflations of local union treasuries occurred in army cantonment construction in the East between 1940 and 1941 when neighborhood locals assessed out-of-town job hunters high initiation fees.

Such abuses are possible under some circumstances among some craft unions and generally among boss-ridden unions. Industrial union fees and dues are generally low, a dollar a month being the usual dues. High dues and initiation fees have provoked extravagant generalizations and fixed beliefs that the evils are general and that they lead out of collective bargaining. But it is beyond the scope of collective bargaining, for instance, to curb certain monopolistic practices of commerce and industry. Those practices have been brought under public restriction and regulation. When like situations develop under labor organization, their correction, if not self-administered, also rests largely in the hands of the public.

Yet some union-management agreements put restrictions upon activities of closed unions. In return for employer acceptance of closed or preferential shops, some unions agree to accept new members. According to a Chicago men's clothing agreement, "the doors of the union shall be kept open for the reception of non-union workers. Initiation fees and dues must be maintained at a reasonable rate and any applicant must be admitted who is not an offender against the union and who is eligible for membership under its rules."[11] A few agreements grant to impartial chairmen the power to lower union initiation fees and assessments they may deem excessive; and the actors' union, Equity, pledges not to raise initiation fees without approval of theater managers.

9. Slichter, *op. cit.*, p. 69.
10. *How Collective Bargaining Works*, p. 837.   11. Slichter, *op. cit.*, p. 72.

Limitations on the Right of Discharge

Another form of job security is protection against arbitrary and capricious discharge. An employer's right to fire is no longer absolute and unquestioned, and under some agreements union approval is required before an employee may be dropped.[12] In general, unions seek protective clauses which specify that a discharged employee must be given due notice, that he must be told the reason for his dismissal, that he must have a chance to be heard and to appeal, and that he must be redressed for unjust discharge. Appeals are usually handled through procedures followed for grievances and described in Chapter 10; a few go directly to arbitration.

Many agreements list causes "sufficient" for discharge. In a few cases, causes are not specified in agreements but in shop rules or union "laws." Under the stereotypers' "law" in the printing trades an "adjudged incompetent" may demand a mechanical test under supervision of his union.[13] Most frequent dismissal grounds covered by agreements are incompetence, glaring recalcitrance or misbehavior, and reduction of the working force. And in closed- and union-shop agreements are found phrases like these: "Persons losing their membership in the Union shall not be retained in the employ of the Company."[14]

In plants and shops where collective bargaining is no longer new, discharges seldom become burning issues. Both men and management are so used to negotiation and adjustment of differences that unreasonable dismissals and overzealous union backing of men let out for cause are rare. But in recently organized industries where militancy and mutual distrust run high, conditions arise under which unions have virtual veto power over dismissals. Under Akron rubber union-employer agreements, all disciplinary discharges are subject to appeal; and some locals have been so aggressive that it was almost impossible for management to dismiss an employee except for theft or drunkenness.[15] Here is evi-

12. Bureau of National Affairs, *Collective Bargaining Contracts,* Washington, 1941, p. 186.   13. *How Collective Bargaining Works,* p. 91.
    14. From agreement of June 20, 1941, between Ford Motor Company and United Automobile Workers of America (CIO).
    15. *How Collective Bargaining Works,* p. 667.

dence of arbitrary power of discharge being succeeded by arbitrary power in the other direction.

This is also evidence that the atmosphere in which collective bargaining is conducted is frequently more important than what the collective bargain provides. Contrasted with Akron's stormy climate is the mutual understanding by union and management of dismissal problems in the hosiery industry. The union refuses "to support inefficiency," and the agreement recognizes the employer's "free exercise of the right to employ or discharge any worker in accordance with the necessity of his or its business." Protection for the discharged employee is a stipulated right to appeal to the impartial chairman. So well has this feature worked out that rarely are more than two or three dismissal cases appealed in a year.[16]

But whether collective bargaining is stormy or serene, its general effect has been to cut down discharges and, by that much, to add to working people's security. In some automobile plants, dismissals were one third of what they were before management and union got together and signed a compact.[17] Where discharges are subject to appeal or some form of ratification, as frequently occurs among large plants or powerful unions, there is a strong deterrent against action except in clear-cut cases. Largely, as a result, the tendency in big industry is to take away from foremen and other subordinates unregulated power to discharge and to place it with higher and more centralized authority.

The Dismissal Wage

Collective bargaining gives a worker some measure of protection against unjust and unexplained discharge. He has no protection against unavoidable discharge for causes which neither he nor his employer can control—but he may be cushioned against it; and in this sense the dismissal wage, otherwise known as separation pay, is a form of security.

Separation pay is a comparatively new clause to labor agreements. It has been relatively rare, and the somewhat spotty figures

16. *Ibid.*, p. 461.
17. *Ibid.*, p. 622.

on it probably do not reveal its true extent.[18] It appears to have grown out of employer pension plans and was awarded to employees of long service who, because of reorganization or technological displacement, were let out before they became eligible for pensions. In the late 1920's the garment trades adopted the device in some agreements. In the middle 1930's railroad brotherhoods negotiated allowances and lump-sum settlements for employees who lost their jobs through consolidation of railway lines. The lump-sum payments were from one to twelve months' pay, depending upon length of service. The allowance, known as "coordination allowances," ran from a half year to five years and comprised 60 per cent of average pay for the year preceding the consolidation.[19]

Greatest employment of dismissal pay is in agreements which the Newspaper Guild negotiates with publishers. The compensation is cumulative at the rate of one week's pay for service ranging from six months to a year.[20] Under such an arrangement, the dismissal wage provides greater insurance against discharge for older employees; the longer they remain employed, the more expensive it is for the employer to let them out.

Preferment—by Seniority or Ability?

Although one of organized labor's aims through collective bargaining is to prevent unfair discrimination, abolition of all preferment is not sought. Unions claim preferment when they demand the closed shop; and questions come up in most business and industrial operations which only preferment can settle. Who shall be promoted? Who shall be transferred? When times are hard, who shall be laid off first? When business improves and more help is needed, who gets preference in rehiring?

Out of these questions arises an issue which is not so heatedly discussed as the closed shop, yet perplexes both union and management. That issue is whether preferment shall be according to ability or seniority.

18. WPA National Research Project, *Trade-Union Policy and Technological Change*, 1940, p. 102.
19. Slichter, *op. cit.*, pp. 132-35.
20. *How Collective Bargaining Works*, pp. 115-16.

Seniority, or length of service in a given industrial unit usually figures in layoffs, rehirings, promotions, transfers and demotions. Its application may be on a company or plant basis, on a departmental or some other plant unit basis, on an occupational basis, or it may be a combination of some of the foregoing. However seniority is applied, labor leaders declare it their worst headache.

Seniority is a comparatively recent issue. Although it long existed on the railroads and in some printing trades, where it is known as "priority," it did not come prominently to the fore until the layoffs and technological displacements of depression days. It was never much of a problem in small shops, but when free collective bargaining reached big mass production industries, where hundreds of employees were laid off at a time, job security through some such measurement as seniority became of dominating importance in labor relations. Long experienced labor relations negotiators assert that under normal conditions no other matter is so important to rank-and-file union membership.

Employers are more willing for seniority to govern layoffs than promotions. They strongly maintain that, in general, usefulness and ability and not seniority should determine who should be advanced and who should be laid off. That, union men reply, makes possible employer favoritism, likewise discrimination against union members. The only true job protection, they say, is seniority; the last to be hired should be the first to be laid off. However, this contention is not unanimous among union membership. When hard times come, younger members favor share-the-work devices; older men prefer layoffs beginning with those at the bottom of seniority lists.[21]

21. Of an examination of 400 union agreements made between 1935 and 1939, 110 specified no layoff procedure, and 110 provided for some form of seniority. In 120 agreements some form of work sharing was laid down, which sometimes was combined with seniority. Of those 400 trade agreements, 200 stated no preference for rehiring, 105 stated preference for laid-off employees, and 78 required some form of seniority in calling men back to the job. No stipulations for promotion were made in 238 of the 400 agreements. Straight seniority, unaffected by other considerations, governed promotions in 30. Seniority with ability being deemed "sufficient" (typical of railway promotions) was laid down in 64. Forty-two agreements provided that, when ability was equal, seniority should govern. Only one agreement specified unqualified ability as sole determinant for promotion. See Slichter, *op. cit.*, tables pp. 106-07, 110-11, and footnote 18, pp. 150-51.

Thus, seniority is almost as contentious a subject in unionism as it is in collective bargaining. In newly oganized industries, young employees are generally the most militant members, yet under seniority rules they would be the first to be laid off. On the other hand, one surprising feature of organizing campaigns in the automobile industry was the number of older men joining up. They were attracted by union promises of greater job security in an industry where layoffs were frequent and retirement came at a relatively early age; and it appears likely that one benefit of union organization in automobile plants has been more security.

Limitations of Seniority

Both unions and employers occasionally exact concessions from the strict application of seniority. When they were turning out automobiles and not war goods, some auto plants compiled preferential lists of the more skilled and versatile workers who could carry on retooling and other adjustments during slack seasons before the appearance of new models.[22] Unions frequently seek exemption from normal seniority provisions for their shop stewards and committeemen, and some agreements specify that these officials be placed automatically at the head of seniority lists; otherwise, it is argued, these men might be the first casualties in a layoff, leaving union members without shop leadership. Sometimes this "weighted" seniority is reciprocal. An agreement with a large employer in the men's clothing industry specifies that "any exceptionally efficient worker or any especially valuable member of the union may be exempt from the rule of seniority."

Seniority seldom gives perfect satisfaction whether figured on an occupational, plant, or departmental basis. Company or plant seniority is far less usual than the departmental variety—and much more heartily disliked both by men and management. Under this system, a man of high seniority laid off in one department may "bump" or displace one of lower seniority in another department; the "bumped" man displaces another employee elsewhere, and so on, down the line. Thus, one layoff may cause many dislocations and a like number of dissatisfactions.

22. *How Collective Bargaining Works*, p. 617.

Displacement of one worker by another through seniority not only sets employee against employee in the same union; on the railroads it sets union against union. In times of layoffs, an engineer may "bump" a fireman who has been promoted from firebox to engine throttle, a conductor may displace a trainman, and the result is dislocation of seniority and ill feeling between the engineers' and firemen's brotherhoods and between the conductors' and the trainmen's brotherhoods.[23]

The railways are typical of strict seniority's application. The younger men go first when forces are reduced, and the resulting tendency is an elderly work force. When there are vacancies to be filled by promotion, seniority prevails, and the only merit consideration is a proviso, "fitness and ability being sufficient." "Sufficient" meaning "good enough," the result impairs efficiency.[24]

Resolving the Contradictions

In general, the seniority rule protects the worker against uncertainty and against discrimination, but it does not protect the employer against inefficiency. It encourages a steady labor supply, but an aging work force. It protects the long-service worker but at the expense of younger workers. It discourages ability and efficiency, and encourages the chair-warmer. It enables the employee to know where he stands, but it thwarts self-advancement.

These are some of seniority's simpler contradictions. A more complicated one is that seniority encourages a worker to remain with one plant or shop. If he moves, he loses seniority and if he gets another job elsewhere, he begins at the bottom of the list, no matter what his competence. Likewise, if for no fault of his own, the employer for whom he has worked goes under, all accumulated seniority counts for nothing. On the other hand, that very fact gives a worker greater interest in the continued success of the concern which employs him than he might have otherwise; and in times of labor shortages it is helpful to employers as a deterrent to job-changing.

A realistic approach to some of seniority's contradictions has been attempted in the steel and full-fashioned hosiery industries.

23. *Ibid.*, pp. 352-55.   24. *Ibid.*, p. 351.

In some steel plants a committee of company and union representatives weighs employees' competencies and lengths of services,
then prepares lists of promotion eligibles and of the order in
which layoffs shall be made.[25] Each employee then knows where
he stands; and by allaying the anxiety, born of uncertainty, such
procedure strengthens a worker's feeling of security.

Some full-fashioned hosiery labor agreements lay down ability
as the first requirement in determining promotions and layoffs.
When other things are equal, seniority determines. In a few
hosiery plants, management and shop committees work out ability
ratings together. When there is a vacancy to be filled by promotion, the five or ten employees best qualified are listed and the one
with the highest seniority gets the advancement.[26]

Such procedures take into account both the protection which
seniority gives and the incentive to efficiency which the merit
system fosters. They are examples of the contribution which enlightened collective bargaining can make to both the worker's
security and the employer's needs. They are likewise examples of
the still infant, but nevertheless promising, stage of union-management cooperation.[27]

25. *Ibid.,* p. 555.   26. *Ibid.,* p. 461.   27. See Chap. 11.

Chapter 9

WORK RULES AND TECHNOLOGICAL CHANGE

UNIONISM GREW and collective bargaining spread with the rise of the industrial age.[1] When machines displaced hands or hand tools, when various stages of the manufacture of an article were divided among many persons, labor operations became more complex and—sometimes because of that complexity—employment became more insecure.

A glass bottle blowing machine increased individual production 4,000 per cent. A continuous operation steel strip mill may turn out hundreds of tons a day instead of a few tons by hand-tending methods. A transcribed selection by one dance band may be played scores of times over many radio stations. These are typical examples of how the machine affects employment.

Technological advance is likely to be more rapid in expanding than in declining industries—and to cause less individual hardship. For the growing industry can command new or increased capital investment necessary for mechanical improvements. Nevertheless, the immediate effects of technological change upon workers and employment even in big industries are frequently unpredictable. In the rubber industry, the 1936 output of automobile tires and tubes was 90 per cent of the 1929 yield, but owing to new machinery and new processes, it was turned out by 50 per cent fewer workers.[2] In the steel industry, technical improvement was particularly rapid between 1935 and 1940. Major steel companies produced 10 per cent more with 7 per cent less labor than in 1937; and although labor costs in 1939 were the same as in 1936, wage rates were 25 per cent higher.[3]

1. See Chap. 1; also, *How Collective Bargaining Works*, p. 899.
2. *How Collective Bargaining Works*, p. 635.   3. *Ibid.*, pp. 510, 567-68.

One of the strangest results of technological advance came in the auto industry. Laborsaving devices cut down employment, but other mechanisms were introduced complicating car making and calling for more labor. One apparently offset the other, for man-hour productivity in 1938 was virtually what it was in 1929.[4]

Machines versus Men and Industries

No one relishes loss of a job. And when one loses his job through no fault of his own, he has natural resentment against the person or thing displacing him. When the agent of displacement is a machine, resentment is mixed with a sense of bafflement; man may compete against man upon something like equal terms, but man against machine is an unequal contest.

Such a contest in one form or another has long confronted working people. They may attempt to conquer the machine by refusing to work with it or by trying to prevent others from doing so. This is the tactic of obstruction. They may try to limit its use either through collective bargaining or by law. Also through collective bargaining or by law they may compel employment of a greater work force than normal conduct of operations warrants. These are tactics of restriction. Or workers may recognize the ultimate uselessness of opposing technological progress and may try to cushion the shock of the change—again through collective bargaining. This is the tactic of adjustment.

Such attitudes toward technological change do not belong solely to working people or to their unions. Employers and industries are often reluctant—or incapable—of further investment; and the desire to keep old equipment in operation as long as possible also checks technological advance. Likewise, they fear and fight displacement. Canal companies tried vainly to prevent the spread of railroads; later, railroads fought competing motor trucks and busses which cut into their revenues. Newspapers warred on radio, and established radio stations tried to ward off the newer frequency modulation. Silk manufacturers allied against rayon, and makers of hair nets stood with their backs to the wall against bobbed hair and bobby pins.

4. *Ibid.*, p. 610.

Employers denounce unions for make-work tactics and for restrictions upon output—practices which are encountered in their own group. A federal law, for instance, helps glass manufacturers by prohibiting the sale or refilling of empty liquor bottles; and manufacturers of almost everything sought protective tariffs. Even government limited production, as when farmers were paid not to produce cotton and wheat. Wherefore, problems which technological displacement places upon collective bargaining cannot be understood if it is assumed, as it frequently is, that only labor organizations impose artificial restrictions upon methods and devices which give greater service at less cost.

Nevertheless, in peacetime, in many an industry, an employer who recognizes a union and negotiates an agreement with it lets himself in for the virtual certainty that installation of labor-saving devices or of more efficient production methods will be questioned and in some cases opposed by the union. And this may be regardless of whether he is arbitrary or considerate toward his working force. Instance after instance can be cited of where unions have stood in the way of technical progress, of where they have "made work" by limiting output or by insisting upon larger work crews than necessary.

Union Attitudes

Instance after instance also may be cited of where union leaders recognized the futility of trying to stop progress, yet were compelled to try it by their rank and file. A man who spent years learning and practicing a skilled trade only to be displaced by a machine can't take much comfort in the thought that more machine production lowers costs, increases demand, and ultimately means more employment. What may mean more jobs in the future means no job at all in the present. It is like losing a leg from diabetes—then being told that sometime diabetes will be controlled and no legs need be lost.

The general attitude of union leadership toward technological advance in time of peace resembles that of some employers toward collective bargaining. These employers announce their approval of the principle of collective bargaining—but they don't like the spread of unionism. President Green of the American Federation of Labor has declared that the American labor movement "welcomes" the machine.[5] President Murray of the Congress of Industrial Organizations has expressed himself as "wholeheartedly" in favor of "every known device that will speed up production and give more production." Also, he thought it "the bounden duty of American industry to see to it that when a machine is put into industry, no man or no woman is laid off."[6] About the same time he wrote, "in the absence of universal collective bargaining, Congressional regulation of the introduction of large technological changes is necessary."[7]

Quite understandably, labor views technological change in peacetime with uneasiness, for whatever the long-range views of its leaders, a union faces immediate and unwelcome problems.

Tactics of Obstruction

Consider a union composed of skilled workers. It succeeds in a fairly thorough organization of its occupation and becomes strong enough to negotiate favorable labor agreements with employers. Then a machine is perfected which makes its members' skill useless. Attended by one factory hand instructed to watch a few dials and to manipulate a lever or two, the machine may perform in a few minutes as much as the union man did in a week. Shoe machinery displaced old-fashioned shoemakers. The teletype virtually eliminated dot-and-dash Morse telegraph operators. Automatic bottle-making machinery did away with the need for the skilled glass blower and his phenomenal breath control.

Under such circumstances, what shall a union do? If it is powerful, if its rank and file has a highly skilled trade and if its membership is thoroughly roused, it may choose to fight. It may try to prevent the machine's use. It may forbid its members to use the machine or to work in any plant where the device is installed. The

5. Addressing the Bond Club of New York City, March 1929. See *Bridge Men's Magazine,* April 1929, p. 228.
6. Addressing the 1940 Convention of United Mine Workers. See *Proceedings of the Thirty-Sixth Constitutional Convention,* 1940, Vol. 1, p. 287.
7. Philip Murray, *Technological Unemployment,* SWOC Publication No. 3, 1940, p. 39.

National Window Glass Workers' Union adopted these tactics before World War I, when window glass blowing machines came out. By 1927 there were more and better machines but the NWGWU was no more, having literally forbidden its members out of jobs.[8] Blind hostility of union lamp chimney workers to machine methods eventually lost to them what was left of the industry.[9] For eleven years, union cigar members fought improved methods of making cigars and lost nearly half their membership.[10]

Although a head-on collision between the hand worker and the machine would seem to be like opposing tanks with bows and arrows, the clash is not immediately suicidal. Union locals of painters in many cities have outright prohibition against use of the spray gun.[11] New York bricklayers still use trowels for spreading mortar.[12] But the general record of experience is that continued opposition to laborsaving devices results either in loss of union strength or in gradual cessation of obstructive tactics.

Tactics of Restriction

Delaying actions rather than frontal attacks against technological advance are more widespread union tactics. These are attempts to curb laborsaving methods and they take the form of artificial restrictions designed to "make work," bans upon certain materials and upon extra manning of machines, and regulation of speed of operations or of output.

Bans and restrictions may be incorporated in labor agreements, or they may be union regulations or "laws" governing their members' working methods, or they may be written into government statutes or municipal ordinances. Outstanding practitioners of all three of these methods are unions in the building construction industry, which is an extraordinary combination of centuries-old handicrafts alongside of new and prefabricated materials and power-driven tools.

The security of old skills being challenged by modern innovations, building trade locals have set up all manner of restrictions

8. *How Collective Bargaining Works,* pp. 720-21.   9. *Ibid.,* p. 709.
10. Sumner H. Slichter, *Union Policies and Industrial Management,* The Brookings Institution, Washington, 1941, pp. 216-22.
11. *Ibid.,* pp. 210-11.   12. *How Collective Bargaining Works,* p. 214.

against laborsaving tools, practices and factory-prepared materials which would otherwise shorten the time they spend on a job. Some plasterers refuse to handle gypsum boards, and Boston plasterers limit the size of their hods. Bricklayers seek to ban hollow tile either by union regulation or municipal ordinance. In some cities all concrete must be mixed on the job. Painters try to persuade city governments to pass ordinances against the use of lead paints in spray guns. Milwaukee carpenters require all hardware to be fitted on the job. Glaziers' unions try to forbid off-the-job glass installation work. New York steamfitters demand all pipe cutting and threading to be done on the premises.

These are a few of a long catalogue of union restrictions in the building trades which do more than they should to make building expensive. Largely because of weakly organized contractors and of strong unions entrenched against change, technological advance has been obstructed in this industry.[13] Also adding to building costs is the fact that frequently these restrictions are by collusive agreement between unions and contractors and some of them have resulted in indictments under antitrust laws. If the remedy for this situation is more law, then legal processes will supersede collective bargaining processes; and courts, and not labor and management, would finally determine how wide a "fair" paint brush should be and how many bricks "reasonably" may be laid an hour.

Make-work rules and restrictions upon the use of laborsaving devices have been familiar practices of craft unions. They have not been so prevalent among industrial unions or in mass production because an industrial union, which includes many occupations, is not vitally concerned with the perpetuation of a single trade or craft.

The Fight Against the Speed-Up

Both craft and industrial unions, however, have warred upon speed-up of productive operations which they deem excessive. Sometimes the given reason for their opposition is to prevent slashes in the work force and to save jobs. Sometimes increased

13. *Ibid.*, Chap. 4.

productive speed is opposed on grounds of health and safety. This is a more persuasive argument, but when union action has blocked increased work loads, regardless of the motive, the effect is to maintain employment opportunities.[14] An unusual collective agreement fixes the ratio of employment to the growth of business. An agreement between New York City doll manufacturers and the Playthings and Novelty Workers, CIO, specifies ten additional sewing machines and operators for each $100,000 addition in annual business. If business falls off, on the other hand, no reduction in machines is authorized.[15]

A traditional union enemy is the stop watch. Labor long regarded it as the herald, if not the symbol, of speed-ups and additional work burdens; and largely through union pressure were passed federal laws prohibiting stop-watch measurements of employees in navy yards and government arsenals.[16] In recent years timing devices have been regarded with less disfavor. Hosiery and women's garment workers' unions clocked their members' operations, and there has been an increasing tendency toward joint time-and-effort studies by union and management.

Where there was no such cooperation in mass production industries, organized workers had their own tactics in combating real or fancied speed-ups. This was the slowdown, a familiar practice in the automobile industry. It may be union authorized or practiced by rank and file in defiance of union officials. A few labor agreements lay down discharge penalties for slowdowns; in others, the union agrees not to engage in them.[17] But, whether authorized or not, the slowdown is an elusive but restrictive tactic.

Tactics of Adjustment

Adjustment by organized labor to technical change involves more than the old maxim of professional politics, "If you can't lick 'em, join 'em." For the union has a rank and file whose jobs

14. WPA National Research Project, *Trade-Union Policy and Technological Change*, 1940, p. 41.
15. Bureau of National Affairs, *Collective Bargaining Contracts*, Washington, 1941, p. 362.
16. See Chap. 6, footnote 31.
17. Bureau of National Affairs, *op. cit.*, pp. 187, 516, 521.

are affected. Its members may be unwilling to master a new task —or if they do, the union may lose them as members. Consequently, many a union has negotiated with employers for the retraining of workers whose jobs have been eliminated by new processes. Examples of this are the old-fashioned printers who learned to operate linotypes, hand telegraphers who were taught the ways of the teletype, and streetcar motormen who were trained to operate motor busses.

In some industries, unions agree not to oppose new machinery and methods. This is the practice of CIO construction workers, as opposed to restrictive practices of AF of L building trades.[18] The first agreement which the United Automobile Workers negotiated with the Ford Motor Company recognized as "belonging solely to the company" the right to determine methods and processes of manufacture.[19] In the garment industry, in which sometimes 250 workers are involved in the making of one man's suit, unions pledge not to oppose new machinery or to restrict output—provided they have a part in planning the new techniques.[20] This involves recognition of production problems and union cooperation with the employer, which very well might be one of collective bargaining's greatest current contributions.[21]

Glass Union Policies

Outstanding for the variety of its object lessons in attitudes toward technological change is the glass industry, sections of which have gone through obstruction, restriction, and adjustment. Once the industry depended upon a highly skilled, highly paid and closely organized craft which was handed down from father to son. It became a mass production industry, composed largely of semiskilled machine-tending workers. Few industries are more thoroughly unionized. In few industries has collective bargaining been more successful and useful. And probably no other industry

18. WPA National Research Project, *op. cit.*, pp. 21-23.

19. Clause 13 of the agreement of June 21, 1941. In July 1942, the Ford Motor Company offered figures in support of its contention that individual productivity in its River Rouge plant has declined since a year ago, before the plant was unionized. See *The New York Times*, July 15, 1942.

20. Bureau of National Affairs, *op. cit.*, p. 531.

21. See Chap. 11.

shows so clearly the results of short-sighted policies and the benefits of far-seeing attitudes toward the machine and laborsaving
devices.

Glass workers' unions which tried to outlaw machines by for-
bidding members to operate them figuratively cut their own
throats. Union restrictions upon output, such as by Ohio Valley
bottle workers who stood around idle after performing a half-
day's quota, were revised to payment for performance.[22] When
bottle-making machinery was first introduced (1904) the Glass
Bottle Blowers' Association (despite its trade association name, it
is a union) decided upon adjustment rather than opposition to the
machine. It was not an easy or a popular decision. It meant transformation of an occupation and giving up experts' pay for factory-
scale wages. It meant keeping pace with a production revolution
in which individual output increased 4,000 per cent and unit
labor costs fell 97 per cent. In thirty-five years between 1904 and
1939, employment rose only 20 per cent, while the value of the
product increased 600 per cent.[23] Fourteen years after the bottle
blowers' union launched this policy, manufacturers of the bottle-
making machines were asking employers in plants leasing their
machines to cooperate with the union.[24]

Printing Unions and the Machine

The printing trades are an example of both adjustment to technological change and of continuance of make-work restrictions.
The appearance of the linotype in the late 1880's threatened to
displace large numbers of hand compositors. Instead of fighting
the machine, the typographical union in effect captured it by requiring its members to learn to operate linotypes and by instruct-
ing local unions to see to it that none but practical—and union—
printers were employed at the keys of the new contraptions. Typographical unions also impose limits upon the amount of type
which one operator may set during work periods.

Restriction of output, however, is a tradition in printing trades
unions.[25] Many of these restrictions and regulations of working

22. *How Collective Bargaining Works*, pp. 704-05.
23. *Ibid.*, pp. 684-86.   24. *Ibid.*, pp. 707-09.   25. *Ibid.*, p. 168.

conditions never reach the stage of collective bargaining but are imposed upon employers in the shape of highly detailed union "laws." The pressmen's locals insist upon having a say about the number manning a press crew; which was partially responsible for the migration of magazine printing plants from New York City.[26] Weirdest of all make-work rules in the printing trades is one governing the acceptance in newspaper composing rooms of advertising plates and of advertising matter which has been set in outside print shops. Under typographical union "law" this matter may be used, provided a duplicate of it has been set up in the newspaper plant—and discarded.[27]

There appears to be some justification for claims that unionization has been followed by greater efficiency in some plants.[28] But there is less justification for claims that while union make-work rules are uneconomic they have little influential effect, for this is virtual denial of the efficiency claim. However, although they may not "make" much work, printing "laws" are challenges to the collective bargaining process and are illustrative of the difficulty of lifting restrictions long after the motives for imposing them have gone.

Railroad Practice

Opposition of a somewhat different sort to technological change has been occasionally displayed by organized railroad labor. Probably no other group of employees in any industry has more legislative protection. The industry itself is regulated by the Interstate Commerce Commission. Employees have had their own labor relations act. They have had laws specifying full crews and regulating the length of trains, and some measurements of arriving at wage payments are a generation old and obsolete.[29]

Technological advance hit railroads hard before railroads themselves did a bit of streamlining. Hydroelectric plants decreased the use of railroad-borne coal. Oil heat, with the fuel conveyed long distances by tankers and through pipelines, also hit the

26. *Ibid.*, pp. 164-66.
27. This restriction corresponds to one in the musicians' union which requires the presence of union "stand-ins" when nonunion musicians perform over radio stations.
28. *Ibid.*, p. 177.   29. *Ibid.*, p. 350.

coal-carrying roads. Trucks, passenger busses and airplanes took toll of railroad freight and passenger business. In two decades, between 1920 and 1940, railroad employment fell from around two million to about one million. Then came a war which was a shot in the arm to railroad traffic and even the Erie declared a dividend. But both management and railroad labor for a long time were in change-resisting moods. Management was hidebound against improvements. Rail labor failed to make concessions that might help weak roads to get along. Though it is as mature as in any American industry, collective bargaining has done little toward rehabilitation of the industry.[30]

Jurisdictional Problems

Technical displacement tosses another unwelcome problem into union laps. Assume that a new process is developed in an industry and that the old workers have been trained to handle the new jobs. By encouraging them to learn a new occupation and in having helped to keep its members employed, the union may find that those workers are now claimed by another union. Two unions now claim the right to bargain for those retrained workers and the employer and employees are hamstrung by a jurisdictional row.

This may happen within one industry, or it may be that a new enterprise arises which is virtually a new industry and renders the old one at least semi-obsolete. During the 1920's streetcar lines in many cities began to be displaced by motor busses.[31] Whereupon arose the question: Were these bus drivers to be classed as chauffeurs, or were they still street railway men? And who should represent them—the International Brotherhood of Teamsters, Chauffeurs, Stablemen and Helpers, or the Amalgamated Association of Street and Electrical Railway Employees? In 1925 the AF of L decided that bus drivers employed by street railway com-

30. *Ibid.*, pp. 377-80.
31. Other technological problems figured in this situation. To meet bus competition, street railways cut their costs and sought operation of one-man cars. For a long time the union opposed one-man cars but yielded in the face of bus competition. And when street railways abandoned electric cars for motor busses, the problem arose whether to hire new bus drivers or to train their old employees.

panies belonged to the street railway union, but for eight years the teamsters refused to accept the decision.[32]

Interunion squabbles frequently arise when new materials come on the market. Appearance of glazed brick and hollow tile as a building material precipitated a long jurisdictional dispute between tile layers and bricklayers.[33] For years the carpenters' union and the woodworkers' union wrangled over which should represent mill operators of woodworking machinery. And for nearly a quarter of a century, carpenters and sheet metal workers quarreled over which trade should handle steel substitutes for wood building materials.[34]

Although such disputes are between unions, they have had injurious effects upon collective bargaining by jeopardizing agreements which employers might make with one or the other of the warring parties.

Conclusions

Industrial efficiency has been both hampered and spurred by collective bargaining. Beyond question, some unions obstruct technical progress. Equally beyond question, some employers improved their production methods to meet increased costs occasioned by union demands. It cannot be said, however, that the former is canceled out by the latter.

The record of collective bargaining shows the futility and the short-range attitude of restricting improved methods of work. It also shows some beneficial results of union acceptance of labor-saving methods. Union "laws" and federal legislation, however, tend to sidetrack collective bargaining processes.

On the whole, unionism has not convinced any large segment of management of its eagerness for technological advance. This may require a change in attitude on the part of organized labor as great as the one involved if employers in general should accept rather than oppose the spread of unionism.

32. Emerson P. Schmidt, *Industrial Relations in Urban Transportation,* University of Minnesota Press, Minneapolis, 1937, pp. 235-36.
33. William Haber, *Industrial Relations in the Building Industry,* Harvard University Press, Cambridge, 1930, pp. 235-36.   34. *Ibid.,* p. 159.

Chapter 10

THE ADMINISTRATION OF AGREEMENTS

A GROUP of tired corporation executives and union officials emerge from a hotel room or an office conference room. They have spent long hours of discussion, argument and persuasion which wore down knotty points and smoothed away rough edges of the contentions of both sides. Accord has been reached over wages, working hours and other conditions of employment—which has been reduced to writing and included in a signed agreement after measuring every word and microscopic meaning.

The document's preamble has a few eloquent expressions of purpose, "to promote and maintain harmonious industrial relations," and "to forestall industrial disputes." The agreement has clauses limiting strikes and lockouts which newspapers hail as harbingers of industrial peace. And so, in popular belief, the agreement marks a successful conclusion of collective bargaining until the time comes to negotiate a new agreement or to decide whether to continue the old one.

Instead of ending with the signing or extension of an agreement, however, the process of collective bargaining has really only just begun. All that goes on between the negotiators, and the terms which they so carefully work over, are only preliminaries; the continuing part of collective bargaining starts when an agreement goes into effect. The preliminaries may have suspense, drama of a sort, and an element of contest which draws public attention. That is the spectacular side of collective bargaining. The unspectacular and more lastingly important side is the day-in, day-out process which keeps labor and management from the public dispute stage.

Only a small proportion of labor disputes can be foreseen.

116

Reorganizations of production may occur, new piece rates may be needed; and no seniority clause ever written can cover every possible shift of employment. Honest differences of opinion may arise over the meanings or interpretations of some clauses in an agreement. In some newly organized industries where distrust prevails between union and management, one side may try to stretch and the other attempt to tighten agreement provisions. Or one or both sides may evade their promises. All of these, and more, may arise unexpectedly; consequently, union and management try to concur in ways and means of settling whatever differences, seen or unforeseen, which may arise during the life of an agreement.

Those ways and means are set forth in the agreements. They may be worked out in great detail in a "legislative" agreement, while an "administrative" agreement sets forth general principles and methods.[1] One may be said to emphasize the letter, the other the spirit, but regardless of their form, virtually all agreements prohibit strikes and lockouts until all specified means of settling disputes have been exhausted.[2]

Grievance Machinery

In the vocabulary of labor relations, the collective bargaining process which goes on after an agreement is signed is termed "administration of the agreement," which merely means how an agreement is carried out. Disputes are usually called "grievances," and their method of settlement is "grievance procedure," or "grievance machinery." But whatever the descriptive terms and whatever the methods for settling industrial disputes, they mean little without inclusion of the human element.

Granted that some specified methods of adjusting differences may be better than others, a more important factor is the state of mind of the disputants and their attitude toward each other. If both sides "would rather fight than eat," or if they aren't willing to make concessions to come to an agreement, or if they won't see the other side, then the most carefully planned and tested griev-

1. See Chap. 5.
2. According to a study of 7,000 union agreements. U. S. Bureau of Labor Statistics, Serial No. R. 1072, *Settlement of Grievances Under Union Agreements*, pp. 2, 10.

ance procedure is virtually useless. An agreement may prescribe a reasonable attitude, but it cannot compel it.[3]

Both legislative and administrative agreements provide for attempted settlements of grievances under joint union-management auspices, and a large proportion call for some form of arbitration if union and employer cannot clear up the dispute. But no agreement can be said to lay down grievance procedure unless it gives an employee a chance to appeal some decision or act a foreman has made relating to him.[4]

Participants to Grievance Procedure

An overwhelming majority of grievances arising in unionized shops and trades are over actions of foremen or over disputes and irritations between foremen and individual workers. Most disputes do not leave that stage; both management and unions wish complaints to be straightened out as close as possible to their place of origin, without calling in outsiders.

In virtually every organized shop, union members choose one of their number to represent them in adjusting grievances with the foreman. In the printing crafts, the "chapel" in each establishment elects a chapel chairman. In the garment trades a "shop chairman" may represent a whole floor. Gangs of from eight to twenty longshoremen, choose "gang stewards." In the automobile industry, there is one "shop steward" for every thirty to fifty workers. Steel and rubber workers either deputize shop stewards or elect from one to three grievance committeemen to represent entire departments of many hundred employees. Constuction work-

3. Extract from the "square deal" clause of the national agreement of the pottery industry: "In the interpretation and application of the wage agreement and uniform scale, both sides shall recognize the intent to establish a fair day's wage for a fair day's work; they shall not insist upon technicalities when the opposite meaning is clear; and when points arise not clearly and literally covered by the list, they shall decide upon merit, and shall not be governed by what the wage scale may specify for something similar. . . . An earnest effort shall be made to avoid the small and insignificant differences which result in an attempt to take advantage of some clause which may have not been just clearly worded to show what was the intent and understanding of the conference." Cited in *Labor Relations Reporter,* March 14, 1938, p. 8; see also *How Collective Bargaining Works,* pp. 557-58.

4. Bureau of National Affairs, *Collective Bargaining Contracts,* Washington, 1941, p. 256.

ers may have stewards to help the business agents, and the basic representative unit of coal miners is the "pit committee," normally of three men.

Whether committeemen, chairmen, or stewards, these front-line representatives of their fellow unionists have two important functions. First, they dispose of scores of petty complaints and disputes which, if allowed to accumulate, might be as serious a threat as a major dispute to smooth conduct of labor relations. Their second function is to detect and report violations in agreement terms. This, in union parlance, is "policing the contract."

Union organization in a mass production establishment generally parallels that of management. There is a steward on every shift for each shift foreman, a departmental steward for each general foreman, a divisional steward for each division superintendent —and so on up to top officers of the local—and even international officers for dealings with higher executives. Most agreements covering plants where the shop-steward system prevails give special recognition to stewards and committeemen. A large proportion confer upon a shop steward the highest seniority rating within his work group so that grievance handling may not be interrupted by layoffs; and under some clauses, a shop steward may be excused from regular work to carry out his special duties.[5] Some agreements forbid shop committee meetings on company time; others authorize them. In general, these variations reflect the degree of union-management mutual trust and cooperation.

In the building trades and in some other industries where work crews are small and scattered, shop chairmen and committeemen are supplemented by a business agent, who is either elected by members of the local or appointed by its officers. Unlike the shop committeemen, he is not an employee but a paid, full-time union official. A business agent has under his jurisdiction a number of shops and outside work jobs where he checks up on working conditions ("polices the contract") and handles grievances which have not been adjusted by shop committees. Under a few agreements, he has the right of unrestricted access to the shop. Under others, his entrance may be limited; he may be forbidden to inter-

5. *Ibid.*, pp. 253-87.

fere with production, or he must obtain employer consent before he visits a shop.[6]

The Processes of Settlement

The diversity and complexity of American industry require many types of grievance procedure. Complaints of workers in itinerant trades who move from one job to the next must be handled differently from disputes which arise in a mammoth industrial plant. Committees of employees may handle such matters, or they may be left to a union's business agent. Management may hire special executives to deal with union spokesmen, or all labor relations may be centered in the front office. Whatever the form of grievance procedure, it is usually the fruit of experience under given conditions.

Undoubtedly, collective bargainers should know what method is best suited to their problems; and anyone who tries to understand labor relations should know how and why some grievance procedures are applied. These procedures are described with considerable detail in the Twentieth Century Fund's volume of special studies of collective bargaining in representative industries, *How Collective Bargaining Works*. Their great variety may be confusing, but examination of them reveals common principles.[7]

Whatever the procedure employed, efforts are usually made to settle a grievance (1) on the spot, (2) on its merits, and (3) on time. If those three principles are not observed, the probable result is—more grievances.

There are many variations in handling grievances, but basically, the sequence of grievance procedure and appeal follows the following four stages.

First, a grievance is taken up with the foreman. It may be by the aggrieved employee, or by a union representative, or by both. The union representative may be a shop steward or committeeman,

6. *Ibid.,* pp. 583-90; U. S. Bureau of Labor Statistics, Serial No. R. 1072, pp. 3-4.
7. Testimony from another source: "We have weighed our experiences with small firms as against big ones to see if there are any basic differences. Our conclusion is that there are not. The principles of union-management relations in a small firm of one hundred and a big one of one hundred and twenty thousand workers is the same." Clinton S. Golden and Harold J. Ruttenberg, *The Dynamics of Industrial Democracy,* p. 82.

or it may be a grievance committee, or it may be the union's business agent. In some industries as high as 85 per cent of all grievances are settled at this stage usually orally.

Second, if the dispute cannot be settled with the foreman at its point of origin, it is considered by a union grievance committee and the superintendent of a department. The aggrieved employee may be out of the picture by now, his side of the case being handled by union officials; and lest he back down from his complaint and leave his representatives holding the bag, some unions require presentation of appeals in writing.

Third, company officials and higher union officers receive all cases which are not settled at the second stage. The company official may be the concern's industrial relations expert, or he may be the president or general manager or someone else from the front office. Union representatives may be heads of the local or top officers of the international.

Fourth, voluntary or compulsory arbitration.[8]

Almost every conceivable variant of these four stages may be found in labor agreement grievance clauses. Two or more steps may be made out of each stage. According to custom in some industries, notably soft coal and steel, the employee takes up his grievance personally with his foreman; then, if he fails to get satisfaction, a union representative or committee discusses the case with the foreman before higher authority is appealed to.

In large plants, the second stage may have variants. The general manager may try to settle the case with union officials before it reaches higher company and union executives. And if the union agreement is with an association or group of employers, as in coal and in some garment trades, another step in the third stage is reference of the dispute to a joint board of an equal number of union and employer members.

The Nature of Grievances

Are the most frequent grievance causes pay, or hours, or working conditions? Are they seniority and layoffs, or cases of discrimination?

8. Discussed in arbitration section, later in this chapter.

No such over-all information exists. Even if it did, probably few serviceable conclusions could be drawn because what might apply to one industry would not govern in another, or what might prevail in one industry at one time of the year would not be found in another season, and even what might apply to one plant in an industry might not hold in another shop.

In the militantly organized Akron rubber factories, working conditions lead the complaints, with wage protests next and seniority matters third.[9] In the automobile industry, likewise militantly organized, seniority difficulties prevailed during times of layoff and rehiring; but when a new agreement went into effect, or after a nonuniform wage increase, the chief grievances were over job classification and wages.[10] In the printing industry, seniority leads the list, with more grievances over the manning of machines than over wages and overtime pay.[11] Seniority first and wage adjustments second were leading grievances in glass and electrical manufacturing.[12] On the other hand, the first grievance of unionized Illinois soft coal miners was over pay schedules with discharge and discipline trailing far behind.[13] Likewise, on railroads, pay rates lead the grievance list with disputes over working time, discipline and allegations of violation of contract coming next in order.[14]

Despite these variations, seniority appears to be the leading grievance in mass production industries.

The Human Elements

Unionization brought considerable dislocation in mass production. Top management adjusted itself to the new conditions quicker than subordinates. Unions found themselves with negotiated agreements but with little disciplined rank-and-file leadership cap-

9. *How Collective Bargaining Works*, p. 675, Table 5.
10. Supplementary information from W. H. McPherson, author of Automobiles chapter, *ibid*.
11. Supplementary information from Emily Clark Brown, author of Book and Job Printing chapter, *ibid*.
12. Supplementary information from Milton Derber, author of Glass and Electrical Products chapters, *ibid*.
13. *How Collective Bargaining Works*, p. 245.
14. *Ibid.*, pp. 262-63.

able of fulfilling them. Provocations by representatives of both sides in the shops increased grievances. The process of training union and management officials in handling grievances is a slow one.[15] In newly organized industries it may take months and even years for subordinate leadership and shop committeemen handling complaints to adopt the collective bargaining spirit shown by higher union and corporation officials.

The man who signed up the most union members or was otherwise active during an organizing campaign does not necessarily make the best shop steward. Nor is an old-fashioned "what-I-say-goes," foreman the most reasonable adjuster of grievances. Both union officials and top management discover a few chickens home to roost when veteran combatants of the "fighting" days are called upon to conciliate disputes. This difference was marked in industrial unions, in automobiles, Akron rubber works, and in steel, which learned that peaceful collective bargaining must be performed not by militants but by negotiators. The problem is particularly acute in the preliminary stages of handling grievances where, as in rubber, "the inexperience and emotionalism of both foremen and union committeemen made adjustment exceedingly difficult."[16]

The union has a problem in the caliber of its shop stewards and minor officials. The democratic way is to elect them, but frequently the type most needed will not undertake the responsibility, and the place goes by default to hotheads unsuited to the give and take of day-in and day-out collective bargaining. In some cases in the garment industry only those qualified by experience and ability are allowed to stand for election. The needle trades' unions pioneered in training shop committeemen in tested methods of adjusting differences and of "policing the contract." Similar educational programs have been launched by unions in autos, steel, flat glass, rubber, and some other mass production industries. A few universities have maintained summer schools for workers and at Wisconsin public funds have long been used for this purpose.

"A serious obstacle to the development of better union leaders," says one United Steelworkers of America official, "is the lack of

15. *Ibid.*, p. 27.   16. *Ibid.*, p. 673.

proper training by management of its own rank and file."[17] Two
other Steelworkers officials have this to say of guides to grievance
handling and other matters of union-management relations put
out by their organization: "We are not too happy over the fact that
these publications are read more carefully and extensively by management personnel than by our own staff, local union leaders and
members."[18]

Nevertheless, handbooks like the Steelworkers guides illuminate
the spirit and philosophy of collective bargaining and are useful
educational material for both foremen and shop committeemen.
When a plant is unionized, many a foreman—and higher supervisor, too—has had to undergo a tremendous readjustment in
outlook and behavior. Many a foreman, and even superintendents
and plant managers who were unable to abandon their former
attitudes, have been replaced. A number of companies like Goodrich and RCA held classes for foremen in problems of union relations and the handling of grievances. A few, like Firestone, hold
that foremen and superintendents are primarily production men
who should not be involved in personnel problems and adjustments of grievances; and these concerns have followed the practice
of many other large enterprises in setting up industrial relations
departments to deal with union representatives.[19]

Forms of Arbitration

There are two kinds of outside intervention in industrial disputes.[20] One is conciliation ("help us to agree") which is usually
employed when management and labor are deadlocked in negotiating a trade agreement. The other is arbitration ("decide for
us") which in peacetime is rarely employed in deadlocked agreement negotiations and is usually the final step in grievance procedure. Most agreements prescribe some form of arbitration—
either voluntary or obligatory—after a grievance dispute has gone
through all stages of discussion and is still unsettled.

Two main forms of arbitration are encountered in trade agree-

17. *Ibid.*, p. 541.   18. Golden and Ruttenberg, *op. cit.*, pp. 107-08.
19. See section on labor relations executives, Chap. 3.
20. For arbitration and conciliation of disputes during negotiation of agreement,
see Chap. 5 for peacetime conditions and Chap. 13 for wartime developments.

ments. One is machinery already set up to handle deadlocked disputes arising during an agreement's life. This is standing or permanent arbitration—ready to operate immediately. The other is temporary or emergency arbitration—resorted to in single unadjusted cases and some time may pass before it is ready to function.

Permanent and temporary arbitration have these varieties:

1. Temporary Nonpartisan
   Referred to an umpire, chosen by
   a. Mutual agreement
   b. Government conciliation body or government official
2. Temporary Bipartisan Board
   Equal union-employer representation, impartial member chosen
   a. By the Board
   b. By a public official
   c. By a conciliation board
   d. From a panel
3. Permanent Nonpartisan
   Referred to a government, state or federal, mediation board
   Referred to an impartial chairman, chosen
   a. By a public official
   b. By a disinterested private citizen
   c. From a panel
4. Permanent Bipartisan Board
   Equal employer-union representation; one impartial member
   a. Named by the Board
   b. Designated in the agreement

Voluntary, Temporary Arbitration

Temporary arbitration, encountered more often in recently organized mass production industries, is resorted to only when both sides are willing to entrust their dispute to an outsider. The standard steel agreement leaves the choice of an arbiter to "mutual agreement"; when steel companies decline to be judged by an outsider because he "knows nothing of the industry," the result is little arbitration.[21] An agreement between General Electric and United Electrical, Radio and Machine Workers of America dilutes this process further with each side promising no more than "considering" to refer by mutual agreement to arbitration.[22]

21. *How Collective Bargaining Works*, pp. 559-60.
22. "In the event no agreement is reached on any matter through direct negotiations, the two parties will then consider referring such a matter to an impartial umpire or board by mutual agreement."

Such provisions may encourage delay, which in grievance cases is generally a dangerous tactic; yet that very delay in choosing arbiters may allow for a relatively harmless amount of verbal fireworks when otherwise a stoppage of work might result. The chief fault of the mutual agreement method is that it is not likely to cover the more serious disputes in which mutual agreement is difficult. And another defect of the temporary arbitration process is that the umpires selected may have little knowledge of the fine points at issue—all of which consumes more time before the grievance is settled.

Permanent Arbitration Procedure

A permanent arbitration setup avoids the delays and irritations of the selection of temporary umpires. Its personnel is, or becomes, familiar with the industry, and each case adjudicated gives it further familiarity. The permanent, bipartisan board is now fairly rare except on the railroads, where it is established by law; the favored referees at present are arbiters from government conciliation services and impartial chairmen.

One of the failings of a bipartisan board is that it is on the borderline between joint handling of grievances and impartial arbitration. Possibly a bit over the borderline is the most important of all bipartisan boards, the National Railroad Adjustment Board. This is a child not of union-management agreement but of federal legislation. Except for its cash awards, its decisions are final and binding, with enforcement resting in the federal courts; and it therefore has somewhat of an official status, although half of its thirty-six members are chosen and paid by the carriers and the other half by railway labor organizations.

Railroad agreements are complicated affairs with many pages of closely packed type and there are more than four thousand of them. The labors of the adjustment board are therefore involved; and the board's practice of handling of grievances and interpretation of contract by ten- and six-man divisions are apt to be long and cumbersome. When the divisions fail to agree, an outside referee is called in, and the case is gone all over again. The awards are targets for complaint by labor and carriers, with carriers the most persistent, and appraisal of the board's work is described as "difficult."[23]

Impartial Chairman

A logical outgrowth of the bipartisan board is the impartial chairman. When boards had equal employer and labor representation, members were often as deadlocked over an issue as were union and management negotiators during successive stages of grievance procedure. This led to the inclusion on the board of an impartial member; and with employer and union representatives incapable of agreement, the impartial member evolved into an impartial chairman and ultimately the sole arbiter.

The impartial chairman is a person of reputation beyond his community—a lawyer or a professional man or an economist who has the confidence both of employers and of labor. He is especially serviceable in recently organized industries in which both management's subordinates and union rank and file are new to collective bargaining, and in other industries where disputes are frequent. There may be times when shop committees well know the solution of a dispute but for various reasons cannot themselves propose it. Under such circumstances, the impartial chairman bears the brunt of the necessary decision.

A successful impartial chairman is the "candid friend" of both sides. Out of 1500 cases decided in ten years by the impartial chairman in the full-fashioned hosiery industry, there was not a single instance of noncompliance or nonacceptance.[24] An impartial chairman helps to preserve the peace and make an agreement work, for his decisions educate shop stewards and foremen in the settlement of future disputes; which in turn ultimately means fewer cases brought up to him for adjudication. Sometimes, however, an impartial chairman can undermine rather than strengthen collective bargaining. If he has an overdeveloped legal sense and is guided more by precedent and rules than by a desire to settle a specific problem, he may clutter up instead of simplify grievance procedure. For grievances which are settled by rules and precedent and not according to their merits still remain grievances.

23. *How Collective Bargaining Works*, pp. 361-64.   24. *Ibid.*, pp. 459-60.

Government Arbitration

Although mediation is the primary service of federal and state conciliation boards, the arbitration of unsettled grievances is an increasingly active side line of these government agencies. The impartial chairman and permanent umpire system applies particularly to industries with union agreements which cover either associations and groups of employers, or big corporations, some of which are as large as whole industries. But other groups cannot afford or have no continuous need for permanent arbiters; and many of them are now submitting their unresolved grievances to government conciliation boards, most of which have separate conciliation and arbitration personnel.

This invocation of federal or state government arbiters is an increasing tendency which appears destined to expand further when labor and management become more and more aware of the impartiality of the awards, which have the effect of court decrees. Of 531 grievances decided in 1939 by arbitrators of the New York State Mediation Board, only two or three decisions were questioned and enforced by legal action.[25]

Advantages and Limitations of Arbitration

In most industries, any dispute arising out of the union agreement may be carried to umpires as long as it pertains directly to employer-union relations and not to internal union affairs. Some agreements limit arbitration of grievances. Under the General Motors-UAW agreement, the impartial chairman may not order changes in wage rates, or decide disputes of speed of operations, or fix penalties in disciplinary, layoff or discharge cases.[26] International "laws" which some trade unions are able to apply to working conditions in their shops are usually exempted from outside arbitration. This is stipulated in 90 per cent of typographical union agreements.[27] Although their agreements usually provide for arbitration of other deadlocked issues, the printing trades have a strong preference for direct settlement of their grievances; and

25. *Labor and National Defense,* The Twentieth Century Fund, New York, 1941, p. 91.
26. *How Collective Bargaining Works,* pp. 606-07.
27. *Ibid.,* p. 153.

where the trade once employed arbitration frequently, it rarely does so now.

Arbitration clauses in coal mining agreements are seldom invoked because of the miners' "direct action" temperament; yet figures for the Illinois field shows that 3 per cent of unresolved grievances submitted were to arbitration.[28] As a rule, the recently organized industry, scarcely out of the brick and tear gas stage of labor relations, needs arbitration the most and is the most reluctant to invoke it. One side may be so fearful of losing to the other that it may be unwilling to jeopardize its contentions—even to the extent of jeopardizing its cause. In the rubber products industry, only one agreement covering a large corporation (Firestone) provides for arbitration of unsettled grievances.[29] If one side or the other is intransigent, arbitration is no more successful than conciliation. It may contribute to industrial peace, but it cannot ensure it.

Both union and management, it is apparent from the Fund's special studies (*How Collective Bargaining Works*), have discovered that decisions reached by direct negotiations are on the whole more satisfactory than the rulings of an arbiter. Whether temporary or permanent, an umpire does not know the trade so well as the parties to the dispute; he may "split the difference" to reach a settlement rather than resolve a grievance on its merits; and the very existence of arbitration machinery may weaken the collective bargaining process by encouraging an attitude of "let George do it" instead of a habit of settling disputes at their place of origin.

Basically, arbitration is a last resort. It is a means of settling a dispute unresolved by collective bargaining. It is a restorative when normal collective bargaining processes fail. It is sometimes useful as a crutch. But as a substitute it has its dangers.

28. *Ibid.*, pp. 240, 247.
29. U. S. Bureau of Labor Statistics, Serial No. R. 1271, *Strike Restrictions in Union Agreements*, p. 16.

Chapter 11

UNION-MANAGEMENT COOPERATION

ONCE IT GETS the wage rates and working conditions it seeks, has organized labor any concern as to whether an employer can meet those terms? What has a union to offer an employer? If employers go under, what is left of unions?

As we have seen, an agreement between union and employer may forestall industrial disputes, but it does not ensure the whole-hearted conduct of industrial relations. The first stage of collective bargaining is reached when employers, either willingly or compelled, sit down and talk with unions. The second stage is reached when unions and employers sign covenants regarding wages and work conditions and agree upon methods of settling future disagreements. This is still an arm's-length stage. A third stage is when management and organized labor discover a partnership of interest. When unions and employers have learned how to get along together, many a union cooperates with an employer either on an informal basis or through joint production committees.

Informal Cooperation

The traditional union attitude was that an employer was capable of looking after himself. Unionism had to fight for its existence against employer opposition. Why, it was argued, should unionism strengthen its opponent? But when employment conditions in a whole industry are affected, many a union has joined with employers to fight a common threat.

Unions have been helpful to employers in legislative matters. Outstanding examples of this cooperation have been the railway brotherhoods which stood side by side with the carriers in opposing or favoring many bills, both in Congress and various state legislatures, which affected the railroad industry. In 1938, rail labor organizations proposed a joint committee to study the whole transportation situation and to report its findings to the President of the United States. The "Committee of Six" issued its report which laid down a national policy for all forms of transportation. It called for revision of tax burdens upon railroads, regulation of motor and air competition and RFC loans to the carriers;[1] and out of these recommendations came, in greatly altered form, the Transportation Act of 1940.

Glass workers have also been powerful lobbyists in collaboration with employer legislative agents. They fought for high tariffs against low-priced glass products from abroad, and they secured considerable state and federal legislation favorable to their industry.[2] They obtained repeal of state laws requiring deposits upon beer bottles; and together with brewery workers, they were active participants in agitation for repeal of Prohibition.

Glass workers' unions also took a hand in inter-industrial competition. They joined with employers in campaigns against tin cans for beer and paper cartons for milk and also in efforts to sell the housewife the idea that glass containers are preferable to tin cans because she can see the product she is buying. The International Ladies' Garment Workers' Union created a joint industry-labor fund to stimulate demand and to advertise the industry's product. Another contributor to a joint promotional and advertising project was the potters' brotherhood.

Informal union cooperation with management has also occurred in the field of intra-industrial competition. A most noteworthy case was in the hosiery industry where the union gave more favorable terms to unionized northern manufacturers which competed with nonunion southern mills.

In production matters many unions have been helpful. Some have aided employers in preparing work forces for unavoidable changes, in maintaining shop discipline and observance of safety

1. *Report of the Committee to Submit Recommendations Upon the General Transportation Situation*, December 23, 1938.
2. *How Collective Bargaining Works*, pp. 715-16.

rules, and in educating their members in economic conditions of the industry of which they are a part. Typographical locals and publishers in many cities have jointly operated schools for apprentices. The pressmen's union has had a consulting service for employers on technical problems. Union photoengravers have conducted their own research. New York electrical workers have advised contractors on economical wiring installations. The hosiery workers' union has sent employers instructors to teach unskilled workers better production methods.[3]

Organized Union-Management Cooperation

Many employers and executives rose from the ranks because of their ready ability to solve technical problems. Is all practical knowledge at the top? Have men at the bench no worth-while ideas about better production methods? Is it possible for labor and management to have a partnership in cutting costs and in achieving greater efficiency?

Organized labor did not take up the question of employer cooperation in earnest until the middle of the 1920's. It was spurred to do so by the crop of "employee representation" plans which blossomed shortly after World War I. Some of these were tied up with scientific management and efficiency programs; virtually all were designed to arouse some employee interest in production and other problems of management, and almost all were related to attempts to forestall or thwart union organization of employees. In the view of many an employer, there was altogether too much union interference with production. Restrictive rules and union laws regulating shop conduct were held obstacles to drive for lower unit costs.

At the 1925 AF of L convention the Executive Council submitted a report which described the spread of employee representation plans and proposed a policy of union-management cooperation. "After collective bargaining becomes an established practice," the report stated, "a union might render service by partici-

3. WPA National Research Project, *Trade-Union Policy and Technological Change*, 1940, p. 110.

pating in finding better methods of production and greater production economies."[4]

Four years later, as a part of its attempt to organize southern industry, the AF of L offered southern employers the services of its engineering and educational departments and union-management cooperation to reduce waste in production and sharing of the resulting savings. Three small establishments took up this offer— a hosiery mill employing thirty, a syrup factory of about the same size, and a food packing plant employing less than twenty.[5]

Partnership of interest, or union-management cooperation has developed in these three general forms:

1. Production committees: shop workers and management meeting and conferring upon collected suggestions for improved production methods. Examples: Tennessee Valley Authority, Baltimore and Ohio Railroad shops, and United Steelworkers.

2. Joint research: independent experts working with management and union representatives. Example: Naumkeag Steam Cotton Mills experiment.

3. Unions as production advisers. Example: Amalgamated Clothing Workers.

Production Committees: War Plants and Railroads

Labor-management production committees, which draw upon the technical knowledge of employees, have the backing and encouragement of the federal government. Their formation in all war plants to plan greater and faster output was urged by Donald Nelson, Chairman of the War Production Board, when launching the expanded war material program March 2, 1942. Although organized labor representation on these committees was not specified, the Nelson proposal is similar to union-management production committees worked out through collective bargaining.

In the fall of 1942, replies to questionnaires received from executives of 181 war plants with 405,634 employees indicated that four out of five union-management production committees were successful. The tabulations were:[6]

4. AF of L, *Proceedings of Forty-Fifth Annual Convention*, p. 35.
5. Jean C. Trepp, "Union Management Cooperation and the Southern Organizing Campaign," *Journal of Political Economy*, October 1933, p. 617.
6. *Factory Management and Maintenance*, October 1942.

Ninety-three per cent found no evidence that labor seeks to usurp managerial functions

Seventy-nine per cent found that these committees improve industrial relations

Seventy-eight per cent believed that worker sense of responsibility for war production had been increased

Fifty-five per cent reported increased production

Six per cent reported strikes in their plants since joint committees had been set up; yet half of this 6 per cent believed in the value of this committee work

By the middle of September 1942, some 3.5 million workers in war plants were represented by labor-management production committees, and Chairman Nelson reported that "acknowledged leaders of labor and management" had asked him to extend such committees to more plants. By the end of October 1944, more than 5,000 had been established throughout the country. They covered nearly 8 million workers, involved the activities of some 50,000 committee members, and were operating in factories, mills, mines, shipyards and lumber camps. The ordnance industry had the largest number—587.[7]

One of the oldest existing union-management production committee systems covers the 45 repair shops and roundhouses and 15,000 shop craftsmen of the Baltimore and Ohio Railroad. Under this plan, members of union-shop committees originally set up to handle grievance cases meet with management officials to discuss improvement of work methods, elimination of waste and other ways of cutting material costs. Such meetings do not take up individual grievances or other matters connected with "policing the agreement" but consider suggestions made by employees for doing the work better and more economically. Suggestions are either accepted or rejected immediately or are held over for investigation and report at subsequent meetings; none die "on the table." In eighteen years of operation—1924 to 1942—there were 11,783 management-shop committee meetings which considered 32,297 suggestions. An impressive number of suggestions were adopted— 27,851, or 86.2 per cent. Rejected suggestions were 2,921; post-

7. *The New York Times*, September 14, 1942; report of address of Donald Nelson to RCA employees; see also *Labor Fact Book*, p. 106.

poned suggestions were 1,214 and still under consideration, 311.[8]

These meetings have given management an opportunity to outline future plans and enlist employee support, and, judged by most standards, the plan has been a success. Employment has been steadier, workmanship has improved, morale and working conditions have bettered. All of this is despite the fact that one of the chief incentives for labor interest in the plan is missing: B & O shopmen's cooperation has not brought higher wages than on other roads, for union policy demands standardized wages on all roads; nevertheless, B & O shops were the first of all railroads to advance wages and restore overtime payment.[9]

Father of the B & O scheme is Otto S. Beyer, for long a member of the National Mediation Board and later with the Defense Transportation Administration. During World War I he experimented with employee-management cooperation at Rock Island Arsenal and devised a plan for conference-table meetings on production matters between labor and company officials. The idea was pushed by railroad shop-craft unions and was under consideration by the United States Railway Administration when the roads were returned to private ownership in 1920.

Next to take up the plan was Baltimore and Ohio's president, Daniel Willard, who had progressive labor policies. The bitter railroad shopmen's strike of 1922 postponed a trial until a year later when Beyer, under retainer from the machinists' union, but backed by Willard, organized the first cooperation meetings at Glenwood shops near Pittsburgh. Glenwood's production was the slowest and costliest and its labor relations were the sourest of any B & O shop, but conditions improved so rapidly in a few months that a 1924 agreement between Baltimore and Ohio and shop-craft unions made the plan effective in all shops of the road.

8. Philip M. Wagner, "It Worked for the B & O," *Saturday Evening Post,* August 22, 1942. p, 22.

9. For further discussion of the B & O plan, see Otto S. Beyer, "Experiences With Cooperation Between Labor and Management in the Railway Industry," *Wertheim Lectures on Industrial Relations,* Harvard University Press, Cambridge, 1929, pp. 10-27; Louis A. Wood, *Union Management Cooperation on the Railroads,* Yale University Press, New Haven, pp. 233-50; Sumner H. Slichter, *Union Policies and Industrial Management,* The Brookings Institution, Washington, 1941, pp. 437-503.

A few other railroads adopted the idea in their shops in the late 1920's and it is still in force on B & O and Canadian National systems. It was abandoned on other roads largely because top management and union leadership lost interest. That interest, according to Captain Beyer, is essential for success of a labor-management cooperation plan. Also, he says, management must regard unions as potential assets instead of liabilities, and it must be willing to accept their help. Furthermore, genuine collective bargaining must be in operation before a cooperation plan can be started, and employees must choose their shop representation without management help or interference. Management must consider stabilized employment as important to maintain as financial credit, and finally, management must be willing to share with employees benefits which arise from cooperative effort.[10]

Planning Committees: Steel

Another variety of the union-management production committee is the joint planning committee developed by the steelworkers' union, which has campaigned vigorously for greater union participation in output problems. Unlike the Baltimore and Ohio plan, in which the shop grievance committee also represents the union on the joint production committee, union representation in steel research and planning committees has no part in grievance adjustment but must be composed "of men who have a knack for handling facts and figures and of men who have ideas about better ways of doing things."[11]

While the SWOC was attempting to organize the steel industry, local lodges which had collective bargaining relations with steel mills were urged to appoint committees to study shop practices and report how production could be improved. Armed with these data, union negotiators then approached company officials to propose a union-management cooperation agreement.

The steelworkers' standard cooperation agreement calls for a research and planning committee of five representatives each

10. Beyer, *op. cit.*, pp. 20-21.
11. Steel Workers Organizing Committee, Publication No. 2, *Production Problems*, pp. 4-5.

from union and management. "The duties of the committee," it states, "shall be to solicit from the employees of all ranks suggestions designed to increase efficiency, reduce production costs, and eliminate waste; to review them; to adopt those that are practical and feasible; and to explain to employees whose suggestions were not adopted the reasons why." All facts and plans relating to production costs are to be revealed to this committee "and its understanding and consent shall be obtained at every step." Other stipulations: all benefits from cutting production costs shall be shared by management and union; and no one shall lose his job through any new installation. If the improvement cannot be established without dislocation, it must be installed gradually so that no discharges are necessary.

In return for their cooperation in a search for better production methods, the steelworkers asked a price: a union-shop agreement.[12] None of the large companies accepted this price but by 1939, when war business increased production, 30 per cent of the 541 employers then having bargaining relations with SWOC had or were negotiating production cooperation agreements.[13] After labor-management cooperation became part of the War Production Board's policy, virtually all of the steel industry may have had joint production committees, but the proportion of those formed through collective bargaining is not known.

Joint Research: Naumkeag Cotton

Joint production committees deal with suggestions for better output. Job assignment and participation in time and effort studies are beyond their regular field. Although older unions are traditionally suspicious of scientific management technique, some unions have engaged industrial engineers to make independent studies and checks of company incentive rates. At the Naumkeag Steam Cotton Mills at Salem, Massachusetts, union and management cooperated in joint research to set up job standards.

Although Naumkeag's two-year experiment in union-manage-

12. Harold J. Ruttenberg, "The Strategy of Industrial Peace," *Harvard Business Review,* Winter 1939, pp. 175-76.
13. Clinton S. Golden and Harold J. Ruttenberg, *The Dynamics of Industrial Democracy,* Harper, New York, 1942, p. 243.

ment cooperation ended in a strike, it cannot be dismissed as an entire failure; and it stands as an object lesson to cooperators not to "drive ahead of their lights" and work without the confidence or understanding of rank-and-file workers. Unable to hold up its end of competition in the late 1920's, Naumkeag sought to increase work loads and asked union approval. An industrial engineer engaged by the union to examine the situation reported that costs could be reduced by more efficient use of labor and recommended new job assignments by joint union-management research.

The Naumkeag company hired the engineer to carry out his recommendations. He formed a research staff of two representatives each from company and union, and their work was supervised by a waste-elimination committee of four members each from company and union—including the research staff. The industrial engineer headed the committee and passed upon all technical questions. Subsequently, outside textile engineers were engaged to standardize certain work operations. Their scientific procedures in many cases ran counter to "we've-always-done-things-that-way" ideas of both management and employees, and compromises were made which failed to standardize some operations. There were some layoffs, more job dislocations and a sizable proportion of demotions. Annual savings achieved by joint research amounted to between $18,000 and $230,000 a year. The company's competitive position was improved, and so was the condition of most workers.

Had it not been for the depression, the experiment might have been successful, but wage cuts which came in the early 1930's soured the rank and file against further joint research, and finally came a strike in defiance of international union officials. Regardless of speculation about what continued joint research might have accomplished, the Naumkeag experiment emphasized two points:

1. The dangers of outside job assignment by engineering principles and the clash between scientific and age-long rule-of-thumb methods.

2. The danger of too much union participation in setting job standards and thereby setting rank and file against its leaders—which raises the point as to whether it is not better for manage-

ment to make these assignments subject to independent investigation and study by the union.[14]

Unions As Production Advisers: Printing and Clothing

Some judgments of collective bargaining collide with each other. The process has been charged with fostering inefficiency and with discouraging worker interest in the job. Union-management cooperation, aimed at correction of this criticism, is opposed because it permits union invasion of managerial problems.

Some unions, particularly in the printing trades, place experts of their own at the disposal of employers. No example exists of any but a strong union engaging in such practice. A union struggling for existence can't have a long-range view, nor can it offer anything likely to jeopardize its immediate standing with its own rank and file. But in industries where employers are struggling for existence, a strong union may be able to straighten matters out. This has been done in certain garment trades, composed of here-today-gone-tomorrow establishments, in and out of the red operations and relentless competition between relatively small firms; and an outstanding example of cooperation is in men's clothing—the services of the Amalgamated Clothing Workers.

The basic principle of the Amalgamated's cooperation with management policy is that inefficient shops mean low wages, long hours and irregular employment. Accordingly, it has placed at the disposal of union employers the services of expert technicians. It has worked out production standards and piecework rates and has advised on new machinery and cost-cutting techniques. It has recommended changes in executive personnel and it has extended credit to manufacturers from its own bank. To induce an antiunion manufacturer to deal with the union, Amalgamated once opened a shop of its own and competed so strongly that the manufacturer saw the light.[15]

14. For fuller discussion of Naumkeag experiment, see Richard C. Nyman, *Union-Management Cooperation in the "Stretch-Out,"* Yale University Press, New Haven, 1924; Sumner H. Slichter, *op. cit.,* pp. 532-60; Francis Goodell, "Joint Research—the Technician's Point of View," *American Federationist,* March 1930; *idem,* "Joint Research at Naumkeag," *American Federationist,* July 1932.

15. For a more extended summary, see *How Collective Bargaining Works,* pp. 406-48.

This activity began in the early 1920's when the Amalgamated helped the firm of Hart, Schaffner & Marx to reorganize its production and become a manufacturer of low-cost clothing in successful competition with nonunion firms. By substituting labor-saving machinery, shifting unskilled tasks from skilled to unskilled workers and improving plant layouts, piece rates were reduced without much loss of income. Moreover, piece rates were revised so as to be based upon total labor cost of a garment rather than of the particular operation.

Through its stabilization plan, which it put into effect in 1939, the Amalgamated has advanced its "cooperation with the employers" philosophy to such an extent that it now determines the trade's major policies and, in a sense, has virtually captured the industry. The main points in that plan are as follows:

1. All tailoring processes of men's clothing production are standardized into six grades. The purpose is to standardize production so that labor costs can then be stabilized. No changes in grades are made without union permission.

2. Fixing of standard labor costs for each grade.

3. Limitation of cutthroat competition and prevention of dealings with nonunion contractors by requiring union approval of the arrangement contractors make with manufacturers and workers.

4. Requiring contractors' associations to fix contractors' prices.

5. Wage adjustments by a stabilization department directly responsible to President Hillman thus ensuring industry-wide policy and discouraging competition between markets.

The legal status of steps one, three and four in the plan are still uncertain although the purposes and accomplishments of the plan may now be more in accord with recent pragmatic "rule of reason" tendencies of the Supreme Court of the United States.[16]

The Outlook for Union-Management Cooperation

Until the United States was catapulted into war, union-management cooperation was small and scattered. It had high mortality in railroad repair shops, two out of four plans giving up the ghost, but indicative of its vitality is the fact that it was still going strong in the Baltimore and Ohio shops where it started nearly

16. *Ibid.*, p. 440.

twenty years ago. It was getting hard-headed application in some steel mills and it had reached extraordinary development in the men's and women's clothing industries.

Cooperation was increasing, not phenomenally but steadily. Although no comprehensive figures exist, it is the impression of most investigators that more cooperation plans were set in motion by unions than by employers; and cooperation seemed to make greater headway when proposed for an ailing enterprise than for a healthy one.

However, nearly two decades of trial and error had shown a half dozen conditions essential for cooperation.

1. Harmonious collective bargaining relations already established, with the union having assured status as bargaining agent
2. Regularized production and employment
3. Abandonment by the union of restrictions against output
4. Joint participation in setting standards of output
5. Sharing of gains resulting from lowered costs
6. Full confidence of both union and management that results of their cooperation will not be devoted to the disadvantage of either

Union-management cooperation is based upon realization by both sides that one cannot get along without the other. That realization is not universal. Required by law to bargain collectively, management does little to assist the spread of unionism, then charges organized labor with failure to appreciate that its welfare depends upon successful enterprise. Good union men, who may have leaders who have predatory ambitions or who would abolish the enterprise system, charge management with antiunion discrimination. When both sides are bent upon destroying the other, it is pointless to expect cooperation.

The enforced partnership of war, however, compelled a suspension of some attitudes which previously had stood in cooperation's way. It is possible that the encouragement of labor-management cooperation by the War Production Board may prove to have done as much for union-management cooperation as the National Labor Relations Act did for the spread of collective bargaining. It is also possible that such cooperation will make both employers and unions more understanding and responsible bargainers. If so, then a new plane of labor relations will be reached.

Chapter 12

GOVERNMENT COLLECTIVE BARGAINING

WHEN GERMANY SURRENDERED on May 7, 1945, there were five million civilians on America's public pay roll. They represented one out of every eleven gainfully employed in the United States— a ratio which must have been much smaller when the Japanese war ended. Around 8 per cent of these public employees, or 540,000, belonged to unions; about 100,000 of them having signed up since 1942 (see table opposite). While some of the craft unions in this sphere, such as postmen, fire fighters and teachers have been going concerns for a generation, the all-inclusive industrial unions composed of clerks, typists, bookkeepers, street cleaners, inspectors and statisticians and the like are comparatively young— on the average less than a dozen years old. Whatever their age, or the character of their constituency, they are all seeking more and more to bargain collectively with the employer, in other words, with government.

Of course, the range of collective bargaining in the public service is automatically circumscribed by the fact that wages and working conditions are generally fixed by law rather than by negotiations between employer and employees. Outside of common labor, and the skilled trades, whose wages frequently accord with the "prevailing rate" in the community, the incomes of public employees are set by state or federal statute, or by municipal ordinance. The legislative branch of government, like the board of directors in a private corporation, is the ultimate, if absentee, boss. The administrator immediately in charge of a department or bureau must operate within the boundary of rules laid down by the law-making body. He can sometimes alter these rules in detail, if not in underlying purpose. But he usually lacks the latitude and

flexibility of decision with which the manager of a private plant
is endowed.

UNIONS AMONG GOVERNMENT EMPLOYEES
(*As of January 1944*)

	Number of Members
Postal Service	
National Association of Letter Carriers (AF of L)	64,500
National Federation of Post Office Clerks (AF of L)	45,000
United National Association of Post Office Clerks (Unaf.)	37,420
National Rural Letter Carriers' Association (Unaf.)	28,066
Railway Mail Association (AF of L)	21,800
National League of District Postmasters of the U.S. (Unaf.)	18,000
National Alliance of Postal Employees (Unaf.)	10,047
National Association of Postal Supervisors (Unaf.)	9,400
National Association of Post Office and Railway Mail Laborers (AF of L)	1,500
National Association of Special Delivery Messengers (AF of L)	1,000
National Federation of Rural Letter Carriers (AF of L)	400
Total Postal Service	**237,133**
Federal Government, General	
National Federation of Federal Employees (Unaf.)	75,000
American Federation of Government Employees (AF of L)	35,500
United Federal Workers of America (CIO)	30,000
National Association of Master Mechanics and Foremen of Navy Yards and Naval Stations (AF of L)	300
Total Federal Government, General	**140,800**
State, County and Municipal Governments	
American Federation of State, County and Municipal Employees (AF of L)	50,000
International Association of Fire Fighters (AF of L)	38,200
State, County and Municipal Workers of America (CIO)	38,000
American Federation of Teachers (AF of L)	35,000
Total State, County and Municipal Governments	**161,200**
Grand Total	**539,133**

Sources: Industrial Relations Unit, Bureau of Labor Statistics, U. S. Department
of Labor; Florence Peterson, *Handbook of Labor Unions,* American Council on Public Affairs, Washington, 1944.

Parallels With Private Enterprise

The origins of collective bargaining in public enterprise are undoubtedly rooted in the same motivations that foster collective bargaining in private enterprise, namely, the search for higher pay, improved working conditions, and the like. The most recent convention of the National Association of Letter Carriers (AF of L) illustrates the identity of aims and wants between public and private employees. The delegates had to address themselves to the Congress and the Post Office Department since the laws of the first and the regulations of the second establish the carriers' rates of pay, hours of work, and the conduct of their duties. Otherwise, the proceedings of the Association's convention were indistinguishable from those of almost any other national union in private industry.

In passing their many resolutions, the delegates insisted, among other things, that time and one half be paid for all hours of work in excess of forty a week, and that double time be paid for work on holidays. They demanded that the weight of mail to be carried out be reduced from a fifty- to a thirty-five-pound maximum. They asked for free hospitalization. They tartly recommended that the Roosevelt Administration "practice what it preaches" and extend the Wagner Act, especially its protection against labor spies and espionage, to postal employees. The delegates informed the Postmaster General that the lack of clean toilets and adequate heat and ventilation at many post offices and substations threatens the "health and morale" of the carrier, a condition that "must be promptly rectified." The delegates also demanded that the present fifteen-day annual vacation be extended to thirty, and sick leave from ten to twenty days. They urged that magazine publishers be compelled to adopt a uniform method of mailing their periodicals unwrapped and flat, rather than rolled, with the name and address of the recipient at the upper right hand corner and placed "so as to be read right side up when put in the carrier's satchel," thus eliminating "extreme strain on his eyes and nerves." The delegates also wanted the passage of a law that would make the owner of a dog who bites a carrier responsible for medical expenses. They asked that an arbitration board, to be composed of three members of the union and three spokesmen for management, be set up as a court of last resort with power to resolve disputes between labor and employer that could not be otherwise settled. Finally, the delegates enjoined the AF of L and CIO to bury the hatchet at once, and to take steps to achieve peace and unity, lest their continuing quarrels imperil the rights and gains of all organized labor.

Numerous similar demands have been put forward during the past two years by such other unions in the government's second largest industry, as the railway mail clerks, who sort and handle the mail on trains, and the post-office clerks who sell stamps, load parcels, keep the records and the like. While all these government unions do their bargaining with local, regional and national officials, and the legislature, the subjects covered can hardly be dismissed as entirely distinct from those which enter into collective bargaining between, say, the machinists' union and the proprietor of a metal-working establishment.

Limitations on the Right to Strike

There is, however, one respect in which the process of collective bargaining in government differs drastically from that in private pursuits, namely, the use of the strike to enforce union demands. It is true, of course, that public employees have occasionally gone on strike ever since 1836 when shipwrights, caulkers and riggers of the Philadelphia Navy Yard walked out to obtain the ten-hour day. Indeed, David Ziskind's prodigious research for his volume, *One Thousand Strikes of Government Employees,* enabled him to record, up to 1940, 1116 government strikes involving arsenal mechanics, teachers, postmen, policemen, firemen, even the state senators of the Connecticut legislature, and many more. But, with the exception of the famous Boston police strike in 1919, few government walkouts have approximated in severity, extent, length and social impact various strikes on the railroads, in coal mines, in automobile and rubber plants and others in private industry. Moreover, while there have been only a little over a thousand government strikes over the past 125 years, the country has sometimes witnessed that many strikes in private industry within a single month. This disparity is not to be explained solely on the ground that the total number of government workers who belong to unions is far less than workers in private industry. In the peace-time year of 1939, for example, 11.5 million private employees were unionized, but less than 0.5 million public employees were thus oganized. In that year, the ratio of membership was twenty-four to one, and of strikes one thousand to one.

All government unions, some of which accepted the strike in their earlier days, now officially eschew it altogether. The experi-ence of the International Association of Fire Fighters (AF of L) reflects the reasons for this change. In 1918, when the Associa-tion was first being organized, some of its locals won their primary objectives, such as reduction of hours of work from twenty-four to twelve a day, by going on strike. But the uproar and hostility that greeted this action, the tragic, menacing vision of a city in flames, a prospect rendered doubly lurid by scare headlines, soon convinced the union's leaders that they had better devise less spec-tacular methods for improving the status of the fireman. Hence the Association's constitution which, for the first five years merely advised against the strike as a two-edged sword, was in 1923 amended to read as follows:

> We shall not strike or take active part in any sympathetic strike, since the work of fire fighters is different from that performed by any other workers, as we are employed to perform the duties of protecting the lives and prop-erty of communities in case of fire or other serious hazard.

Internationals Enforce the Ban

The Association in 1938 revoked the charter of a Canadian affiliate that violated this mandate. Furthermore, to woo com-munity good will, the Association now grants a charter to a local only after a majority of fire department members have signified their intention of joining the union. A special representative from the Association's national headquarters in Washington is then dis-patched to inform the mayor or city manager: that the Association forbids strikes; that it is strictly nonpartisan and will not pro-mote the career of any political candidate; that the union will cooperate at all times with the fire chief not only in handling his labor relations but also in efforts to improve the service; that the Association is an active affiliate of the National Fire Waste Council, the United States Chamber of Commerce, the National Fire Protection Association, and that it collaborates with the National Board of Fire Underwriters and all other organizations interested in fire fighting and fire prevention.

The Association's strike ban is duplicated everywhere among unions in every zone of the public service. The National Federation of Federal Employees (Independent) declares in its constitution: "Under no circumstances shall this Federation engage in or support strikes against the government." The American Federation of Government Employees (AF of L), as if in responsive reading, affirms: "We oppose and will not support strikes against the United States government." It has gone on record against picketing. Its particular rival, the United Federal Workers (CIO) thus rounds out the refrain: "While the United Federal Workers of America recognize that strikes and picketing may be used legitimately to secure the objectives of organized labor generally, it realizes that these methods are not applicable or desirable for government workers and therefore does not use them."

At other levels of government, unions repeat the same pledge. The constitution of the State, County and Municipal Workers (CIO) contains the emphatic clause: "It shall not be the policy of this organization to engage in strikes as a means of achieving its objectives." But this is modified by the ruling that when a local affiliate contemplates strike action, it must first notify the national officers of its intention and then be guided by their advice and decisions.

The very word strike is spurned by the American Federation of State, County and Municipal Employees (AF of L) which says in its constitution: "The methods of obtaining the objects of this federation shall be by petitioning, by creating and fostering sentiment favorable to the proposed reforms, by cooperating with the state and local officials, by promoting legislation and by other lawful means."

Substitutes for Strike Pressure

This emphasis of unions in public employment upon no work stoppages mirrors community opinion against government strikes far more than it mirrors any clear-cut concepts as to what organizations of public employees may or may not do. Actually in the public service a hybrid form of collective bargaining has grown up. Instead of exerting the economic pressure of the lockout, public management draws on the real or implied powers of the state to oppose or curtail collective bargaining, or to keep it within bounds once accepted. Instead of the economic pressures of the strike, the unions exert political, publicity and psychological pressures.

In constant lobbying, in pleading their cause in the press, in passing the word along that Administrator X, who considers and acts on grievances, is a decent upstanding person, while Administrator Y, who spurns the grievance committee, is a Simon Legree, the unions have sought a substitute for the strike. To some old timers in the labor movement, wedded as they are to the idea of applying economic force, the attempt of the government unions to find a substitute for the strike is nonsensical. By the same token, opponents of collective bargaining for public employees assume that the strike is its necessary complement. Both sides make the same error. They deny the immense usefulness and adaptability of collective bargaining without resort to its most powerful weapons, the lockout and strike.

A more legitimate criticism of government collective bargaining is that, in its present stage of development, it has hardly begun to exploit the potentialities of mediation and arbitration, either voluntary or compulsory. Yet in anything that so directly involves the public interest, the intervention of the third party, the neutral, the umpire, would seem particularly apt. On the whole, however, appropriate machinery for mediation or arbitration does not yet exist. The lack of clear-cut official procedures of conciliation, of tribunals to settle disputes between public unions and public managements remains a primary reason why collective bargaining in government often seems so confused.

More Administrative Machinery Needed

That collective bargaining in government, however, needs its own administrative and judicial apparatus for mediation and arbitration of wages, hours and work conditions that cannot be resolved by negotiation between the parties is shown by the experience of Local 277 of the State, County and Municipal Workers (CIO). Early in 1942 this local, which had enrolled most of the employees in the Public Works Department of Newark, New Jersey, asked for a fifteen-cent-an-hour wage increase. The Commissioner, Joseph M. Byrne, not only refused to bargain collectively with Local 277 but also demoted five garage mechanics, dismissed fifteen sanitation workers, and suspended seventy-one others for union activity. Since the Wagner Act expressly excludes all government employees from its jurisdiction, Local 277 could not appeal to the National Labor Relations Board for relief from "unfair labor practices." The union did, however, request the Mayor of Newark to intercede, but he failed to "persuade" the Commissioner to deal with Local 277—so did the Governor of the State, the State Mediation Board, the United States Conciliation Service. They were all unable to get the Commissioner to move from his position that no municipal department can or should bargain collectively with its employees, or sign an agreement with their union. In a last effort to achieve a meeting of minds, the United States Conciliation Service appointed a fact-finding panel to make an impartial investigation of the dispute and render a report. In its findings, the panel was constrained to point out that the Commissioner had summarily refused to lend any assistance whatever.

The members of Local 277, against the advice of their national officers, then went on strike and the National War Labor Board next entered the scene. It held a hearing in Washington to determine whether or not it had jurisdiction in cases of a dispute between state and local governments and their employees. The union spokesmen asserted that the Board should intervene for two reasons. In the first place, they said, the WLB was empowered under Executive Order 9250 to settle all disputes involving any industries and any employees that might hamper "effective prosecution of the war." In the second place, said the union representatives, the WLB, in the exercise of its stabilization mandate, had declared in the New York Title and Guaranty Company case that since it had authority over voluntary wage adjustments, it also had jurisdiction over all wage disputes. The union claimed that Local 277's ruckus with the Commissioner fell under the Board's double jurisdiction: (1) the settlement of wartime disputes that had not yielded to collective bargaining, mediation, and the like; (2) the disposition of disputes arising from demands for wage advances.

To substantiate its argument, the union pointed out that state, county and municipal employees are also war workers. It affirmed that the driver of a city-owned bus that takes munitions makers to their jobs is as much a war worker as they; that the turbine oiler in a city-owned electric light and power plant supplying war factories is as much a war worker as those manning the assembly lines; that the pick-and-shovel crews who keep state highways in repair, aiding the transportation of war equipment from plant to port, are likewise war workers. The union further contended that at a time of total war, with its mobilization of all human and material resources, it was unrealistic to separate public from private employees.

The union also submitted evidence to prove that, from the standpoint of wage stabilization, the public employee was not getting fair treatment. Union statisticians offered statistics showing that two fifths of all state, county and municipal workers earn $1,000, or less, a year; that the national average income of these civil servants is between $100 and $110 a month; that living costs from August 1939 to December 1942, date of the WLB hearing, had risen 20.7 per cent thus substantially cutting the "real wages" of public employees. In the light of these circumstances, the union asked the WLB, what could public employees do when faced by a Commissioner Byrne who had said flatly, "I'll not mediate, conciliate or arbitrate" when Local 277 requested negotiations looking toward a fifteen-cent-an-hour wage increase? Unless the WLB took jurisdiction, the union concluded, what other recourse did any public union have when up against an official who simply rejected the very notion of collective bargaining?

Federal Powers Limited

The Board pondered these questions for five days and then said that it could do nothing. To justify its failure to act, the Board invoked the theory that state governments and their subdivisions (counties and municipalities) are sovereign in their own areas, and that the federal government lacks the power to encroach upon the rights of the states. Hence, the Board reasoned, as an agency of the federal government, it lacked authority to "finally determine" controversies between cities and their employees, except when a "dispute between a local government and its employees . . . might reach such a point of disturbance as to impede or interfere with the successful prosecution of the war. . . ."

Standards Often Low in Public Employment

Nine days after it handed down this decision, the WLB—as if uneasy over the consistency of its action when measured against its inherent purposes—felt called on to release a supplementary "opinion." In it, the Board declared:

Although in the instant case the National War Labor Board has decided that it is without power to take jurisdiction of controversies involving the employees of local governments, nevertheless, the Board is keenly aware of the very serious labor problems confronting the country because of the fact that a few officials of a minority of local governments have adopted such uncooperative and antagonistic attitudes in their dealings with organizations representing government employees. . . . Government today is the largest employer in the country. . . . The health, safety, and comfort of our people, is dependent, in large degree, upon the quality of service rendered by public employees. . . . Efficient and clean government cannot be maintained in the face of low standards of working conditions, substandard wages, petty political discriminations, and a "take it and like it or quit" attitude on the part of public officials. . . .

The War Labor Board has not made an exhaustive study of prevailing wages among government employees, but such data as are at hand adequately support its taking judicial notice of the fact that large numbers of public employees are not paid enough to maintain a standard of living of health and decency. In fact, it is rather an interesting commentary that the people of the country acting through their elective representatives, have imposed, during recent years, such relatively high standards of labor conditions upon private industry but at the same time have maintained such low standards in public employment.

This attitude on the part of the public becomes even more interesting when it is observed that in recent years they have directed their governments to invade more and more those fields of economic activity which heretofore were dominated almost entirely by private industry. . . . The refusal of many government agencies or political subdivisions to even discuss grievances and employment problems with labor organizations representing their employees, is provocative of much ill-will . . . and results in the perpetuation of many injustices and discriminations. The solution of these problems rests primarily with the electors in the divisions of government concerned.

Have Cities a Right to Bargain?

Despite the WLB's exhortations, it remains a fiercely contested point as to whether or not a city has the right to bargain collectively with its employees and to sign contracts that stipulate wages, hours, the union shop and the like. The Institute of Municipal Law Officers has not retreated from the stand it took in 1941 on this issue. It then asserted that a municipality may not enter into a labor contract in the absence of express enabling law endowing it with the authority to do so. "Cities are creatures of limited powers," said the Institute, "having only those specifically delegated by constitution, charter and statute, and power to sign such collective bargaining agreements has not been expressly delegated to cities, except in a very limited way by the state of Washington."

The Institute has also stated that a city cannot be a party to a collective bargaining pact because: (1) this would be against declared public policy, (2) municipal employees can't strike and in the Institute's view the use of the strike and collective bargaining are inseparable, and (3) they are, in legal and economic terms, different from employees in private industry.

Those who oppose this view answer that cities conduct their business constantly under the doctrine of implied powers. Many courts, indeed, have found that the municipal corporation can draw on three classes of authority: (1) that granted in specific words; (2) that fairly or necessarily implied; and (3) that essential to accomplishing its avowed objects.

The courts have further held that cities may legitimately invoke implied powers to hire "outside" architects, and attorneys, to make assessments for local improvements, to purchase lands on which to erect school buildings, to construct waterworks and a long list of other things. It would seem that, today, harmonious labor relations are crucial to the efficient transaction of a city's business. Hence, to achieve that end, the power to utilize collective bargaining, and written agreements flowing from it, may be both "fairly" and "necessarily" implied, as "essential" for attaining the very purposes for which the city, as a public corporation, exists.

Proponents of collective bargaining for public employees argue further that, while federal and state statutes which provide for collective bargaining exclude public employees, this exclusion does not justify the Institute's inference that public employees are not entitled to the privileges of collective bargaining. As a matter of fact the Michigan, Wisconsin and other labor relations acts tend to safeguard the rights of civil servants to bargain collectively. When a Michigan city contended that it was exempt from that part of the state act which requires mediation of labor disputes on the ground that the legislature could not regulate a municipality's labor relations, the supreme court of Michigan rejected this view. The court said:

It is a matter of general public concern, and well within the police power of the State to attempt to prevent disputes between employees and employers not only in manufacturing concerns and factories but also in public utilities, whether privately or publicly owned and operated. The nature of the ownership will make no difference in the deleterious effect of the labor dispute on the general public. The act was intended to alleviate labor difficulties in general and not only in disputes in privately owned factories and utilities.

In the third place, say proponents of collective bargaining, while it is correct that civil servants differ from private employees in certain legal and economic respects, notably that the former's incomes are set by law, this logic in part begs the question. The economic drives and aspirations of public employees are identical with those actuating other workers. "The desire of government employees for fair and adequate pay," President Roosevelt said, "for reasonable hours of work, safe and suitable working conditions, development of opportunities for advancement, facilities for fair and impartial consideration and review of grievances, and other objectives of a proper employee-relations policy, is basically no different from that of employees in private industry. Organization on their part to present their views on such matters is both natural and logical. . . ."

A Typical Test Case: New York's Transit Workers

Whether or not a city can sign a contract with a union with members in both private and public employment has been the center of a four-year litigation (still going on) between New York City's Board of Transportation and the Transport Workers Union (CIO). The union has exclusive collective bargaining contracts with the Fifth Avenue Coach Company and other private corporations. It had similar agreements with the IRT and BMT subway lines until New York City acquired them, adding them to its own Independent subway system. When it took over the IRT and BMT properties, the Board refused to extend the union's old agreements.

In arguing against the union proposal that it again become sole bargaining agent for what are now city owned and operated subways, the Board points out that it is basic for a civil servant to have the right individually to petition for redress of whatever grievances he might have, and that Section 3 of the Civil Service law specifies that "no public officer shall require an employee to waive" any such right. The Board therefore deduces that this prevents it from recognizing the union as sole bargaining agency, since this would erase the individual's right to ask that his dissatisfactions with his job be allayed. But the union claims this reasoning ignores the salient fact that both the Wagner Act and the New York State Labor Relations Act stipulate clearly that exclusive bargaining shall never be construed to prohibit the presentation of individual grievances—in other words that sole bargaining rights coexist with, rather than conflict with, the right of an individual to speak for himself if he has any complaints.

Examples of City Bargaining

The continuing development of collective bargaining in local and other government fields in the face of such legalistic obstacles testifies to its inherent vitality. To measure the sweep of the movement it may be useful to examine the provisions of thirty-two pacts negotiated by AF of L and CIO unions with municipalities during 1943 and 1944. They were all signed in cities of 100,000 or less, with the exception of Philadelphia. Only eight out of these thirty-two agreements expressly exclude strikes and lockouts either by explicit reference or by reaffirmation of the particular union's avowed "no strike" policy. In the remaining twenty-four contracts, this topic was not mentioned. It was inferentially "left open," except in so far as the unions—in accord with their constitutions—have renounced the strike weapon.

In general, the workers covered are mechanics, janitors, laborers, street cleaners, attendants and the like. But six of the agreements embrace such white-collar groups as technicians, teachers, clerks, bookkeepers and stenographers, as well as foremen and superintendents of maintenance and repair crews. It is noteworthy that eleven of the documents call for the union shop, i.e., that all persons hired in the department concerned must be or become members of the union within thirty or sixty days after being employed and must remain in good standing. Indeed, three of the union-shop agreements provide that an employee is to be discharged if he fractures union rules. Three other agreements call for a hybrid type of union shop under which employees are encouraged to join the union, but are not in any way penalized should they desire not to do so. Nine of the agreements recognize the union as sole collective bargaining agency for its members but carry no proviso that employees must belong. In some instances, the employer permits a union representative to visit the department, investigate working conditions, and adjust disputes. Still others set up periodic conferences between the heads of city departments and the union leaders to establish "fair and equitable" working schedules.

Administration and Enforcement

Moreover, six of the agreements specify the checkoff for union dues and assessments, and in a seventh case this is made compulsory. Virtually all these contracts name as grievances to be settled between union spokesmen and the responsible administrator, such matters as reduction in pay, demotions, suspension, and layoff. Discharges must be accompanied by a written and detailed explanation of reasons wherefore and hearings are held to ascertain whether or not such terminations were justified. Sometimes changes in job classification and dismissals are threshed out by the top representatives of both union and public agency and are also frequently referred to arbitration.

More than half of these agreements also parallel their counterparts in private industry by calling for arbitration. They provide for an impartial arbitration board to be composed of a union spokesman, an appointee of the city council, and a third "outsider" to be jointly selected. Frequently, the United States Department of Labor is asked to name a neutral if the partisans can't agree on a choice.

Again reflecting practices in private industry, the wage and hour clauses in these agreements range from the requirement that all pay must conform to rates set by the budget to job classification structures as detailed and elaborate as those in an automobile factory. Any variation from the normal pay envelope has to be negotiated. Time and one half is standard. So, too, are the forty- or forty-eight-hour work weeks, and seniority on a departmental basis. Curiously enough, some of the contracts add elements to the seniority idea that are not always found in private plants. Instead of "plain and simple" seniority, ability, experience, and number of dependents are to be considered also in determining promotions. However, in tune with customary procedures, straight seniority prevails in layoffs, rehiring and transfers. The seniority of veterans and war workers is strongly safeguarded in nearly all the contracts. They furthermore contain provisions for vacations with pay (one week after one year's service), sick leave (ten days annually), double time for Sunday and other holiday work, for creation of safety regulations and changes in civil service retirement plans. Finally, like their prototypes in private industry, the agreements usually run for a year or two, and can be modified or abrogated by either of the signatories upon thirty- to sixty-days written notice.

Bargaining by Federal Agencies

In the province of the federal government, too, the content of collective bargaining increasingly resembles that in private spheres. Contracts dealing with wages, salaries, hours and working conditions, along with grievance machinery, are to be found in the TVA, the Inland Waterways, and the Alaska railroad. The first two, of course, are government-owned corporations. The third is an appendage of the Interior Department.

Less similar to collective bargaining agreements in private industry are the pacts in force in the Securities and Exchange Commission, the United States Housing Authority and the National Labor Relations Board. On the whole, these agreements—like many in state and municipal service—tend to be more informal. Mainly they call for consultation with the union to devise methods for handling grievances, and promotions, and generally for filling vacancies. Furthermore, in some spheres of government, a considerable amount of extracurricular bargaining over wage rates and working conditions exists. This kind of bargaining has been practiced for a long time in navy yards, arsenals, the Government Printing Office, the Bureau of Engraving and Printing and in activities of state and municipal governments where skilled craftsmen are required. While rates and hours are set by civil laws and regulations, they are often "bargained out" with the unions and prevail even if no written contract ensues.

Collective bargaining in government everywhere illustrates efforts to solve problems by mutual consent against the background of the administrative peculiarities and special legal powers of the government as employer. Hence in Inland Waterways, where no civil service merit system existed before the union appeared on the scene, a complete closed shop is to be found. But on the Alaska railroad, the agreement—signed with the Big Four railroad brotherhoods—gives the union no control over labor supply since the closed shop is prohibited by the Railway Labor Act. And, though this agreement sets forth in detail the wages for engineers, firemen, telegraph and telephone operators, trackwalkers, and even desk clerks and bellboys at the government's hotel in Curry,

pensions remain, under the Railroad Retirement Act which sets annuity standards, that no collective bargaining can alter.

On the other hand, the TVA from the outset was not restricted by pre-existing laws or civil service regulations. It was given carte blanche to fashion its own industrial relations policy proclaimed by its board of directors some ten years ago after consultation with AF of L and other unions. That policy first took the form of a declaration of intent to grant the TVA's 70,000 employees the right to organize unions of their own choosing and to bargain collectively. The TVA program marked a double innovation: (1) from the first, employees were called in to help formulate over-all working standards; and (2) this approach was consciously designed by the TVA administration to offset claims that unions have no rightful place in government, that they should not be allowed to affiliate with any outside labor organization, and that government employees anyway should do their collective bargaining through legislative and political channels. Three assumptions lay behind this approach: (1) that employees have a stake in the enterprise, and a "know-how" to contribute; (2) that their good sense and feeling of responsibility render them as zealous for the integrity of government as any top-ranking administrator; (3) that national policy itself, through the Wagner Act, encouraged collective bargaining. In 1940 these precepts, after considerable experimentation, were crystallized into TVA collective bargaining agreements with fifteen unions.

They reflect the more advanced principles of the management-union relationship. They embody everything from joint setting of pay scales to labor participation in improving production standards, techniques, and devices. The TVA as an independent government corporation, with wide latitude for entering almost any germane economic activity, is the forerunner of similar ventures. In its collective bargaining arrangements it is also likely to become the model for all "government in business."

State Bargaining Lags Behind

At the moment, collective bargaining in the state government field would seem to be less well advanced than in the municipal and federal areas. One explanation is that many state legislatures have a preponderance or a strong minority of assemblymen and senators from the rural and small town communities. While they are upon occasion amenable to pleas to raise the pay of other government servants, as individuals, they tend to be inimical to unions. They have often let it be known that they won't vote for added compensation if state employees have any truck with unions. Nevertheless, both the AF of L and CIO have succeeded in organizing locals in various state capitals. In Lansing, Michigan, for example, the State, County and Municipal Workers (CIO) lobbied through the legislature a new pension system for all state employees.

Some authorities on collective bargaining doubt the value of having the legislative branch of government, acting as it does upon the advice of the various civil service commissions, prescribe job categories, duties and incomes. They believe that the legislatures are too far removed from the day-by-day operations of departments and bureaus, that the lawmakers, indeed, know but vaguely what particular agencies are supposed to do, and are rarely familiar with their problems and personalities. It may well be that the very size and complexity of today's government functions render the legislative method of coping with personnel practice at once obsolete, haphazard and too remote to serve either the equities or efficiency. No subway, no water supply system can be conducted with the utmost dependability if, in effect, workers have to run to the legislature every time they want a grievance settled.

Improvements Under Discussion

To remedy this deficiency, and to legitimize a natural child of collective bargaining, two steps are being seriously considered at public management and public union conferences. The first is to empower by law every appropriate public manager to negotiate and sign contracts with unions within limits to be established by the legislature concerned. The second is to create within every civil service commission, at city, state and federal levels, an industrial relations unit. Its members would advise, and act for, the executive directly in charge in much the same manner as an industrial relations director of a private corporation. If private industry needs this type of assistance, the government can surely use it to advantage.

The sharing of authority and jurisdiction among administrative officials further suggests this approach. In New York City, for example, an expanding Department of Welfare may ask for additional space. But buildings are allocated, rented, approved and remodeled by the real-estate bureau in the Board of Estimate. The Department of Purchase handles all desks, filing cabinets, typewriters and other supplies. To remove a telephone from one sub-bureau to another is a process that must be okayed by the Budget Director. By the same token, government employees who have civil service status, or who are appointees, find that their duties constantly interlock with those performed in other departments, and therefore cannot submit their complaints merely to the head of a particular department. In such cases a personnel expert, attached to the Civil Service Commission's industrial relations unit, and familiar with the routines in each division, could be assigned to handle employee grievances by consultation with the head of each department involved.

There is no rule or rote, no magic formula for collective bargaining in the government, or anywhere else. Collective bargaining is an immensely flexible instrument that can be changed to meet changing needs. Certain techniques which the unions find useful, or even indispensable, in private industry cannot be as expeditiously applied to the public service. The closed shop, for example, originated in the desire to prevent the private employer from introducing nonunionists into the plant to undermine union standards. However, with the government employer, these standards—whether set up by statute or by collective bargaining or by a blend of both—are public, uniform, and fixed over a certain span of time. Under such circumstances, the closed shop—viewed as a method for protecting union standards—has far less reason to exist.

However, as government functions multiply, and ramify out from the function of policing toward the administrative and proprietary, the same underlying forces that sponsored collective bargaining in private enterprise will become more and more manifest in public enterprise. The similarity, even the identity, between collective bargaining agreements with private industry and those with the government would seem to confirm this trend.

Chapter 13

IMPACT OF WAR

SHORTLY AFTER THE START of the national defense program in June 1940, the United States strike curve began to go up very rapidly, coinciding with a sharp rise in employment. Bitter, prolonged strife between many managements and many unions broke out even as blueprints for guns, tanks, planes were being transformed into new martial might. The Allis-Chalmers dispute, for example, dragging out for three months, held up production of twenty-nine types of machinery urgently required by the expanding Navy. Other industrial clashes in other plants and mines and shops and shipyards, some marked by rioting, similarly hampered output of materiel for our armed forces and for export to Britain.

Neither the commissioners of the United States Conciliation Service nor the "trouble shooters" working out of the Labor Division of the National Defense Advisory Commission and its sequel, the Office of Production Management, were able to arrest this trend—a trend complicated by the upsurge of jurisdictional feuds between the AF of L and the CIO. Hence in March of 1941, President Roosevelt established the National Defense Mediation Board to strengthen the hand of Conciliation Service emissaries and their prototypes in the OPM. The Board was composed of four labor members (two AF of L, two CIO) ; four industry members suggested by various business associations and three public members, all appointed by the President.

The Board, as its name implied, was supposed to mediate labor-management disputes, acting as official friend and informal counselor to assist the contending parties to iron out their differences. If mediation failed, the Board could fall back on voluntary arbitration. The Board furthermore sought to enlist public opinion behind its findings, using the threat of its own official condemnation to bring recalcitrant managements and unions into line.

The results of this approach, combined mediation and voluntary arbitration, were often noteworthy. At the same time, the Board developed the plan of asking strikers to return to work, and employers to restore the conditions that existed before the dispute flared up, while the Board looked into the merits as prologue to making its recommendations for settlement. By October 1941 this practice had been generally accepted. It had been accepted to such an extent that virtually all workers, involved in a controversy pending before the Board, stayed on the production line instead of going out on the picket line. But this harmonious state of affairs didn't last very long.

Voluntary Mediation Fails

In June of 1941, Communist leaders of the United Automobile Workers local (CIO) at the North American Aviation Company, pulled the employees out on strike, violating an interim agreement with the Board, and scorning its "get back to work" adjurations. Using his powers under the "unlimited national emergency" he had previously declared to exist, the President directed the Secretary of War to seize the plant and operate it. Upon orders from the International officers of the UAW-CIO, the strikers resumed their jobs, and the plant was promptly restored to private management. But the Board's prestige was shaken.

It was soon to be shaken again. In the early fall of 1941, the Board recommended a maintenance-of-membership clause to settle a dispute between the Federal Shipbuilding and Drydock Company and the Marine and Shipbuilding Workers (CIO). The company rejected this proposal. The Board once more had no alternative but to appeal to the President for help. He directed the Secretary of the Navy to take over the company's facilities and run them. Thus, the Board which had started out as a voluntary mediatory branch of government, under the exigencies of the occasion had to resort to compulsory arbitration, or settlement by force. Simultaneously, it presented a picture of impotence. When up against stubborn resistance to its findings, the Board was stalemated since it lacked enforcement authority of its own. To achieve compliance, it could invoke the ultimate powers of the state only by appeal to the President.

It might have continued indefinitely, however, if it had not been for John L. Lewis and his United Mine Workers. They wanted to extend to the so-called "captive mines" owned by the United States Steel Corporation the same closed-shop provisions that prevailed throughout the coal industry proper. When the dispute that ensued from this issue reached the Board, it refused the miners' demand. The President reinforced the Board's position by stating that the United States government would never impose the closed shop upon any employer. At Mr. Lewis' behest, the CIO members thereupon withdrew from the Board, wrecking it.

The Industry-Labor Conference of 1941

With the Board's extinction a new wave of strikes billowed over the country. In the House and Senate bills to clamp down draconian controls over unions, and over industrial relations generally, were filling the legislative hopper. To thwart these pending measures, to quiet public resentment over work stoppages, and to set up new policies and new machinery for the peaceful resolution of disputes, the Administration in November 1941 prepared to call a conference between industry and labor. Pearl Harbor activated the original program which had shown signs of bogging down and three weeks later the conference was convened in Washington. It was attended by twelve industrialists and twelve labor leaders (six each from AF of L and CIO). William H. Davis, Chairman of the defunct National Mediation Board acted as moderator and Senator Elbert D. Thomas (D.) of Utah as his associate.

For six days the conference was deadlocked over the question of union security. Employers urged that union status in this respect be frozen for the duration, as it was in World War I—in short, that the unions should cease asking for the closed shop, while employers would retain it wherever it already existed. Both AF of L and CIO leaders, however, were afraid to go along with this idea. They sensed that the public would not long tolerate use of the strike for enforcing unionism's demands for the closed shop. They feared that unless they could continue to press for the closed shop and its variants in every other way, they would find that the draft, labor turnover, and employer opposition might weaken particular unions to such an extent that they would emerge from the war considerably damaged, if not almost extinguished.

After some wrangling on this subject by all the conferees, the President announced that agreement had been reached on three major counts:

1. That strikes and lockouts would be relinquished for the period of the war;
2. That all disputes would be settled by methods that would not hamper war production;
3. That a new National War Labor Board would be established to handle management-labor conflict whenever the parties failed to reconcile their differences by other means.

Some critics still denounce the late Mr. Roosevelt's handling of this conference. They assert that no authentic agreement had been achieved, and that Mr. Roosevelt was something less than forthright in announcing a concert of opinions when none existed. They claim that he was even more ill-advised to ignore Congress in this effort to formulate wartime labor policy. They further maintain that none of the conferees from the National Association of Manufacturers, the U.S. Chamber of Commerce, the AF of L or CIO had authority to bind their respective organizations to comply with the policy embodied in the President's three points. Moreover, these same critics complain that the conferees were not instructed by the President to submit the new policy to their memberships for ratification. In short, even today, they insist that the entire policy was in its origins inconclusive, an improvisation thrown together *in vacuo;* and that since it lacked Congressional participation, it lacked a sound basis for public support.

On the other hand, Administration defenders declare that there was a rough-and-ready working agreement, at least on the three major points proclaimed by the President. They argue that, after all, the Japanese had bombed Pearl Harbor, and that time was of the essence in producing war weapons—a process that could have been slowed down to an incalculable extent by strikes. The situation, they say, called for speedy action to prevent strikes—speedy action of a kind that could not await Congressional debates which, when they center around the inflammatory issue of industrial relations, are invariably protracted. The President, acting under his war powers, had every Constitutional right to adopt whatever course he thought would best serve the nation's war needs. Finally, they maintain that outside of William H. Davis and Senator Thomas, all the others at the conference were duly elected officials or designated emissaries of their organizations, having all the delegated authority implicit in these positions.

War Labor Board Established

The tangled problem of union security was omitted from the Presidential pronouncement. Employer spokesmen afterwards insisted that they had never, directly or by implication, agreed to let the solution of this contested point rest with any government agency. Labor spokesmen claimed that it was at least inferred. In any event, when on January 12, 1942, the President issued Executive Order 9017 establishing the National War Labor Board, it was empowered to deal with every type of dispute that "might interrupt work that contributes to the effective prosecution of the war."

Like its predecessor, the National Defense Mediation Board, the new Board was, and remains, the only government agency that wholly functions on a tripartite basis. To be sure, there are advisory boards and committees similarly constituted in the WPB, OPA, WMC and elsewhere. But the NWLB is the single government agency in which both policy-making and operations are from start to finish in the hands of labor, industry and public representatives each with the same voting power.

At present, the NWLB is composed of four regular public members (with one vacancy) and four alternates, all of whom serve full time and are appointed by the President. Similarly, there are four regular and four alternate industry members, and about fifteen substitute industry members. The regulars and alternates are named by the President but the substitutes by the WLB itself.

By the same token, there are four regular and four alternate labor
members, half from the AF of L and half from the CIO, appointed
by the President, and some fifteen substitutes named by the WLB.
All industry and labor members are selected from a list of nomi-
nations made by their various major national organizations such
as the National Association of Manufacturers, the U.S. Chamber
of Commerce, the AF of L and the CIO.

The industry members never, and the labor members rarely, put
in full time on the Board. There is a constant rotation of regulars,
alternates, and substitutes from these groups. The Board's tremendous work-load compels it to subdivide its personnel into
sections of two each from industry, labor and the public, with a
total of six thus comprising a quorum. On high-policy questions,
however, and in important cases which, in their results, create
policy, full-dress Board sessions are convened.

The Board officers consist of a chairman, and vice chairman,
chosen by the President from among the public members. At general headquarters in Washington, an executive director coordinates
the activities of the Disputes, Legal, and Administrative Management Divisions, along with the Information Service. Under his
supervision also falls the extremely important Wage Stabilization
Division which conducts elaborate economic research to guide the
Board in arriving at wage decisions. The Wage Stabilization Division came into being when the range of the Board's activity was
vastly enlarged, under Executive Order 9250 issued on October 2,
1942, to carry out the Anti-Inflation Act of Congress. This entrusted to the Board the task of stabilizing wages as part of the
Administration's anti-inflation program. Hence, in addition to
settling disputes, the Board had to see to it that no adjustments
in wage rates (or in most salary rates under $5,000 a year) could
be made without its sanction.

The Board Decentralized

To cope with the tremendous new volume of work arising from
its wage stabilization powers, the Board had to decentralize. As
a disputes agency it could operate from Washington, naming any
extra personnel it needed for work in the field. But as a *combina-*

tion disputes and wage stabilization entity, this procedure soon proved to be impossible. Indeed, for the first year following Executive Order 9250, the Board was called on to handle 109,000 cases of voluntary wage and salary adjustments alone.

In February 1943, the Board therefore divided the country into twelve regions, each served by a Regional War Labor Board to which have been delegated virtually all the powers of the parent body in determining both voluntary and disputes cases in wages as well as resolving industrial discords from other causes. In region 1 are Connecticut, Maine, Massachusetts, New Hampshire, Rhode Island and Vermont. In region 2 are northern New Jersey and the whole of New York. In region 3 are southern New Jersey, Pennsylvania, Delaware, the District of Columbia and Maryland. In region 4 are Alabama, Florida, Georgia, Mississippi, North Carolina, South Carolina, Tennessee and Virginia. In region 5 are Kentucky, Ohio and West Virginia. In region 6 are Illinois, Indiana, Minnesota, North Dakota, South Dakota and Wisconsin. In region 7 are Arkansas, Iowa, Kansas, Missouri and Nebraska. In region 8 are Louisiana, Oklahoma, and Texas. In region 9 are Colorado, Idaho, Montana, New Mexico, Utah and Wyoming. In region 10 are Arizona, California and Nevada. Region 11 is Michigan. In region 12 are Alaska, Oregon and Washington. In region 14 is Hawaii.

As another step in decentralization, the National Board has created tripartite commissions to cope with the special geographic and industrial perplexities in such industries as lumber, tool and die making, nonferrous metal mining, trucking. Like the regional boards, these commissions, which are set up along industry lines, can make final decisions in cases within their purview, subject to appeal by the parties, or to review by the National Board on its own motion. In addition to the commissions are permanent panels namely, the Air Frame Panel, the Steel Panel, the Telephone Panel and the War Shipping Panel. Like the commissions, they are also set up along industry lines but they do not issue directives or orders. Instead they only recommend to the National Board methods for the disposition of cases. Dispute cases are generally referred to tripartite panels for hearings and recommendations.

These panels usually consist of one representative each from the public, from industry and from labor. Sometimes, with the consent of the participants, a case may be referred to a single hearing official who is either a staff member or a person selected from the list of public panel members. The overwhelming majority of dispute cases are handled by the regional boards who themselves appoint the panels and hearing officers. Under this arrangement the National Board itself was transformed into a supreme court for industrial disputes and wage stabilization, devoting itself to appeals from its "lower courts" (regional boards and commissions) to the processing of major cases, and to the formulation of directives and general orders as guideposts to over-all policy.

The Board's Jurisdiction Defined

The WLB did not long retain intact its original all-embracing power in the stabilization sphere. To lighten its administrative chores, it in effect exempted from its authority all establishments with eight or less employees. In some fifty districts and localities, however, the Board has required employers of eight or less to secure its approval for wage changes. In November 1942, the Director of the Office of Economic Stabilization transferred to the Secretary of Agriculture the task of stabilizing wages for the nation's 2.5 million farm laborers. Three months later the President (under Executive Order 9299) removed from the Board's jurisdiction some 1.4 million railroad and airline employees, giving to a National Railway panel the duty of stabilizing their incomes. Moreover, the WLB shares with the Wage Adjustment Board in the Department of Labor jurisdiction over some 2 million building trades craftsmen. The wage decisions of all other agencies, however, must conform with stabilization rules laid down by the WLB.

Such nonprofit institutions as community chest funds, foundations, or cemetery companies, as well as employees of institutions devoted exclusively to religious, charitable, educational, or literary purposes, have been requested to conform to the over-all stabilization policy. Nevertheless, the field remaining to the Board would seem to be broad and formidable enough. In the domain of stabilization it has not only to pass on wage and salary increases jointly agreed on by employer and employees but also must adjudicate disputes arising from pay-envelope issues, as well as finally to resolve every other kind of industrial conflict within its jurisdiction—a jurisdiction which covers an estimated 25 million employees. Unlike virtually all other United States labor laws, the Wage Stabilization Act contains no specific numerical exemptions.

What Is a "War Industry"?

From its very beginning the Board's jurisdiction has been frequently questioned. Many employers involved in disputes coming before the Board maintained from the first that their companies were not engaged in "war industry" within the meaning of Executive Order 9017, i.e., that they had nothing to do with the "effective prosecution of the war." However, the Board had early taken control over disputes covering employees in hotels, laundries, dyeing plants and stock-brokerage houses on the ground that these undertakings did have at least an indirect influence upon the conduct of the war. It was not until March 1943, when the Board handed down its ruling in the Reuben H. Donnelley Corporation case, that it really crystallized its position on this subject.

The case involved a dispute over salaries between the company and a group of its salesmen who solicited advertising for the classified section of telephone directories. On the face of it, this pursuit was seemingly far removed from any impact on the war effort. The Board, however, assumed jurisdiction since, after much soul-searching, it had once and for all concluded that any dispute, irrespective of its character, which may result in strike or lockout, has some actual or potential effect upon "the more effective prosecution of the war." It has subsequently supported this view by pointing to the "fallacy" of seeking to differentiate between "war industries" and "nonwar industries" at a time when all material and human resources are mobilized for all-out war. The Board asserted that the attempt to set up any such "classifications would necessitate the assumption that employees in industries and businesses defined as nonessential to the war effort are free to strike and lock out. Such . . . premises would be shocking to the American people because they expect, and have the right to expect, that for the duration of the war, all labor disputes are to be settled by peaceful procedures." Moreover, in its decision on the Donnelley case, the Board went out of its way to make doubly clear its stand on this entire issue.

The passage of the War Labor Disputes Act of June 5, 1943 once and for all "confined" the WLB's jurisdiction to disputes affecting the war effort. Up to that time, the Board's scope was as broad as the war powers of the President himself, since its authority derived from Executive Order 9107 and, as such, represented a direct delegation of Presidential prerogatives. As a matter of fact, however, the War Labor Disputes Act buttressed the Board with legislative sanction to do virtually what it had been doing anyway on its own discretion. The Act extinguished the last expiring doubts about WLB powers—not only to "decide the dispute" but also to specify the "Terms and conditions . . . governing the relations between the parties."

WLB versus NLRB

There was, however, still another and different area of jurisdiction that the WLB had to define—and on a trial and error basis—namely, its relations with the National Labor Relations Board. For when the WLB began carrying out its mandates, it found this other agency already exercising dominion over certain types of industrial dissension. The Wagner Act provided for the NLRB (1) to make employers "cease and desist" from attempts to prevent their workers from organizing unions of their own choosing, and (2) to determine by means of elections, or otherwise, what union the majority of employees wanted to represent them in collective bargaining negotiations.

The NLRB, of course, is in no way concerned with the content of a collective bargaining agreement nor with efforts to interpret it, or enforce it. In brief, the settlement of disputes over the terms and conditions of employment are outside the NLRB's province. In contrast, the WLB—charged with the responsibility for adjusting all wartime labor disputes—soon discovered that these included points of collective representation and unfair labor practices which were NLRB territory. While the NLRB is a permanent peacetime body, designed to ensure freedom of economic action to employees, the WLB is an emergency tribunal, designed to help ensure maximum war production. Their jurisdiction at some points overlaps. They have been able, however, to devise techniques of collaboration that have averted the threat of what might have been a saddening and confusing squabble over jurisdiction, with bad effects upon labor law and labor relations.

Since the NLRB's authority and methods are carefully prescribed by Congress, and minutely crystallized by day-to-day practice over the past ten years, it was mainly up to the more flexible, relatively unhampered WLB to work out a proper *modus vivendi*. The executive order creating the WLB contains the injunction: "Nothing herein shall be construed as superseding or in conflict with the provisions of the National Labor Relations Act." Hence the WLB—even though it proclaimed the theory that its own *raison d'être*, uninterrupted war output, gave it virtually unlimited jurisdiction—in practice left the NLRB area of activity untouched, with some few exceptions. Over and above the executive order's instructions, the WLB policy in this regard reflected the effort of its public members in particular to do nothing that would impair NLRB standing, or thwart its processes.

Testing the Issues in the Courts

The first WLB proceeding that caused it to share jurisdiction with the NLRB occurred in the Virginia Electric and Power Company case. In 1937 this utility had signed a contract with an organization of its employees, an alleged company union, known as the Independent. A year later, the Amalgamated Association of Street and Railway Employees (AF of L) submitted charges of unfair labor practices before the NLRB which then directed the company to dissolve the Independent, as demonstrably its own creature. However, the Circuit Court of Appeals reversed the NLRB finding in November 1940, and thirteen months later the Supreme Court referred the entire case back to the NLRB to redetermine the issues. At about the same time, the Amalgamated asked the NLRB to name it as the bona fide collective bargaining agent since it had enrolled a majority of the employees. But in accord with NLRB doctrine this request was withdrawn in the light of the Supreme Court's adjuration to go into the whole business all over again. Meanwhile, the Independent had obtained an extension of its original contract with the company, highlighted by a pay boost. At this juncture, the members of the Amalgamated lost patience and voted to strike unless their union was immediately recognized. The WLB stepped in to settle it.

It may be noted that in this kind of situation, one that cropped up throughout the 1941-1943 period, the time element was crucial. To the NLRB, with its tempo set to the metronome of peace, the lapse of months, or even years, was secondary to the need to ensure to employers the right to contest NLRB action in the courts. If this NLRB pace was too slow for employees in peacetime they could always resort to the strike, or other devices to get the employer to concede to their demands. The WLB, however, if it were to deliver on its assignment to prevent work stoppages from hindering war production, presumably could not afford the luxury of such delays. Then, too, the Amalgamated which as an AF of L affiliate had given up the strike for the duration, was up against the Hobson's choice of either conforming to NLRB's long drawn-out methods, or going back on its word, unless the WLB could intercede. The Amalgamated in fact pointed out to the WLB that the sheer length of the NLRB litigation had exasperated its members, impairing their morale and efficiency. For this reason, too, it urged the WLB to draw on its emergency powers to dispose of the case quickly.

But the WLB, attached as always to the mediation modality, rejected the union's plea. Instead the WLB set up a mediation panel, hoping that this would arrange matters by mutual consent. This expectation was not fulfilled. The WLB then recommitted the issue to the NLRB with the request that it "expedite" the case. Simultaneously, the WLB told the Virginia Power and Electric Company and the Amalgamated to continue operations, pending the outcome. Eight months later, the WLB—finding no other alternative—directed the utility to disestablish its company union.

Labor Urges More Speed

Visibly the WLB's behavior in this case was not calculated to hasten the settlement of wartime labor disputes. Both AF of L and CIO members, enraged by such dilatory devices, clamored for more affirmative—and speedier—action. Their attitude on this score was related to the fact that every week thousands of new workers, potential union members, were entering war industry. Labor shortages were raising wages, without benefit of union influence, especially in instances where the union was still struggling to gain employer recognition. To lure these new workers into the fold, the unions had to have at least official collective bargaining status. Otherwise, they couldn't claim credit for higher wages. Even more important, since the unions had forfeited the strike for any purpose, whether for recognition or more pay, the antagonistic employer, in their view, held all the trumps. He could postpone recognizing the union for a year or longer by the simple expedient of insisting upon Wagner Act procedure.

This meant that even after the NLRB had ordered him to deal with the union, no sanctions could apply until a Circuit Court of Appeals, upon pain of contempt, sustained the NLRB ruling. He could stall further by taking his case to the Supreme Court. In the meantime, newcomers to his plant would be impressed by the union's inability to accomplish anything to their advantage. The AF of L and CIO warned the WLB that either *it* would have to contrive more rapid remedies, while sharing jurisdiction with the NLRB, or assume complete jurisdiction on *its* own.

NLRB Powers Strengthened

Apparently persuaded by this line of reasoning, the WLB married the Wagner Act to wartime disputes in the Ohio Public Service case. The company, banking on a favorable opinion from a Circuit Court of Appeals review, refused to bargain with the union that had won an NLRB election, thus tying the situation into a knot less gracious than Gordian. On this occasion, however, the Board played the role of Alexander—and cut it. It informed the company that it must immediately recognize and bargain with the union. The WLB further served notice that whenever the

NLRB certified a union as the correct collective bargaining agent, this step would be final and binding upon the WLB unless the older agency modified or reversed its own rulings or "appropriate judicial authority" did either or both. In other words the WLB became, on its own discretion, an enforcement arm of the NLRB. It should be noted that in pursuing this course, the WLB tended to deprive the employer of the right of judicial review of an NLRB administrative order—a right guaranteed by the Wagner Act. Yet the WLB faced the necessity of either altering the enforcement methods of the Wagner Act under which the Fabian tactics of employers were putting workers into a restive and bellicose mood, or removing this kind of unrest and thus assuring continuous output of war weapons. The WLB chose the path of restricting employer privilege.

The precepts laid down by the WLB in the Ohio Public Service case were extended to questions of discharge for union activity, and some minor issues where WLB and NLRB jurisdictions infringed upon each other. The net result of their concurrent jurisdiction during the war has been to uphold and reinforce NLRB authority and prestige.

WLB Tried to Nourish Voluntary Bargaining

In wartime, collective bargaining must be conducted within the framework of government policies, decisions, and directives. But within these limits the WLB sought persistently to preserve and amplify collective bargaining. Its very procedure reflects this concern. Under the terms of the WLB's own charter, it is only after a dispute cannot be resolved by means of collective bargaining, and after the mediation efforts of the U.S. Conciliation Service have proved unavailing, that the Secretary of Labor certifies the controversy to the WLB. (Less frequently, the Board— after consultation with the Secretary of Labor—may assume jurisdiction on its own motion.) The course that a dispute takes once it reaches the Board is charted by its Committee on New Cases which may refer the dispute to further mediation, or to a fact-finding panel, or to a single investigator, or to voluntary arbitration—in short to explore and exhaust every conceivable avenue of settlement by further negotiations between employer and employees. "It is in the operation of this Committee," said William H. Davis, then WLB Chairman, "which tries to exploit all possible means of voluntary agreement, that the Board's basic concern for collective bargaining is most effectively expressed."

The Board soon discovered, however, that there was one form of dispute in which settlement by the parties was not feasible. This was the union security conflict which had destroyed the National Defense Mediation Board, and had been the subject of such acrimonious debate at the industry-labor conference to which the WLB owed its immediate origin. On the one hand, the Board could not order this kind of union security without generating more trouble than it cured because of employer opposition to an extension of the closed shop during wartime which had been fortified by the President's statement that the government would never foist the closed shop on any management. On the other hand, the Board's public members were committed to the belief that authentic collective bargaining was impossible without a stable, responsible union. They were further convinced that the war emergency placed a special hardship on labor leaders since it deprived them of the chance to use the strike for satisfying the wage and other demands of their adherents.

Then, too, the Board's public members favored a system that would carry the employer-union relationship as quickly as possible through the early contentious period, when the union is weak and struggling, to the more peaceable, cooperative period when the union is a going concern. It is axiomatic that only when a written agreement with a union to which the majority of employees belong has formalized collective bargaining, can labor leadership put the stress on administration as against organization. The public members believed that once the questions of union recognition and security were out of the way, leadership could concentrate not only on applying the clauses of the contract but also on assisting management to cut down on absenteeism, and labor turnover, and otherwise help to keep production high and regular.

"Maintenance of Membership" Proposed

The maintenance-of-membership idea grew out of efforts to find a compromise in the open-shop versus closed-shop squabble. The maintenance-of-membership clause in a collective bargaining agreement does not require an employee to join or belong to a union. If already a member, he is given opportunity to withdraw within a specified period of, say, from fifteen to thirty days. But if he does not so signify his intention to quit, he must remain a member of the union throughout the life of the contract. Hence, maintenance of membership becomes a mechanism which enables the union to keep up its numerical and dues-paying strength. Considerable experiment was needed before the present and standard maintenance-of-membership form finally emerged. Over the first six months, several different varieties were ordained by the Board. Early in April 1942, for example, the Board directed the International Harvester Company to incorporate a maintenance-of-membership clause in its contracts with a number of AF of L and CIO unions at its eight plants in various parts of the country. It was to take effect only if a majority of the union members involved voted in its favor. Ninety per cent of them marked "Yes" on secret ballots in elections held under Board auspices at each of the eight plants. However, this type of voting procedure was abandoned since elections were too costly. To hold them on a national scale, not only put a strain on the Board's budget but also placed too onerous a burden upon its administrative machinery.

The Board faced its next important test on maintenance of membership when seeking to dispose, once and for all, of the almost perennial dispute over union security between the Marine and Shipbuilding Workers (CIO) and the Federal Ship and Drydock Company, a U.S. Steel subsidiary. It was this company (see above) which had rejected the National Defense Mediation Board's recommendation for a maintenance-of-membership plan, causing the President to have the company's plant seized and run by the Navy. A month after Pearl Harbor, however, the plant had been restored to private management. When early in 1942 this controversy came before the Board, it specified a new maintenance-of-membership provision. It stipulated that a union member who did not remain in good standing, i.e., refused to pay his dues and abide by the union's working rules, and the like, should be discharged unless "as a condition of continued employment" the employee should then agree "to request the company, in writing, to deduct from his pay his financial obligations to the union."

The Plan Is Modified

In dissenting from this majority decision, rendered by the Board's public and labor members, the employer members declared that they would find such rulings more palatable if every individual employee were allowed a definite time, after the Board's directive, in which to resign from the union if he didn't wish to be bound by the maintenance-of-membership proviso. This employer proposal for an "escape period" was adopted by the Board in the Ryan Aeronautical case in June 1942. A similar escape clause was soon combined with a new feature that no employee can be coerced into union membership. The Board added this ingredient when it handed down a maintenance-of-membership award in the S. A. Woods Machine Company case in August 1942. Then, carrying this principle to its logical conclusion, the Board stressed its determination to guarantee the worker complete freedom of choice. In November 1942, it passed a resolution designed to protect a union member covered by a maintenance-of-membership clause from both union and employer interference with his liberty to withdraw within the fifteen-day period without risking his livelihood. The Board's resolution stated in part:

Any employee may withdraw from his union without losing his job at any time prior to the effective date of the maintenance-of-membership clause . . . irrespective of any rules, regulations or constitutional provisions of the union involved that would otherwise make such withdrawal ineffective. . . . Employers shall refrain from attempting to influence employees to resign from the union and from adopting other means or methods of interfering with the voluntary action and free choice of the employees.

Finally, the Board rounded out its union security policy in the Harvill Aircraft case in February 1943. It then declared that no company can be permitted to take advantage of labor's no-strike

pledge in order to rescind, in wartime, a union shop already established by a prior contract arrived at by collective bargaining.

The evolution of the maintenance-of-membership modality
through its various stages typifies Board insistence upon fostering
and extending the framework within which collective bargaining
can be conducted, despite the limitations of the war emergency.
Moreover, the WLB has provided that whenever any union member has been deprived of "good standing" and he objects, the controversy is to be submitted to the arbitrator who presumably will
review the case on its merits. In short, the War Labor Board has
implemented its belief that collective bargaining depends, in large
measure, upon a stable and secure union. It applied maintenance
of membership as a compromise between the open and closed shop
to ensure this kind of union security and stability. In other words,
the Board has used maintenance of membership to maintain collective bargaining by maintaining unionism.

Will Membership Maintenance Survive?

It remains, of course, a moot point as to whether or not maintenance of membership will survive—either under government pressure or voluntarily—now that the war is over. Many employers are
against it. Some oppose it because they think it is merely an
oblique kind of closed shop, or at least its inevitable preface. Still
others oppose maintenance of membership because notably when
bracketed with the checkoff, it allows unions to accumulate big
treasuries that would enable them to finance long "waiting-it-out"
strikes. On the other hand, the desire of labor leaders for the
complete closed shop is not satisfied by maintenance of membership. In its favor, however, is the fact that it has all the earmarks
of a workable compromise. It both gives to and takes away from
opposing desires: management's wish to be entirely free to hire
and fire, and labor's wish to protect its organization by "sewing
it up tight."

Unionism's success in holding and even expanding its ranks
during the war, would seem to have been due at least partly to the
widespread application of maintenance of membership. At the
same time, it lessened the union's ability to coerce into affiliation

the few mavericks who, for their own reasons, did not want to sign up. The opportunity to exercise such feelings of independence not only has high intrinsic value but also can serve as a check upon union leadership. The chance to quit without fear of being penalized can become a good gadfly, a protest against a leadership indolent, irresponsible, or incompetent.

While the wartime merits of maintenance of membership have not automatically ensured its continuance in peace, they have made its use at least tolerable, especially in instances where the strength of the union and management is closely matched; and, in a dispute over union security both groups would find it more expedient to compromise rather than to slug it out.

More Wage Rationalization Will Survive the War

The commotion surrounding wage stabilization has tended to obscure a very crucial development in collective bargaining: the "speeded up" encroachment of unionism, under government aegis, into domains customarily regarded as management's own. It is this doctrine—far more than the question as to whether or not the Little Steel formula allows five or ten or fifteen cents an hour as a wage increase—that will largely determine the peacetime climate of collective bargaining. It is likely that now that the war is over, WLB control over wages will vanish. Perhaps, however, WLB will be stationed on the pay front, during a time of transition, to prevent too sharp a deflationary movement of wages in peace in the same way that it prevented their too sharp inflationary movement in war. WLB's fate as a disputes agency remains anyone's guess.

There can be no doubt, of course, that what the WLB has accomplished in helping to rationalize the American wage structure by plant, industry and region will have its effect on peacetime pay practices, as such. But even more significant are the methods and procedures by which it has been attained. It is these means rather than the end which represent a deepening and broadening of the collective bargaining function.

From the first month that the WLB undertook to stabilize wages, whether by correcting maladjustments, or inequities, or substandards of living, or whatever, it discerned that the wage pattern in many plants reflected a haphazard and fortuitous, rather than a planned and comprehensible, series of relationships. In the larger companies the WLB frequently found six or seven hundred wage rates, many of which covered only a single individual. Indeed, the five subsidiary companies of the U.S. Steel Corporation together had approximately 26,000 different rates. The underlying reason, of course, is that most of our wage structures "just growed," like Topsy. They embody the vestigial remains of an earlier day's personnel practice.

The rate of pay was based on the market value as this filtered through the employer's estimate of an applicant's ability. But with the great growth of industrial establishments the setting of rates for particular jobs became capricious, especially when one man's work was compared with another's. As the big factory replaced the small shop, as plants had thousands rather than dozens on their pay rolls, an intermediate group of foremen and supervisors had a hand in shaping pay schedules. Often wage differentials were used to ward off unionism. When rates that seem to have neither rhyme nor reason exist, the suspicion that management intends to reward for something more than the work done tends to flourish. The belief, as often false as true, arises that the employer purposely creates variations in individual rates to undermine the union, to build loyalty to himself in exchange for pay favors. All this fosters resentment among a labor force. Indeed, in the West Coast Air Frame cases, the Board pointed out: "In our opinion there is no single factor in the whole field of labor relations that does more to break down morale, create individual dissatisfaction, encourage absenteeism, increase labor turnover, and hamper production than obviously unjust inequalities in the wage rates paid to different individuals in the same labor group within the same plant."

Job Classifications Set Up

Since such conditions constantly promote disputes, the WLB was time and again compelled to remedy "unjust inequalities in the wage rates," which were on the whole incorporated in crazy-quilt systems of job classification. A job classification, of course, is a category of jobs and positions similar in nature and content and in the amount of knowledge, skill, experience and responsibility required. It involves more than a title; the classification itself should be clearly defined and described. In theory, where jobs differ, there must be different classifications: typists, stenographers and secretaries are not to be lumped together into a single catalogue, but must be separately listed into three groups. Payment for each classification may be made on a *rate* basis under which everyone in this category gets the same wage or salary; or payment may be made on a *rate-range* basis whenever a job classification contains a number of rates varying from a minimum of, say, 75 cents an hour to a maximum of $1.00 an hour for the same job.

When it came to stabilizing wages within a plant, the WLB found that altogether too many job classifications, notably those with rate ranges, were an admixture of the arbitrary and the anarchic. This lack of logic aroused among the workers feelings of being unfairly treated—feelings intensified by the competitive bidding for labor among employers, by changes in process accompanied by changes in rates, by a general impression on the part of the individual worker that he wasn't making out as well as others.

Before the war it had been traditionally management's prerogative to fix rates and rate ranges within a job classification. But under war conditions this practice was raising such havoc with labor morale and productivity that the WLB decided that if the workers themselves, through their unions, could participate in fixing rates and rate ranges a great deal of management-labor conflict would be eradicated at the source. Hence, in more than three hundred cases the Board directed managements and unions to negotiate the elimination of intraplant inequities—different rates of pay for jobs entailing the same skill and experience. To gain this goal, the Board has ordered what amounts to a complete re-examination of the content and character of every job in a company.

Wage Structure: a Joint Responsibility

More importantly, the Board directed that this project be jointly undertaken by management and the union. This crystallized and quickened the trend toward union participation in fashioning wage patterns. Obviously, to transfer to collective bargaining the very creation of the wage-rate structure, with its critical influence on costs and profits, is to let the union invade a province previously pre-empted by the comptroller, the engineer, and executive management generally.

The WLB decision in the Big Steel case set forth this doctrine in its most detailed and dramatic form. The Board commanded the management and the union to collaborate in the effort to: (1) describe concisely and simply the nature and characteristics of each job, (2) place jobs in their proper relationship to each other in terms of what has to be mechanically done and the human capacity needed to do it, (3) group jobs which are similar into a single cluster or configuration, and (4) set the appropriate rates for every such alignment, or job classification.

Although encouraged by the WLB as a wartime measure, this practice of developing with the union the exact ranking of jobs within the hierarchy of a plant's occupations, of assessing each job's relative standing in the production scheme, of establishing the sums to be paid for that job, has now hardened into a widely accepted procedure. While this circumscribes the authority of management, it has certain practical advantages to the employer. The union, once it becomes a responsible party to the fashioning of any job classification system cannot protest, save in minor details, when that system is put into effect. As a partner in a common venture, it is deprived of any rightful ground on which it can object to "unfair" or "arbitrary" behavior on the part of management. A primary cause for labor complaints is by this means virtually abolished, the more especially since it does much to fulfill labor's instinctive demand for "equal pay for equal work."

The Merit Increase Plan

It is not alone in devising techniques of this kind that the

WLB, in its ardor to promote collective bargaining, has moved the unions further into management's bailiwick. In the General Electric Company case, along with others, the Board has given the union opportunity to share with management the obligation to administer the system under which an employee advances from one pay level to another: the so-called *merit increase* plan. Formerly, the question as to whether or not an employee should get a raise was decided by management alone. It similarly forged the standards by which an employee's performance was to be judged. In the past, if he failed to get an increase on the "merit" basis, he had no recourse, except grousing and charges of sycophancy which may have relieved his feelings but did nothing to swell the size of his pay envelope. The foreman, as the person immediately responsible, often became the object of mistrust. Worker pique over real or alleged supervisory partiality impaired morale.

The labor movement's own remedy for this condition was a proposal to take the matter entirely out of management's hands by means of automatic wage and salary increases. These were to be founded not upon a debatable competence but rather upon length of service. Management opposed this idea as an undue trespassing upon its own historic ground and because it impaired efficiency.

However, in much the same way that the WLB designed maintenance of membership as a compromise between the open and closed shop, it resolved this conflict by designing a new variety of merit increase plan. Under this scheme, management ostensibly reserves one of its old prerogatives and itself "decides" whether or not an employee is entitled to a raise. But in all other respects, union participation prevails to such an extent that management's exercise of its former privilege becomes all but meaningless. The four corner posts that support this new WLB policy are: (1) joint management-union negotiation to set up the criteria (skill, diligence, initiative, etc.) with which to measure the value of an employee's contribution; (2) periodic review of an employee's work, a review in which the employer applies the criteria, as jointly fashioned by management and union, to ascertain whether or not a worker is eligible for a pay boost; (3) notification of the union concerning the action taken; (4) use of grievance machinery if disagreement arises over the equity of the award, or failure to give an increase. The last does much to cancel out the one franchise that management usually keeps for itself.

Bargaining Area Further Extended

Naturally, the wage rates paid within a job classification, and the persons chosen for increases substantially influence the conduct of any business. By opening up both fields to collective bargaining the WLB has endowed the unions with a new stronghold over a company's basic operating decisions. It is probable that now that the war is over, the unions will never yield this vantage ground without a stubborn fight.

The WLB has extended collective bargaining to include still other issues divorced from the customary concept of the "workman and his hire": dismissal pay for example. Until early in 1945 the WLB denied labor's demands for both on the ground that they were merely gratuities, and that this form of management philanthropy could not be exacted either by government decree or collective bargaining. However, in pleading their cause the unions pointed to comparable safeguards awarded to industry, such as the excess-profits carry-back provisions. Impressed by this argument, the WLB reversed its policy. It declared that labor as well as management was entitled to certain bulwarks against insecurity. Hence, in the "pivot" Big Steel case, the Board instructed the parties to that dispute to negotiate the form and details of a dismissal pay schedule along lines suggested by the Board itself. Although this WLB decision was limited to a group of steel mills and although the Board has rejected severance pay as a blanket policy for all war workers, its action in Big Steel is regarded by labor leaders as the hole in the dyke through which dismissal pay demands for workers in other industries can, and must, flow.

In World War I American labor was still struggling to achieve the right to bargain collectively. To be sure, the Taft-Walsh War Labor Board, created by Woodrow Wilson, secured from management a recognition of labor's right to organize and bargain collectively, but that right was not generally fixed by law until the

advent of the Wagner Act in 1935. In World War II, with this
right firmly established, the unions were much assisted by government intervention to enlarge the scope and significance of collective bargaining. In pledging to give up the strike for the duration,
the unions gained new privileges that may well be permanent.
Surely the WLB's day-by-day rulings have become, in large
measure, the scaffolding for our labor relations in the peace. In
this respect it may be recalled that the final powers of government
which were invoked in war to enforce WLB decrees will be supplanted in the postwar period by unionism's use of the strike.
There will not be, of course, the acute labor shortage which
rendered the strike such a potent threat during the war. But employers who expect that a time of labor plenitude will render the
strike an ineffectual gesture reckon without the Wagner Act .

Under the administration of this Act, the discharge of employees engaged in collective action, such as a strike, may result
in reinstatement and often some costly back pay. Disregard of
National Labor Relations Board rulings in this respect can
culminate in an injunction against the employer—an injunction
which, if breached, becomes contempt of court with criminal
penalties of $1,000 fine and one year in prison.

Postwar Collective Bargaining

Hence, even though the existence of pools of unemployed in
the postwar period may weaken labor's *economic position,* and
its ability to maintain high wages, its *collective bargaining methods and procedures* will not be in any essential impaired. On the
contrary, they have been amplified and solidified by WLB action.

The war has enabled unionism to draw on collective bargaining to cover in a single stride many intermediary steps in its evolution from hired help to something akin to partnership in United
States industry. Certainly unionism as a genus has more to say
now in the conduct of a business than at any time preceding Pearl
Harbor. A process that ordinarily might have taken decades has
been compressed into four short years. That much of it has been
synthetic—a forced rather than an organic growth—can hardly be
denied. Much of it bears all the earmarks of precocity. Yet this
whole development, even if a wartime adolescent, is more likely

to grow up into adulthood in peace than to regress toward infantilism.

It must be remembered that all through the years unionism, via collective bargaining, has been whittling away at management sovereignty over hiring and firing, seniority, wage scales, and related concerns. Attempts of unions to acquire control over the labor supply, or to revise employment rules, or to install grievance machinery, have been consistently resisted as menacing management prerogative. Yet business has survived, and even flourished, after these once sensational reforms had lost their novelty and become a habit.

The ruling idea in today's economic thought is that prosperity is based on full employment, full production, internal price-cost equilibrium, and high levels of purchasing power. The stake of both labor and management in all four is beyond doubt. What a company decides in the way of work schedules, production quotas, and wages and prices is a concern of labor as of management. If employer and labor leader act on this assumption of mutuality of interests, collective bargaining may be applied to a whole range of industrial problems hitherto untouched by bilateral action.

During reconversion, for example, the introduction of new machinery may be a subject for management-union negotiation. Wage rates may be set to reflect the speed with which costs of installing new equipment are amortized. Similarly, the opening of a new plant could mean that piece rates would be arrived at only after consultation with the union. To install or to discontinue the more elaborate incentive systems, entailing time and motion study, will be decided to an ever increasing extent by collective bargaining. It may be that profit-sharing, in its multifarious forms, will derive from joint fixing and policing of production standards and wages. It can be argued that the substantial expansion of collective bargaining during the war has done much to make the fate of the profit motive depend upon its becoming the motive of labor as well as the motive of management. Even if war-induced developments in collective bargaining are not a *fait accompli,* they are the catalysts of long-term trends, an inescapable legacy that will influence the direction and dynamics of our industrial relations for many years to come.

Chapter 14

THE HUMAN SIDE

COLLECTIVE BARGAINING is usually thought of in terms of such economic questions as wages, or in terms of such organizational questions as the apparatus of management and the set-up of the union. Equally important, however, are the psychological attitudes animating not only the rank-and-file workers but also the leadership on both sides. It is these attitudes which establish the atmosphere, the emotional tone within the plant; and will also, to a large degree, determine the whole future of collective bargaining in the United States.

As our industrial establishments keep growing in size, the worker on his job often lacks a sense of "belonging," of being significant. He feels isolated and restless. Off the job he tends to reach out for distractions which merely intensify an underlying discontent that often derives from monotonous mechanized work. These symptoms can hardly be ignored with the comfortable platitudes of "I have faith in the fundamental soundness and common sense of the American worker," or "what the worker wants is to be told what to do and then get paid for it." The fact is that while modern industry continues its miracles in "production engineering," its "human engineering" continues to lag behind. Yet this human engineering, this fitting of the worker into his job environment with something like the efficiency that marks the installation of new machinery, is the first indispensable step toward industrial cooperation.

For the worker's conviction that he doesn't count, that he isn't appreciated, that he is a faceless man in the factory setup threatens the ability of both management and union leaders to use collective bargaining as an instrument for achieving that cooperation. Yet their ability, as key figures in our society, to stand and deliver in the days ahead, to validate their claims to leadership, depends greatly on how well they elicit the active, rather than the passive, cooperation of the workers. Experience in wartime plants has again verified the axiom that this kind of cooperation between employer and employee cannot be left to chance.

Paradoxical as it may seem, the more apparently spontaneous the teamwork in a shop, the more it has to be planned for and cultivated by giving careful attention to the "human side," to the psychology of labor. This means a year-round program to surround "the job" with human satisfactions, to foster interest and pride in it, to rediscover the individual by helping him find meaningfulness in work. Naturally, in the light of present-day industrial conditions, with its large-scale enterprise, this is an immensely complex and difficult task. Both its complexity and difficulty would seem to be confirmed by many studies into human cooperation over the past one hundred and fifty years.

Learning to Work Together

These inquiries make out a persuasive case to the effect that, since the industrial revolution, our advances in science, invention, and technology, our complicated techniques for turning out goods, have placed new stringent demands upon the human capacity to work together.

Perhaps the most impressive and exhaustive investigation of this subject ever undertaken was that of the amazing French engineer turned sociologist, Frédéric Le Play. In traveling widely over the Continent some hundred years ago, Le Play believed that he had seen a diminishing ability to work together among people in industrialized localities. To discover if this were really true he set himself the project of observing and recording systematically, in case-book fashion, the social and economic situation in various parts of Europe. His explorations covered twenty-six years, and took him from the Ruhr to Siberia, from Narvik to Lisbon. His findings are set forth in six huge volumes (*The European Workers*) which, by one of those inexplicable accidents of history, remain the great neglected masterpiece in the documentation and analysis of human attitudes in response to socio-economic conditions.

Le Play first describes the simpler communities in northern and eastern Europe where the dominant economic activity was farming, or fishing, supplemented by a little village handicraft. In such places he found that the individual was familiar with virtually every segment of the economic process and participated in it to greater or less degree, i.e., peasants brought to the village bootmaker hides they had taken from livestock they had butchered themselves. Moreover, the bonds of family and kinship, the lack of mobility, helped to relate the individual more firmly to his "job." The capacity to cooperate, whether in gathering a herring run or a harvest, was at a high level.

Members of such communities pulled in harness less by compulsion than by impulse. Theirs was a natural concert of interest, sponsored at first by necessity, and later crystallized into custom. The aims and ambitions of the individual and the rules and ideals of the economic framework were virtually identical. The individual participated, not only because he wished to do it, but also because his environment induced participation automatically. He counted. He belonged. (If Le Play had visited America during the period of his investigations, 1829-1855, he would have found much of that same free-flowing cooperation in our pioneer settlements with their "bees" for corn-husking, log-cutting, cabin-building, house-raising and the like.)

Mechanization and Morale

However, when Le Play moved from such simple communities to the more urban and industrialized areas, he saw that, while the living standard was on the average higher, the individual's status, especially in relation to his means of livelihood, was less integrated, and less secure. In his own words, Le Play classified some of these communities as "shaken," and others as "disorganized." Yet both displayed the same characteristics relevant to our own times. There was increasing separation between those who owned and directed economic activity and their employees. The latter complained that the former were getting remote and unreachable. The ties of blood were no longer as binding when the farmer's son from Normandy tended a loom in Marseilles. The implicit authority of a local "social code" was supplanted by abstract law, and magistrates also remote. A deep, urgent desire for novelty everywhere prevailed. The coal miners in England, France, Germany and Belgium were as uprooted and aimless as they were wretched and impoverished. The "new masters" of the rising middle class were becoming more and more removed from contact with their employees, and were less imbued with the feelings of noblesse oblige, of social responsibility, that had often characterized the squires, the margraves and the counts they had replaced in power and prestige.

Le Play concluded that the historic economic relationships which from birth had trained the individual to cooperate were collapsing, and that—unless this trend could be arrested—the State, the supreme State, would emerge as the single entity capable of preventing final disintegration as a result of this chaotic competitiveness within the industrial community.

The investigations of Le Play and many others imply that it is impossible to obtain spontaneity of cooperation in work without reverting to simpler forms of social and economic life. That way is closed to us. Even if we were sure that it was the right way the question remains as to whether or not there is ever a road back.

The immense significance of such findings persists as a guidepost for the twentieth century's human relations. They show that, historically, collaboration within a working unit must vitalize the economic effort. But in our modern power-age society we have tended to lose sight of this fundamental requirement. Whether this has happened inadvertently, or not, is beside the point. The basic fact is that every industrial establishment is expected by its employees to provide them with: (1) the means to satisfy their economic needs and wants, and (2) the media for creating and preserving organized cooperation.

The school of economic determinism has achieved widespread and tacit acceptance for its view concerning the mechanistic nature of "economic" man. Yet in even the most pecuniary system, the accumulation of money is not important in itself. It is rather the standing and authority, comfort and security, which wealth can impart which are important. In this sense, we don't earn money. We earn status, power, ease, distinction. Aristotle said that man is a political animal. Marx said he is an economic animal. Yet far more crucial to present day human relations in industry is the perception that man is essentially a social animal. He is activated by a deep-seated and continuing drive for constant and intimate association in work with others.

In America, over the past generation, that drive has been intensified by change in the composition of the labor force. First of all, labor consists almost entirely of the native born, since immigration steadily dwindled from 1919 forward. As a result of conditioning in the American milieu, it expects more, its standards are higher. It contains more people who have had high-school and even college educations. Those in this latter group can be most effectively used only when asked to think, when given responsibility. They respond to special training, as shown by their enthusiasm for the speeded and improved upgrading methods popularized by the government's wartime training-within-industry program.

But there is another factor in the job attitude of this group. If the worker is intelligent and reasonably well informed, he frequently is not content to remain a member of his crew, or gang, even if he becomes "team leader" by virtue of natural ability. His aspirations to get up in the world have no adequate outlet. He feels in a rut. He sees that promotions are, after all, limited. There can be only one foreman to a section, one superintendent to a department or plant. Hence the worker, spurred by ambition and the desire to utilize his education more fully, often turns his attention to building a career in the union. During the past decade especially, thousands of better educated men, consigned to factory work by the depression, have come up from the shop to be union officials.

However, while a minority can attain personal fulfillment in this fashion, the underlying problem remains, both in the plant and in the union, namely, what can be done to furnish the rank and file with similar ego satisfactions? They want to feel important, too.

The Primacy of the Person

Both management and union leaders, in negotiating collective bargaining agreements, often make the mistake of thinking that only the economic demands have to be heeded. Yet often the reason employees are not "loyal" or "productive" may be that, while at work, they are not accorded sufficient recognition as people actuated by the authentic American ambition "to be somebody." The primacy of the person is not only the philosophic mainspring of democracy, it is also the core of successful plant relations.

The way in which the boss greets the worker, or an assignment to a task calling for special facility of hand and eye, or a phone and calendar on the desk of the assistant foreman, or being consulted by the front office, can be quite as important as the size of the pay envelope. The individual who believes that the exercise of his skill is not recognized for its full worth is without social function at his job. He works in a void. What he does to earn a living lacks point and direction. The boresome and repetitive nature of much present day production fosters such feelings to an appreciable extent. Even an assembly line crew, which in their operations may achieve a spirit of camaraderie, may as a group be convinced that their contribution is not genuinely appreciated.

Everyone with experience in today's industrial relations has time and again observed the seemingly irrational complaints that alike puzzle supervisors and shop stewards. Grievances over a lighting arrangement, or over the quality of food in the cafeteria, can all mask a more profound malaise. While these may take the form of dissatisfaction with wages, hours, and working conditions, the sources of unrest and disputes often lie deeper, in the worker's certitude that what he does is not recognized. Even on the economic plane, the worker is as often concerned with the relation of his wages to those received by others as with the absolute amount he himself may earn.

Diagnostic Skills Are Needed

From this general approach, as F. J. Roethlisberger points out in his *Management and Morale,* an industrial establishment is not merely a confluence of raw materials, equipment, and production methods. It is also a system of sentiments; a system that embraces an interrelationship between top management, supervision, technical specialists, office employees, together with workers at the bench or along a conveyor belt. In seeking to assess the attitudes generated by this system both management and union leaders can acquire a higher skill in the diagnosis of "what is wrong and what is right" in any particular set of employee demands which are to be resolved through collective bargaining.

The three ingredients for the acquisition of this skill have been, in another context, well summarized by Dr. L. J. Henderson in *The Study of Man*. He says:

In the complex business of living, as in medicine, *both* theory and practice are necessary conditions of understanding, and the method of Hippocrates is the only method that has ever succeeded widely and generally. The first element of that method is hard, persistent, intelligent, responsible, unremitting labor in the sick room, not in the library: the complete adaptation of the doctor to his task, an adaptation that is far from being merely intellectual. The second element of that method is accurate observation of things and events, selection, guided by judgment born of familiarity and experience, of the salient and the recurrent phenomena, and their classification and methodical exploitation. The third element of that method is the judicious construction of a theory—a quasi-religious dogma, but a modest pedestrian affair or perhaps I had better say, a useful walking-stick to help on the way—and the use thereof. All this may be summed up in a word: The physician must have, first, intimate, habitual, intuitive familiarity with things; secondly, systematic knowledge of things; and thirdly, an effective way of thinking about things.

For management and union leaders to develop this kind of skill and to apply it to collective bargaining means a slow, sweating accumulation of data from the employees themselves. It means careful observation of behavior in the shop. It means interviews. It means the slow sifting of evidence to differentiate the apparent from the real. It means a genuine drive to elicit what is actually on the worker's mind. It means that customary preconceptions of how labor "ought to feel" must be set aside for examination into what labor does feel and think. The assumption that by virtue of his position as head of a company or as head of a union a man has this knowledge is not as valid as is generally believed.

Intuition in this field may sometimes be supplanted by the scientific method which has yielded such advances in the physical world, the world of penicillin, electronics, radios, and atomic energy. It has been suggested that, as an aid in gathering such evidence, both management and union leadership might, to their separate and mutual enlightenment, adopt essentially the same cross-check interviewing practices used with such success by public opinion polls.

Plant Psychology and Leadership

Certainly, without comprehension of the psychological factors behind the employee's economic demands, neither management, nor union leaders can be fully prepared to play their parts around the collective bargaining table. In this, as in other areas, the art of leadership is not merely command. It is rather the ability to express in action the needs and aspirations of those who depend upon that leadership. In essence this means an exchange of ideas and sentiments at once clear and frank. However, the sheer size of much modern enterprise, its famous "unmanageable" units, together with the illusion that the wage or salary is always paramount in employee attitudes, have tended to block off the lines of communication both between the management leader and workers in the plant and the labor leader and the members of the union.

Yet to formulate and maintain the nexus between labor's psychic urgencies and the operations in the plant is today's challenge to tomorrow's collective bargaining.

In short, collective bargaining when it comes of age is not only a medium of settling the terms of employment but also a medium for shaping techniques that will stimulate and strengthen the individual's capacity to cooperate. Surely since a man spends the greater part of his waking hours on the job he can with propriety expect to be made spiritually at home there. Other influences in modern existence move in a counterdirection, rendering him more or less rootless. This in turn fosters that planlessness in living which is often reflected in what is commonly called "labor unrest." On the other hand, when the worker has a solid base in a job that by his own criteria signifies something more than a certain amount of money each week, he is not only a more productive employee, he also becomes a personality rather than a cog, a cost, or a commodity. His suspicion and hostility toward management, which originate in feelings of alienation, are then superseded by feelings of rapport.

The union leader is not immune to the same sort of suspicion and hostility. Frequently, the more articulate he is about what Labor (with a capital L) wants, the less he knows about it. The same sense of separateness which, for the worker, turns the company into a cold abstraction turns the union into a distant, and even sore, necessity. The act of consciously building morale by transforming the usual shop surroundings into a place for the worker's self-fulfillment as a human being can enable both management and union leaders to lay hold of new tools for understanding and handling the human material with which they work.

Workers Are People

The famous probings into labor's psyche at the Hawthorne plant of the Western Electric Company merely point the way toward a vast virtually unexplored field of inquiry. At Hawthorne psychologists and other trained investigators conducted controlled experiments in a social laboratory to impale upon the needle of their research the tangibles and intangibles that make up "morale." For nine years the reactions of employees to almost every conceivable circumstance and change in their employment environment were observed, measured, tested. Responses to a switch in foremen, to alterations in temperature, in lighting, in size of the crew, in inspection, in tempo of production, in shifts from one job to another, were scrupulously observed and recorded by means of comparative output in a tremendous variety of situations; as well as by means of physical examinations and careful interviews. The result, as one irreverent critic put it, was the discovery that "workers are people." Notwithstanding such levity, surveys of this type have brought forth extremely valuable insights into labor's aims and hopes and desires on the job, and may range from the simple informal discussions and attitude samplings to the most elaborate accumulation of "mental set" data.

The effort to develop and amplify *esprit de corps* in the work force can be undertaken jointly by management and union heads, each from his own standpoint and major interest. It might be possible to pool the information thus obtained as a groundwork for a policy to be mutually fostered. It is just as short-sighted to leave the intricacies of sound psychological adjustment entirely to foremen and shop stewards as to leave up to them entirely the settings of wage rates. As prologue to the creation of any such policy, of course, the comments and suggestions of foremen and shop stewards would usually be indispensable.

Leadership in the Battle for Union Recognition

If a recognition of the human side of collective bargaining is crucial in the case of the rank and file of workers it is even more so in the case of leaders—both of management and men. The success or failure of collective bargaining in the long run will be largely the resultant of this personal equation.

In the case of union leaders, especially, the three distinct stages in the development of collective bargaining call for three different traits of personality: (1) the fighting stage, when the union is battling for recognition; (2) the stage of negotiations, when both sides meet across the bargaining table; and (3) the administrative stage, when both are called upon to make the collective bargaining agreement work in the daily welter of practical shop detail.

In the first stage even the language of collective bargaining is saturated with the metaphors of warfare. There is battle and truce, strategic retreat and tactical maneuver. Pickets who move in cars from one plant to another are "mobile columns." Strikers "besiege" a factory. A firm that opposes unionism is, *ipso facto*, a "citadel of the open shop." Often management thinks of itself as having been forced to yield temporarily, and therefore is merely waging a rear guard action until the proper time when it will retrieve lost ground by launching an all-out counteroffensive. By the same token, the union often thinks of itself as fighting for its very existence, of needing more and yet more concessions and gains to fortify itself against inevitable attack.

What this terminology reveals is an underlying concept of conflict, sometimes covert, sometimes open, and often violent and bloody. Unless this whole psychology of coercion is replaced with that of mutuality of interests, not as lip service, or a pep-talk platitude, but as down-to-earth reality, our postwar labor relations can become a "darkling plain where ignorant armies clash by night." Unless leadership can concentrate less upon rights and more upon responsibilities, less upon power and more upon persuasion, less upon abstract precepts and more upon immediate particulars, collective bargaining will continue to be trammeled by the fears of faction, and its potentialities as a constructive force making for high production and secure, well-paid jobs will never be fully released.

A Revolution in Emotions

Yet the very vocabulary of combat points up a condition often glossed over: the introduction of collective bargaining into a plant means a great upheaval, and a continuing change, in the very human relations between employer and employee. It is a revolution in emotions. The very drive to unionize a plant is a farrago of unsettling factors, socially and personally. It breaks up old routines of association, habits, loyalties which, whether good, bad or indifferent, are nevertheless the living texture of a going concern. In the place of the familiar *status quo* are new disintegrating influences that persist for some time—until the situation is more stabilized around new routines of association, habits and loyalties. Once the union comes on the scene, there is the shop steward to divide handling of grievances with the foreman; the worker's allegiance is split between the union and the company.

Moreover, the organizing campaign which initiates the first stage of collective bargaining itself intensifies conscious antagonisms, and releases hidden hates and aggressions. Any organizer who knows his business exploits the worker's feelings first of all. The organizer assures him that the union will get him more money —an appeal that not only implies that the employer is not rewarding him justly but also is sure fire in a society where standards are mainly pecuniary. The organizer also offers the solidarity and companionship of the group. Instead of standing alone the worker will have behind him both the help of the local and the resources of the big national union with its lawyers, publicists, lobbyists, and other specialists. The organizer, further, paints some lurid portraits of management, from straw boss to chairman of the board.

Under this dispensation, for example, the foreman almost always becomes a tyrant to his subordinates and a sycophant to the "higher ups." Top management's every act of consideration becomes merely the seigneurial gestures of a benevolent despotism. Absentee owners, the invisible "they," are depicted as callous and soulless money grubbers. Parades, mass meetings, slogans, strikes, fiery speeches, cartoons, the swapping of real or alleged discriminations at the union hall all amplify and reinforce the organizer's sales talk. The management, the other side, is the enemy, the source of the worker's discontent, the personification of attempts to withhold from him his due as producer, his dignity as democratic man. In this atmosphere, the worker often identifies management with the forces in his environment that have deprived him of prestige he craves, of fulfillment in love and friendship, of financial security. Management is the scapegoat on which he can vent his accumulated vexations and thwartings.

On its part, management is often dismayed, and not a little frightened, by the display of vindictive attitudes that rise to the surface during an organizing push. In its own mind, at least to its own satisfaction, it has sought to do the fair and decent thing. But under assault it generally goes on the defensive. It tries to rationalize any mistakes in its past behavior, and to justify its faults. Employees are no longer members of one big happy family. They are rather a bunch of ingrates, stupid enough to be lured by the pied pipers of unionism who also want to run the business. Anger begets retaliation and mutual mistrust is the progeny next in line.

Leadership in the Negotiating Stage

The recognition of the union by itself does little to allay these feelings. It may merely crystallize them. Hence the second stage of collective bargaining, that of negotiations around the conference table, may be colored by a residue of mutual alienation and suspicion.

The more prolonged and bitter the struggle, the deeper are the concealed estrangements and antagonisms. Although the rational is by now supposed to supplant the emotional, this happens mainly in textbooks. An old order of things has been disturbed, and even shattered. A new order of things is emerging, but not yet crystallized. Besides, any break with the past, especially so drastic a break as the commencement of collective bargaining, is marked by apprehension of the unknown.

Whatever their facades of confidence, leaders of both management and union are uncertain about what is going to happen next. The former asks himself, in effect, "If the union wants so much today, what more will it want tomorrow?" Moreover, his reaction to the onset of the union may vary from Kismet-like resignation, to grudging acceptance, to a determination to keep resisting it, come hell or high water. It is rarely one of open-handed welcome, and almost never that of unalloyed rapture.

The union leader, despite his garlands of victory, is not sure of where he's going, either. His first obvious job is to consolidate the gains already achieved; his second, to deliver on the promises strewn with a lavish hand during the heat of the campaign; his third is to be warily vigilant toward a management that has warded off the advent of unionism until it proved impossible to stop. Beyond that, he doesn't know. He has to wait and see. Hence, even when negotiations are conducted with apparent amity, or at least with regard to the amenities, these may only hide the hostilities of armed armistice. The management leader is concerned with keeping union encroachments to a minimum, and the area of his own personal choices and prerogatives as wide as possible. The union leader is concerned with solidifying and enhancing the union's status, and his own ability to keep in office. Both are nervously alert to anything that resembles an effort to chip away at the other's jurisdiction.

When the contract is finally signed, its administration, the third stage of collective bargaining, may be plagued by the carryover of the same discords which existed during the organizing and negotiation stages. If, for example, a foreman who is off his feed is short tempered with his section crew, the union leader may see in this a management plot to provoke workers into the retaliation of strike, or slowdown, and thus discredit the union's capacity to live up to its compact. If the management leader hears of a stoppage over a seemingly trivial grievance, he promptly sees in this a plot by the union to "keep the men always stirred up."

Crusader into Diplomat

However, under a leadership that prefers facts to fantasy, negotiation and administration can be the retort in which conflict is transmuted into collaboration. Both functions require a quality of leadership totally different from that called for when the union is contender and the management champ in a fight with no holds barred. Instead of oratory, the union leader soon discovers that he has to gather and ponder data on wage rates, and in general become more the diplomat than the crusader. Instead of being monarch of all he surveys, the management leader finds that he has to give up a share of his authority, and become in general more co-optor than boss. Tolerance instead of zealotry, self-discipline instead of self-assertion, restraint instead of belligerency—these are the qualities called for by the new arrangement.

In this regard, moreover, many earnest men in the ranks of both management and unionism have learned that in negotiation they have had to discard preconceptions of "what ought to be" in favor of what is; namely, a new set of human relationships that need constant, concrete guidance. They have learned, too, that resort to "principles" is less practical than resort to the operational approach of taking a long, hard look at what actually makes the wheels go 'round. They have learned that to concentrate on the specific details of wages, seniority and the like builds infinitely more good will and teamwork than the most eloquent excursions into parochial philosophy, that the vital momentum of any organization resides in its small, hour-by-hour routines. This means that behind the negotiations of such leaders in management and in unions is always the perception that their success or failure will be determined by how well they have provided for genuine participation by their respective surrogates and followers. With this mental set as the basis for harmony, they can proceed as peace-makers whose first duty is to compromise and accommodate, rather than warriors whose first duty is to conquer and aggrandize.

Security for Management

As in other peacemaking pursuits, definitions of purpose and procedure at the outset can avoid a great deal of trouble later on. If there is union security, for example, there is no reason why there shouldn't be management security. Just as the union has the right to be protected against depletion of numerical strength, so, too, has management the right to be protected against inroads upon its power to perform its duties efficiently.

A certain area of management authority is generally taken for granted by everybody concerned. Its right to determine policy on the products it turns out, its finances, the purchase of materials, sales, advertising and promotion, the location of machinery and work stations, and the like are rarely contested or even questioned. There is a second area where management directly shares its rights with the union, as in the settlement of grievances (see page 117 *et seq.*). But there is a third area of rights subject to in-direct union ratification, and this is often the most difficult to nail down. Management's right to discharge is a case in point.

A typical provision in a collective bargaining contract may read: "The right to discharge for cause is the sole responsibility of the company, except that union members shall not be discriminated against as such." Yet a statement of this kind can cover so much ground that it defeats its own purpose. Hence management, on the basis of its own experience and that in other plants, often specifies in advance what the exercise of its discharge privilege is going to mean. To narrow the field of potential discord, it further obtains from the union a pledge that, after verifying the facts surrounding a particular severance, the union will support the management in a discharge made for such activities as: (1) direction of a strike contrary to contract provisions, or stimula-tion of curbs on output against existing shop rules; (2) assault of a supervisor if this can be traced to an employer-employee relationship within the plant; (3) theft; (4) obscene behavior on company premises; (5) constant clowning that is not corrected after sufficient warning; (6) serious injury to a fellow employee by means of assault and battery, or an accident arising from carelessness; and (7) willful damage to company property.

In this, as in other areas of management rights, not all contingencies can be listed. Any such attempt would turn the contract into an encyclopedic structure of minutiae, so rigid that it would fall of its own weight. On the other hand, to set forth salient points can provide a valuable working hypothesis. By staking out the territory of its discharge function, for example, management not only reduces the amount of possible friction but also retains unequivocally its duty to maintain discipline. In other words, management, while making the discharge decision on its own, does not divide authority with the union; but rather—in the interests of fair play and good will—permits the union to review the action as a check upon arbitrary action. Naturally, reasons for discharge may be extended, or compressed, or otherwise revised in the light of new experience in the shop. A wise union leadership usually encourages, rather than retards, such management efforts to clarify its own responsibility.

Such authorities in industrial relations as George W. Taylor, now Chairman of the War Labor Board, believe that in preparing the contract it is one of management's primary obligations to delineate its own functions in this fashion, if collective bargaining is to be more than a one-way street. Certainly the creation of management's own magna chartas is going to be one of the major perplexities to be ironed out in postwar collective bargaining.

"Accentuate the Positive"

Up till now, however, the management leader has on the whole preferred to rely on his implied rights under the common law concepts of master and man, and owner of the premises. He has tended to feel that he is in a safer position if he doesn't permit such rights to be questioned as concrete topics for collective bargaining, or even for discussion. Up to a point, of course, this view arises from lack of clarity as to what are the present-day warranties of management. To cope with this problem, aggravated by the wartime intrusion of unionism to spheres formerly management's own, some industrial leaders are considering a thorough job analysis and re-evaluation of the managerial function in their enterprises.

Conceivably, the adoption of this technique would enable the management leader to depend more upon proof of his essentiality and usefulness, and less upon his claim to certain prescriptive rights. The result could be the development of a positive, rather than a negative, attitude toward collective bargaining. Instead of seeking union insecurity, he can concern himself with designing management security provisions in the contract.

For his part, the union leader wants, above all, the guarantee that his organization will endure. Once this is assured, he can devote himself to what the union can do to improve output and lower cost. He can become more market-minded than dues-minded. But to date neither management nor union leadership, with some few exceptions, has done very much thinking in these terms. The first has usually adhered to the view that the worker's job is to execute management's decisions, not to assist in making them. The union leader is usually worried over whether or not management will seize some occasion to reduce the union's potency and standing.

However, once the security of management and union is out of the way, once the boundaries of that security are mapped out, and methods of adjudication set up to handle borderline disputes, the leadership of both sides is freed to concentrate on the creative and constructive. To be sure, like any other human institution, collective bargaining will always have its irreducible amount of friction. Even in the most ideal context it is no gateway to Utopia, but rather a highway that can be comfortably and cooperatively traveled at least when the leadership knows the direction it is taking.

Leadership of management and union in collective bargaining, as in any other form of authentic democratic leadership, entails not the ability to dominate, or exercise power *over* people, but

THE HUMAN SIDE   205

rather the creation and use of power *with* people. The first type
of leadership is interested primarily in the result. The second
type is interested both in the result and in the process by which
it is attained. This latter outlook is peculiarly germane to collective
bargaining which is, beyond all else, a process. It is a dynamic
evolutionary process calling for many minute adjustments in the
details of association among men at work. These adjustments
bring forth a "taut ship" only to the extent that in matter and
manner they reflect employee participation all along the line.

Briefing for Negotiations

Among experienced management and union leaders, this participation is made to precede negotiations and carry over into the
administration of the agreement. Otherwise, the application of
contract provisions, however correct technically, or sanely reasoned, will lack the efficiency of consent—the consent of the governed. In a mature collective bargaining structure, the management leader, before negotiation is under way, consults with all
members of his staff who will be applying the contract, from personnel director to foreman, and invites their advice and suggestions on the points to be covered in the pending agreement. If
foremen, for example, help to institute a change, they can be
counted on to put it into effect with more understanding than if it
were something imposed from the top down. Some management
leaders have found that "blow-by-blow" reports on the progress
of negotiations can with advantage be made the agenda of special
foremen meetings.

Similarly, the union leader creates, from the information given
him by the rank and file, a précis of demands, convenes special
sessions of union members to inform them of how the negotiations are getting along, and submits for their approval the resulting agreement. When management and union leaders fail to elicit
the participation of their constituencies, of supervisor and worker,
the latter—simply because they have been left out, because they
don't know "what the hell's going on there"—are apt to keep
sniping at each other. They haven't shared in the establishment

of a new state of affairs. Yet this sense of having shared in the drafting of the treaty of peace can usually do more to get the contract accepted wholeheartedly than anything else.

Leaders in management and unions have further found it profitable to coach foremen and shop stewards, or committeemen, in what the agreement really says. Necessarily, any such instruction means patient, step-by-step exposition of how the contract is to be applied in handling a complaint over a dark corner, or dull tools, or a slow jerry-driver, or lack of upgrading opportunity. Some management leaders have inaugurated training programs and reference manuals to educate supervisors for their roles under the new regime of collective bargaining; union leaders have done the same for shop stewards. Frequently, foremen and stewards attend meetings addressed jointly by management and union spokesmen who outline the agreement and answer questions from the floor. This kind of "briefing" does much not only to avert difficulties arising from opposite interpretations of the same document, but it also enhances the feeling that "it's our show" among those who have the most to do in translating contract provisions into flesh-and-blood performance.

To extend participation still further somewhat elaborate ceremonies are sometimes used. They can dramatize the cessation of hostilities, help expunge the vestiges of resentment aroused during the organizing drive, and otherwise set the psychic tone and pacific temper of the new collective bargaining dispensation. One such method for evoking a spirit of good will and concord has been developed by officers of the Commonwealth Edison Company of Chicago and the officials of Local 1361, an affiliate of the Brotherhood of Electrical Workers (AF of L). In the spring of 1944 their first collective bargaining pact was signed in the union hall in the presence of union members summoned for the occasion. Company executives and union leaders affixed their signatures to the agreement while on the platform. Negotiators from both sides were introduced. Management and union representatives pledged themselves to conform in letter and spirit with the rules laid down by the contract. The very appearance of management leaders at union headquarters seemed to testify to the fact that a new era of employer-employee relations had arrived.

Elsewhere, ratification rituals are less solemn, more convivial. They are not only attended by company executives, supervisors, union officers, shop stewards, and rank-and-file members of the union but also are accompanied by such refreshments as barrels of beer which assist fraternization. However, such rites to demonstrate that the hatchet is buried, and to foster feelings of rapport, are still confined to a small vanguard of management and union leaders.

Leadership in the Administrative Stage

In the administration of the agreement, a similar concern for the human element may be even more crucial, more particularly since the administrative phase of collective bargaining is an "on the spot" phenomenon. It is here perhaps, more than in any other phase of collective bargaining that the leaders in management and the union have to prove daily their capacity for leadership. The union leader discovers that it is one thing to whip up emotions and something else again to calm them down and canalize their flow along constructive channels. He has to plan carefully, be patient, and be guided more by his head than his heart. For many union leaders this is an almost complete *volte-face*. The man who is a top-notch organizer, and even a shrewd horse trader around the collective bargaining table, often finds it difficult to harness himself to the nondramatic pursuits, even the drudgery of making the gears of a new social mechanism mesh in smoothly. The management leader discovers that he has to relinquish the pleasant ways of command. He has learned to hold his temper, perhaps get rid of it altogether, while everything he wants to do within certain spheres, is appraised, debated, even opposed. To a man whose habit patterns are formed by issuing orders, whose very career perhaps was built on his ability to make quick judgments and decisions, this new more cumbersome arrangement—unless mastered—can be a short cut to gastric ulcers.

Moreover, the subordinates of management and union leaders

take their cues from the men on top. If the supervisor has reason
to believe that the front office would like to "put a crimp" in the
union, he doesn't need explicit instructions. "Just because 'those
guys on the belt' have got a union, do they think they don't ever
have to shake the lead out of their pants, or that the conveyor is
located in the men's room?"

Similarly, if the shop steward is convinced that the union leader
would like to keep needling the management, he doesn't need to
be told what to do. "The tool crib is too far away, isn't it? The
food is so lousy at the company cafeteria that everybody's getting
heartburn. The foreman's just a wolf, he doesn't keep his mind
on his work at all, why yesterday he was making passes at that
pretty Polack girl, and she's going to quit if he doesn't stop, a
good worker, too."

Translating Principles into Practices

In short, to administer the agreement effectively, management
and union leadership by their own behavior and precepts have to
go out of their way to translate cooperative principles into hour-
by-hour practice. The agreement, at best, is a joint bill of rights,
and a frame of reference. It cannot possibly begin to anticipate
the many modifications needed daily in the shop.

For example, the whole seniority question—triply complicated
in view of pending renegotiation and reconversion and the return
of veterans—is a major test of this kind of leadership in both
management and unions. To the management leader, of course,
seniority stipulations often seem an evil, or at least a nuisance.
In his opinion they conflict with his authority to seek out and stimulate special talent and diligence, and thus reflect adversely upon
his competence as an executive who, after all, is obliged to run
an efficient enterprise. To the union leader, of course, seniority
provisions symbolize a minimum of job security for his adherents.
He may, or may not, be aware that unemployment derives from
technological, seasonal or cyclic causes over which the particular
firm has no real control. But, within the limits of a collective bargaining arrangement with that company, he is anxious to preserve
the highest possible degree of job security.

The rank and file of the union as a rule prefer seniority to mean that "the last man hired is the first fired, and the last to come back" and that "the man longest on the job is entitled to the first promotion." The management leader often feels that insistence upon this latter interpretation in particular cramps his style since it prevents him from encouraging and awarding individual initiative, and may "level out" workers into a deadening uniformity that can decrease the efficiency of the enterprise.

Birth of a Working Compromise

Hence, in negotiations over the seniority issue as it relates to advancement within the company, a compromise of this kind is frequently reached: seniority will be recognized as the determining factor only when merit, ability and capacity are equal. This is a simple idea to put on paper. But soon an ambitious someone in the shop asks for a promotion. He claims that, after all, the seniority clause really means that it is to be the determining factor among all those who are capable of doing the work in the grade from which promotions are to be made. He argues further that if employees weren't thus capable they couldn't have held on to their jobs.

The union may press for acceptance of this view. But if it prevails, the seniority clause becomes, in effect, just another straight seniority program and differences in merit, ability and capacity are ignored. In short, a clause intended to give primary emphasis to ability and the like, and secondary emphasis to length of service, can be turned into a strict seniority affair. On the other hand, management may by itself decide that employee X is the most capable, in view of merit, ability and capacity, and therefore promote him. But in this instance seniority may be given no weight at all, while management's exercise of its unilateral judgment may arouse charges of favoritism, and other resentments.

If management and union leaders really expect to see to it that ability is to come first, and seniority second, they find that to effectuate this intention is not as easy as to express it. The daily administration of collective bargaining agreements is rarely facile; yet to sidestep it is to let the contract freeze into a device for congealing confusion. Quite a few management and labor leaders have been able to work out a solution that combines seniority with ability as criteria for promotion. They start off on the assumption that it is rarely practical to gain general accord as to who is the "best" employee in the department. They have observed, however, that it is comparatively easy to get everyone to concur on the six or seven ablest workers out of, say, a hundred. The management and union leaders, after consultation with foremen and shop stewards, suggest that a list of, say, seven of the most competent be made up and placed in a new category of "in line for promotion." Then the supervisor in charge can apply seniority within this chosen group to make sure that the proper, secondary consideration is granted to length of service. After all, this was what the management and union leaders were driving at when drawing up the contract. Moreover, this method has the advantage of keeping envy down and ambition up since the average employee can more readily visualize himself as belonging to a top group of seven than to a solitary unit of one, the more especially if that one is selected by management alone.

It is this sort of joint "follow-through" to vitalize the phrases of the contract, to adapt it to the prismatic personnel adjustments that constantly crop up, that remains the most overlooked—and most crucial—part of the collective bargaining process. To perceive that this is the most important part, and to act on that perception, would seem to be the index of modern leadership in both management and union circles.

Leadership and the Future

The moral crisis of our time is, in large measure, a crisis in leadership. Today many Americans lack a very strong belief in the vision, integrity, and ability of the two sides of our industrial leadership—both managerial and unionist. In this regard it should not be forgotten that from the crash of Black October 1929 until the very late thirties, the business leader was "in the doghouse." Somewhere around 1940 he moved out and the labor leader took his place. There remains a widespread cynicism in regard to both —not only in the ranks of labor but also amid other sections of the "phantom public." These attitudes are the traumatic scars seared by the depression upon the national unconscious. The "public-be-damned" intransigeance of a John L. Lewis or a Sewell Avery further impairs confidence in prototypes less stubborn, willful and reckless.

As steps toward regaining public respect and support, management and union leadership can together do much to abolish feather bedding and other restrictions of output, along with the high, rigid price that results from the high, rigid wage. All these derive fundamentally from fears of job scarcity and job insecurity. To allay such fears, management and union leaders at a particular plant are able to develop, within the limits of the national economic situation, programs that can make the work at hand something more for the employee than putting in eight hours a day as often as he can in order to "eat regular." Instead of being merely an irregular source of nutriment, the worker wants from his job four basic values: (1) the kind of security that is rooted in steady employment, year in and year out; (2) a chance for advancement; (3) treatment from the boss, supervisor and associates that causes him to believe that he has a personal stake in the success of the enterprise; and (4) the sense of dignity that flows from the assurance that what he contributes is going to be justly assessed and appreciated.

In the collective bargaining of the postwar period, American labor cannot be expected to settle for less.

Report and Recommendations

Chapter 15

REPORT AND RECOMMENDATIONS OF
THE LABOR COMMITTEE

1. THE ROLE OF COLLECTIVE BARGAINING

THIS REPORT REPRESENTS a cross section of inquiry and thinking on the part of management, union and public members of the Twentieth Century Fund's Committee on Labor, assisted by staff personnel.

Central to the present report are these basic findings: (1) that collective bargaining, as an instrument of public and industrial policy, is here to stay; (2) that like any other social invention, collective bargaining is subject to abuses that at times can be as vicious as its uses are generally valuable; (3) that efforts to deflect the aims and destroy the purposes of collective bargaining may foster social tensions of a kind that threaten the equilibrium of our economy; (4) that collective bargaining can be, and should increasingly become, a technique to help ensure a larger and more regular output of goods and services, to maintain high levels of purchasing power, to establish clear lines of communication between employer and worker, to inspire and intensify their joint responsibility and responsiveness to their common interests, and the interests of the national community, and to promote that industrial self-government which, inside the plant, as within the community, is democracy's safeguard.

The Uneven Growth of Collective Bargaining

Collective bargaining began in the United States about one hundred years ago and was carried on intermittently until the 1890's when in the form of a few strong crafts it sank its roots down deep into United States soil. It was not, in fact, until 1891 that the term collective bargaining was first coined (by Beatrice Webb, now Lady Passfield, in a speech before London's Fabian

Society) and promptly popularized in this country by Samuel Gompers, founding father of the American Federation of Labor.

The entire history of collective bargaining has been marked by uneven, ragged development, differing in various industries and periods and places. There is no single uniform pattern discernible either in the past or the present. If we take around 1890 as a starting point, for example, we find that in the glass industry managements and unions began to work out, slowly and often painfully, a policy of collaboration by means of collective bargaining. In essentials that policy, with some setbacks, and disruptions, has endured to the present day despite technological changes and equally drastic changes in the forms of unionism itself. In the flint glass and container sections of the industry, for instance, there grew up a mutual affirmation of collective bargaining as an instrument that could advance the interests of both sides. From time to time, the unions involved have voluntarily undergone wage cuts when persuaded that the long-term advantage of employer and worker required this action. After more than half a century of collective bargaining experienced employers and labor leaders agree that it has helped to stabilize the industry by equalizing wages; that it has been flexible enough to permit downward as well as upward adjustments in pay; and that with some exceptions it has served to prevent strife during two generations of violent industrial outbreaks elsewhere.

In contrast the steel industry, in which employers resisted collective bargaining vigorously, and successfully until around 1937, had been (up to that time) the scene of unceasing employer-employee tension and bitterness. Unlike the situation in glass, collective bargaining as currently conducted in the steel industry has virtually no roots in historical intra-industry practice. Both the Amalgamated Association of Iron, Steel and Tin Workers and the kind of mills that gave it its peak strength of 8 per cent of the workers in the industry, were obsolete by the early 1900's. Until the passage of the National Labor Relations Act and the unionizing campaign waged by the Steel Workers Organizing Committee (now the United Steelworkers of America), both Big and Little Steel had regularly frustrated attempts to establish collective bargaining. It is in that industry that a process was built almost from scratch over the past few years.

Hence the labor policy of the Roosevelt Administration with its Section 7(a) in NIRA, and its Wagner Act, cut across a patchwork of collective bargaining customs, attitudes, time spans. In general the New Deal broadened and intensified collective bargaining where it existed, and helped to extend it to places where it had not appeared before. Over the past decade, the principle of government encouragement (of the right of workers to bargain collectively) has become part of our national law. In large measure as a result of this government support, the labor movement has grown from less than 3 million in 1933 to more than 12 million in 1944. At the same time, collective bargaining agreements cover several million additional workers, since benefits achieved by the union accrue to the unorganized as well.

During the war, the intervention of government in settling industrial disputes tended to narrow the scope of collective bargaining in some respects but also widened it in others. Certainly the interposition of government may have developed some useful patterns that can carry over into the peace. Up to a point, at least, the restrictions on free, unhampered collective bargaining were offset (1) by a wider appreciation in both management and union circles of the effect on the larger public of strikes and lockouts, a point of view dramatized by their threat to the national security during the war; (2) by an enlarged understanding on the part of the populace in general of the critical importance of stable and harmonious industrial relations. Still another result of wartime's government controls over collective bargaining was the accumulation of wage data to an extent never before thought desirable or practical. This body of knowledge has laid the groundwork for the wartime attempt to rationalize wages, to introduce a clear, ordered, comprehensible relationship among the many wage rates and wage scales that make up a particular wage structure.

Of first importance, in this respect, was the effort to substitute job evaluation, to be jointly undertaken by managements and unions, for caprice and intuition in determining a job's worth. There can be little doubt that this war-stimulated method and all it signifies for arriving at the "fairness" of wages will be preserved in the peace. In brief, the only constant about collective bargaining is that its substance and techniques are in a perpetual state of flux and change.

In any event the act of collective bargaining is neither novel nor untried. Yet, outside of the printing and building and metal trades, men's clothing and women's wear, coal mining and the railroads, glass, and some smaller industries, collective bargaining has hardly built up a backlog of mature experience for guiding future developments; and even in these spheres there is ample room for further growth in effectiveness, if not in coverage.

While from the century's turn there were small scattered unions in automobiles, electrical equipment, rubber processing and other major mass production industries, large-scale collective bargaining in these areas is only a few years old. Elsewhere, as in aluminum and some metal mining, collective bargaining virtually began with World War II. Moreover, the 12 million wage and salary earners who belong to the AF of L, CIO, railroad brotherhoods or other independent unions, are concentrated in manufacturing, mining, transportation and construction.

Almost untouched by unionism are over 3 million agricultural laborers, domestics, and the majority of people in "white-collar" occupations. Of the nearly 6 million employed in wholesale and retail merchandising, about 4 per cent are covered by collective bargaining pacts. Among the 5 million in government service, and the 2 million in public utilities (with the exception of those employed on common carriers) unionism has made only nominal inroads.

Collective versus Individual Bargaining[1, 2]

The fact that less than one third of the total working force in

1. In view of the fact that collective bargaining is now an instrument of public policy, it seems to me that this section would be stronger if it were less of an argument between advocates of individual and advocates of collective bargaining, and more of an explanation of the factors which have given rise to the phenomenon. The material is all right, but it is the way in which it is presented that I do not like. It seems to be trying to justify something which needs no justification.— FRAZIER D. MACIVER

2. It seems to me that the discussion of collective versus individual bargaining

the United States is unionized is often cited to "prove" the individual bargain superior to the collective bargain. Advocates of this view affirm that the relatively small percentage of workers in labor organizations suggests that employers can be counted on to give the worker a fair deal; that the latter is reasonably sure of a maximum pay envelope without the loss of time that results from going out on strike, and without deductions for dues and other insignia of unionism. To be sure, some employers, on the basis of the individual bargain, provide wage standards that equal, and even surpass, those in unionized establishments. On the whole, however, the reverse is true. During the past forty-three

---

attempts to put the case for collective bargaining too much in terms of deficiencies of individual bargaining. This does not seem to me to be necessary. One can make out a persuasive case for negotiating rational wage structures through collective bargaining, even though individual bargaining works fairly well as a method of setting wages.

When one considers an individual workman bargaining with a large enterprise, the individual seems pretty helpless. This is only part of the picture. Increases in the productivity of labor raise the demand for labor and these increases in demand seem to get translated fairly completely into higher wages. All enterprises, big and little, really compete for labor and bid up wages in order to get and hold men. Between 1880 and 1930, the percentage of workers in the United States who were organized into unions was rather low. Business was in the saddle and ran the country pretty much as it wished to run it. During this period, however, real per capita incomes rose about two and one-half fold. The amount of capital per worker increased nearly threefold. Even though capital increased much faster than workers, the share of property in the national income, according to the investigations of Kuznets, remained virtually unchanged. Property got a little more than one fifth of the national income in 1880, and a little less than one fifth in 1930. In view of the great increase in capital per worker, the failure of the share of property to increase is somewhat surprising. When Douglas compared the movement of real wages between 1890 and 1926, he found that there was substantially no difference between the increase of union wages and the increase in other wages. Furthermore, such data as are available show that in periods of revival nonunion wages rise a little sooner than union wages.

All of this is not necessarily an argument against collective bargaining and I do not interpret it as such. Collective bargaining does many things besides modifying wages. Industry produces men as well as goods and collective bargaining affects the minds of men which industry produces. Furthermore, it is possible that the pressure of trade unions may accelerate technological change and thus increase the productivity of labor. The data which I have cited, however, indicate quite plainly that the forces which operate in free markets are capable of producing large wage increases. They refute the statement in the report to the effect that the freedom of the unorganized worker "is all but meaningless." It is neither wise nor necessary to attempt to make a case for collective bargaining in terms of an alleged failure for wages to rise when individuals bargain with large corporations. Incidentally, there are many industries in which large enterprises ordinarily pay higher wages than small enterprises.—SUMNER H. SLICHTER

years (1900-1943) surveys and reports of state and federal agencies, of research foundations, of factory inspectors and individual investigators, and of management associations, all support the conclusion that the union, or collective, bargain not only means higher pay as a rule but also has done much to protect the worker against arbitrary discharge, to promote his safety and his health, and to help improve conditions of the unorganized.

There are, however, still other arguments in favor of the individual bargain—arguments put forward in all sincerity by those who would deny the value and validity of collective bargaining. They claim, for example, that under a system of individual bargaining every worker is on his self-reliant own. The expression of his particular ability is not hampered by the leveling influences of unionism. He sets a price on his labor. The employer also sets a price on it. By higgling, they can reach an accord. Otherwise, both applicant and the person who does the hiring can look elsewhere.

Like any other folklore handed down after its social context has largely vanished, this contention contains a partial truth. In establishments such as a corner, independent drugstore, or an odd-job shop, or small office, where knowledge of the process and the economic status of employer and employed is not too far separated, or where differing functions and differing rewards can be clearly understood, the individual bargain can often be arranged on an equitable basis. Otherwise, its equity is dubious. The underlying assumption of a bargain is the equal, or roughly equal, economic strength of the bargainers. By and large, however, this assumption hardly accords with the present-day structure of United States industry. Today less than 0.1 per cent of United States firms with thousands on their pay rolls employ more than 15 per cent of all workers. It hardly can be said that a man with a wife and two children, and small savings, bargains on equal terms with the personnel director of a multimillion-dollar corporation.

This bargaining weakness has nothing to do with whether or not the wages paid are high or low. In the 1920's, for example, the flourishing automobile industry, anxious to attract a healthy, vigorous labor force, paid comparatively high wages, at least on an hourly basis, even if seasonal layoffs tended to level off annual earnings. But this high wage scale, to an overwhelming extent, reflected management purposes. The average unorganized worker had no control over it. Until large-scale unionism entered the industry in the mid-thirties, the worker had no medium, save complaint to a straw boss, by which he could directly influence the wages he received. So, too, among our smaller concerns which employ up to three hundred workers (a category which comprises some 50 per cent of United States industry), the individual, unorganized wage earner as a rule is all but impotent as bargainer. While a highly skilled craftsman, or foreman, may arrange a bargain which rewards the relative scarcity of his ability, the vast majority of the unskilled, nonunionized workers are virtually voiceless in determining the amount of their pay.

Typically, a management examines its production costs, its selling price, the dividends it wants to pay, and fixes a particular wage scale. It may be fair, or even generous. It may be penurious. But there it is. And for the ordinary, unorganized job seeker it is often a take-it-or-leave-it affair. Except in times of labor shortage he lacks alternatives. There has been a frequent oversupply of labor, defined as people looking for jobs and not finding them, for quite a few years in the recent past—except for World War I, the 1922-1929 period of the boom, and from late 1941 up through the war's end. To be sure, the worker remains free to sell his services in the way he thinks best. But since he and his family are, as a rule, but a few weeks removed from poverty, or even hunger, this freedom is all but meaningless. The pressure to take what he can get becomes overwhelming. On the other hand, the employer can usually afford to wait, not only because he has superior financial resources but also because the normal employment situation is that of more job applicants than jobs. Finally, the worker, especially when unskilled, rarely knows his real worth. He lacks information about prevailing wage rates, about material costs, and interest, rent, taxes, depreciation and the other items of overhead that go into setting a wage.

In the effort to have something effective to say about the setting of a wage, and to achieve higher living standards amid the ever changing environment of United States industry, workers have sought to replace the individual bargain with the group, or collective bargain. By trial and error, they have discovered that to serve their own self-interests, they would have to stop competing against each other, and act in concert. Only in this way could they obtain some measure of control over the labor supply. They have observed, moreover, that the employer could readily discharge Bill Smith if he objected to existing arrangements; but if ten or a hundred or a thousand Bill Smiths joined together in a union, and could threaten to withdraw their labor power simultaneously, the employer could not discharge them all, without risking serious loss. By pooling their ability to work, by submitting to the discipline of their own group, in which they had voice and vote, workers have learned that they could counterbalance the employer's exercise of complete authority. They could pay their own officials to spend time to keep in touch with conditions in other plants, to acquire knowledge of the industry, and of labor's legal rights; to guide organizing activity, to conduct negotiations with skill and insight. They could even hire other specialists such as economists, lawyers and publicity men. They were thus equipped to deal with employers on a plane of greater equality. Quite as important, unionism endowed them with a new sense of dignity, of status, of counting as human beings. Every step that served to democratize plant procedures would extend their franchise as citizens of industry.

Only against this background is it possible to appraise realistically the phenomenon of collective bargaining. It is a trinity of economic wants, political pressures and psychological urgencies, the one reacting reciprocally upon the other.

The Stakes of Collective Bargaining

Collective bargaining is the process by which union members through their representatives market and help manage the labor skills and energies that employers need to buy. The amount of money to be paid for work, the number of hours it is going to take, the conditions under which it is to be performed, all make up the bargain. Its terms are, as a rule, set forth in a trade agreement which may be merely a one-page memorandum or a five hundred-page document adorned with footnotes. Like any other bargain it usually is a compromise between what the union demands and what the employer, whether an individual, a partnership or a corporation, is able or willing to grant. At all times it is wise to keep in mind the triple nature of a collective bargaining agreement which is something more than written embodiment of a mere bargain, and is rather a business compact, a treaty, and a code of honor, all in one.

The negotiation of a collective bargaining agreement by means of conferences around the table is, of course, merely prologue. To interpret and enforce that agreement on the factory floor are tasks less dramatic, but more important. A grievance which may seem trivial to a foreman may be an obsession with the worker, and the correction of that grievance a point of honor with the shop steward. It is the day-by-day adjustments of everything, from lack of paper towels in the men's room to a revised wage scale arising from a new time study, that put collective bargaining to the test. There are few legal precedents for policing a collective agreement. Its success or failure depends upon the mutual trust, good will and intelligence with which management and union can surround a controversial point. To apply collective bargaining competently, to use it even reasonably well, requires hard work— hard work for management and union alike; and, like most hard work, it is easier to evade than to carry out.

The stake of both is crucial. Management's stake is to achieve a self-disciplining labor force, marked by faith in the enterprise, and the desire to contribute to its success. Labor's stake is the building of ever larger security, and ever larger participation in shaping the ways of work. In the months ahead the aims of both can add up either to unprecedented teamwork, or unprecedented turbulence. It is up to every management and every union to decide which it is going to be. In this connection the Committee cannot emphasize too strongly that the recent war telescoped many employer-employee relationships that normally would have taken longer to develop. Like many hothouse growths, these are less hardy than others sprung from the customary environment.

Good Administration Crucial

The Committee therefore suggests that the key to postwar industrial harmony is to be found in the intelligent, equitable and patient administration of collective bargaining contracts. Under wartime pressures many new ones have been signed, and many old ones drastically revised. A major peacetime task will be to make such agreements yield cooperation instead of conflict. The Committee affirms that, in the first place, all such agreements should be adaptable to the changing conditions of the reconversion and postwar periods and that they should outline procedures for joint discussion and review of such questions as: alterations in the rates when operations are modified, or altogether transformed; job classification; the use of merit-rating and incentive systems; seniority; re-employment of veterans; devices to spread the work, adjustment in hours, and related issues. In short, the aim of the present collective bargaining agreement should be to provide managements and unions with specific techniques by which they can jointly and more effectively cope with shifts in machinery, markets and man power that are involved in our return to a peacetime economy. At the same time, management should see to it that the post of industrial relations or personnel director be made commensurate with the importance of his function; that the status and salary attached to such positons equal that for executives dealing with finance, production, and sales. By the same token, negotiating agents for the unions should be similarly equipped.

Collective bargaining is as diverse in form as enterprise itself. A single employer may bargain with a number of workers, as in the case of a restaurant proprietor and the waiters' union. A group of employers, such as building contractors, may bargain with a group of building trades such as carpenters, painters, bricklayers, and the like. An all-embracing association of employers, like that of the coal mine operators, may bargain with all their workers through the almost all-embracing United Mine Workers of America. Whatever the combination, collective bargaining is inseparable from independent unions; for the latter is fundamentally a business institution engaged in the cooperative selling of man-hours.

Indeed, collective bargaining is the essence of unionism, and the essence of unionism is to substitute group strength for personal weakness in arranging an employee's conditions of work. From the employer's side, collective bargaining—to justify itself—must become an instrument of union collaboration and responsibility.

2. THE ECONOMICS OF COLLECTIVE BARGAINING

Almost every collective bargaining negotiation soon or late resolves itself into a wage debate; for it is the size of the pay envelope that, soon or late, comes to occupy the center of the stage. The chief reason that management and union try to achieve a meeting of minds is to resolve points of conflict over who gets what out of total profits, actual and potential. Despite irresponsibles on the right and the left, United States unionism remains primarily concerned with the share the worker can get from the earnings of an enterprise. Indeed, organized labor is not interested in control of an enterprise, as control, but rather in participation to the extent that labor's stake can be safeguarded and advanced. This participation may extend from the joint establishment of apprenticeship rules to the use of union time-study experts who cooperate with management to fix basic standards of pay under wage-incentive programs. In any collective bargaining, both management and union are called on to face a vast array of economic issues, often obscure in origin and impact. Too often they rely—at best—upon a spirit of give and take, rather than upon the marshaling and examination of pertinent data.

The Need for Facts

Indeed, in approaching their joint problems, managements and unions are, in many cases, deficient in facts. A desire to get the controlling facts, to ascertain an accurate ratio between labor costs and company earnings, are characteristics of informed sophisticated bargainers. This whole approach presupposes a certain ripeness of judgment, a willingness to explore mutually, that as a rule go with maturity in the management-union relationship. It is the inexperienced bargainers of the immature union who ask for the moon. It is the unschooled bargainers of an unseasoned management who deny that the moon exists.

However, even among our more mature labor and employer groups, few guiding precepts—other than rule of thumb—are to be found. Hence collective bargaining too often becomes a compromise based upon approximations and upon the financial and forensic power of the two parties rather than upon scientific verifiable evidence. As in quoting scripture, almost any text may be used to support a point. A rise in the cost of living, for example, may furnish the union with its most telling argument; or, again, it may be an increase in per capita output within the plant; or a general round of raises granted by a rival firm. In periods of prosperity, the union seeks to push up the existing scale, carrying out the Gompers adjuration of "more, more, now." In slack or depressed times, the union tries to conserve its gains. Actuated by the same underlying motivations the employer's argument is opposite but of the same caliber. Management may resist union contentions by pointing to wage scales higher than those at a comparable factory; or to heavy investments in new machinery required to keep up with the competitive pace; or to a tax burden uncommonly high.

Neither side seems disposed to accept the bad with the good. A union that, during a span of full employment, wants wages tied to living costs, or profit percentages, finds little merit in this proposal during a time of deflation. The converse also holds. And obscured by the positiveness with which management and union spokesmen, on national and local planes, put forward their respective claims, is the most important consideration of all, namely, that there is no single "law" of wages. Despite the clichés and hysteria that surround the subject there is nothing so fixed and immutable about wages as to inspire some new Carlyle to describe economics as that "dismal science."

Nor is there any such thing as a "wage level." Rather, there are many different and separate wage "laws" and wage "levels." They vary with the locality and its customs, with the rise of one industry and the decline of another, with managerial efficiency, with new inventions, with the use of modern or old-fashioned equipment, with the degree of competition, cutthroat, or none at all, with the waxing of demand and the waning of the supply for labor, and many other elements. A particular wage level is therefore an accretion, building up like a bed of coral from the skeletons of polyps. It is a social, organic growth. Finally, it reflects that national economic environment which conditions the behavior of managements and unions far more than both generally perceive.

Importance of General Economic Conditions[3]

It should be obvious to even the most "let's mind our own business" executive, or labor leader, that it is impossible to escape the influences exerted by the interplay of general economic forces which impinge upon any particular collective bargaining process. The sooner this is realized and translated into action, the more collective bargaining can contribute to national well-being. It is, of course, grotesque to assume a complete analysis, by every management and every union, of the effect of the general economy upon their industry, or plant, or vice versa. There are, however, certain guiding principles that can be put into practice. First among them to be re-examined, not out of a spirit of altruism, but in a mood of tough-minded self-interest, is the concept of promoting the general welfare.

When management cuts production and lays off workers but maintains prices; when unions restrict output or oppose technological innovation; when management and unions together enter into collusive understandings to fence off, as their very own, a particular economic territory, they may be promoting their own welfare while undermining the interests of the rest of the community. But in the long run they are menacing their own well-being, their own survival, which in our kind of delicately interblended economy are inseparable from the general welfare. They are disre-

3. This and the following several sections deal almost exclusively with cost-price relationships. It seems to me that there are other questions, such as opposition to technological innovation, restrictions of opportunities for work through overtight apprenticeship rules and intake rules, etc., that could be expanded and made more important.—FRAZIER D. MacIVER

garding the imperatives of the twentieth century by pretending to fit them into the economic categories of the eighteenth and nineteenth. They are relying upon an outmoded approach in an economy where the interdependence of all segments makes it impossible to rely upon individualistic action alone.

A basic fact of our time is that we no longer live in the laissez-faire realm of free and automatic competition glorified by Adam Smith. Interference with the movement of prices in accord with what was once regarded as the "natural" law of supply and demand, occurs frequently. Yet the only competition that means very much is price competition among producers. The whole theory behind "free enterprise" is based on the assumption that every producer is compelled to sell his wares at a price as close to his costs as he can. Otherwise, the theory goes, if he allows the gap between costs and sales price to widen unduly, some rival—content with a smaller margin of profit—will capture the first producer's market by offering the same commodity at a lower figure.[4]

However, in much of large-scale industry, this kind of competition does not prevail, either in peace or war. In steel, copper, glass, chemicals, electrical and farm equipment, and heavy machinery,

---

4. This description of the pricing process of American industry strikes me as lacking somewhat in realism. Actual prices are considerably more flexible than published quotations indicate. Many special allowances are reflected in price quotations and in many markets the quoted price is simply the point at which bargaining starts. Nevertheless many companies need to do a better job of pricing their products. In endeavoring to strike an optimum compromise between margins and volume, the pricers in each enterprise tend to be unduly influenced by margins. This is natural because margins are more definite than the conjectural volumes which might be gained by a reduction in the price. Hence the price is set too high for maximum profit and maximum employment. More thorough market analysis and better directed market analysis will bring actual prices closer to the prices which would be most profitable. The price policies of American business enterprises during eight or nine years before the war were affected by impediments to the starting of new enterprises and the growth of new enterprises. New and growing concerns exercise a very wholesome effect upon prices because they are trying to carve out markets for themselves partly at the expense of older and larger enterprises. Reforms in the tax laws and in the institutions of the capital market will help raise the business birth rate and improve the quality of business births. All of the discussion of price policies in the report relates to an area not covered by the investigations of the Committee and concerning which the Committee has no special information. I agree, however, with the observations in the report that collective bargaining should not become an instrument for supporting rigidities in the prices paid by consumers.—SUMNER H. SLICHTER

for example, prices tend to be artifically fixed. Even during a depression, producers in such fields prefer to preserve the price structure, and accept losses that arise often from tremendous reductions in sales. During the summer of 1932, for instance, the steel industry was limping along at around 14 per cent of its operating capacity. More than 70 per cent of its plant, and more than 50 per cent of its workers, were idle.

But so devout was the addiction to the doctrine of keeping prices up, that from the boom peak of 1929 to depression trough of 1932, steel prices fell only 23 per cent. Conversely, American farmers who at that time sold their crops in a genuinely competitive market (a market which illustrated the competitive principle underlying the historic supply-and-demand equation) had to put sales first and prices second. In 1929, corn was selling at ninety-four cents a bushel. In 1932 it was selling for thirty-one cents a bushel. Over this same period, moreover, marked by a sharp decline in farmer's purchasing power, the prices for farm machinery remained virtually static, even though effective demand for it dropped off some 65 per cent.

Along with agriculture, there are many units in trade and fabrication where an unrestrained play of prices may exist. On the other hand, over important sectors of the economy, prices are set, pegged, administered, whether by government edict, the Pittsburgh Plus fiats of giant corporations, or antichiseling agreements of trade associations, or the bargaining pressure exerted by unions. Instead of being free-flowing and flexible, such prices are sticky and inflexible. They have given rise to the suggestion that success in American business today means the survival of the least competitive.

The Dangers of High Prices

That this trend is dangerous for the future prosperity can hardly be denied. Wherever prices can be predetermined, independent of the rise or fall of effective demand, the temptation to maintain the price at a high level is generally stronger than the perception that this rigidity, if put into practice throughout the country, would lead to economic stagnation and collapse. The hazard in any such situation is that a company, bent on retaining a previous price structure, in the face of declining demand, produces less and less while layoffs in its own plant swell unemployment. Moreover, it is not only the specific company that is affected by pursuing a policy of price rigidity; supplying and feeder enterprises are likewise affected and in turn curtail their own operations. In short, even where prices are administered, the paramount consideration must be to administer them to call forth full, practical operating capacity.

The same principle applies to the process of setting prices for labor. *Both management and union must be aware of the danger of "pricing themselves and their product out of the market."* In this connection, collective bargaining becomes a crucial instrument for sparking and stimulating the capacity use of our materials, our machines, our man power. This function is especially important in view of the fact that the basic decisions of our time are group decisions, corporate decisions, union decisions, farm bloc decisions, and not the solitary decisions of individual sellers and individual buyers.

But whatever the degree of competition, whether semimonopolistic with prices virtually frozen, or cutthroat competition of free-for-all prices, *the underlying aim of collective bargaining must be to summon forth the utmost use of our resources.*[5] Hence

5. The observation that the underlying aim of collective bargaining must be to summon forth the utmost use of our resources is a challenging one. It raises the question of the relationship between collective bargaining and the expansion of employment in growing industries. The terms negotiated by a union and the employers in an industry determine how many jobs the industry will be able to provide. How does one determine the proportions of the total wage force of the country for which each industry should provide jobs? How does one induce employers and unions to make their bargains with the national interest in full employment in mind? It could be easily possible for collective bargaining to convert increases in the demand for the product of a given industry entirely into higher wages, thus preventing it from producing any expansion of employment. It may be too much to ask that thousands or tens of thousands of collective bargains, covering in each instance only a small fraction of the labor force, be made with reference to their net effect upon the utilization of resources in the country as a whole. Nevertheless, some kind of a yardstick seems to be needed to distinguish between collective bargains which are in the public interest and those which are not in the public interest. For wages such a yardstick can perhaps be found in a comparison of wages in different industries and different occupations. An unbalanced wage structure, whether produced by collective bargaining or in other ways, will produce wage-distortion unemployment by

*when management and union get together to make a bargain, they
should keep in the front of their minds that their arrangements
will influence the price of the product which must be sold to a
third party, the consumer.* The consumer doesn't sit down to approve the price; but he may reject it later when he does his own
kind of "bargaining." He may refuse to buy, or perhaps won't buy
as much as he would otherwise if the price were more favorable
compared to other claims on his income.

In other words, collective bargaining must do more than ever
before to validate the precept that mass production is the Siamese
twin of mass purchasing power. One can live only as long as the
other is alive. That our wheels keep turning only when our workers can keep spending is a lesson bitterly learned in the depression
and one that we will fail to heed at our peril in the postwar
economy.

Collective Bargaining and Maximum Production

In that economy, collective bargaining must be more consciously
invoked by management and unions to serve a double purpose:
(1) to regularize prices without letting them rise too high, and
at the same time to aid in the abolition of sweatshop practices
which may "anchor" prices but at the risk of reducing purchasing
power; (2) to relax the rigidity of prices found in imperfect competition by putting production and employment first, rather than
curtailing output to maintain a pre-existing scale even when up
against falling demand. Price and wage administration today must
move toward the same goal as that achieved by the automatic
competition of the free (or nearly free) market, namely, the complete and continuing use of what we have in materials, machines,
man power.

Only by coming to grips with this reality of our price-wage
equation can the practitioners of collective bargaining prepare to
translate into action the economic philosophy that alone makes
sense in an age of assembly lines and efficiency engineering. That
philosophy is one of high continuous production, high profits in

---

attracting an excess of labor to industries and occupations where the terms of the
labor bargain are unusually favorable.—SUMNER H. SLICHTER

return for genuinely venturesome capital, high wages at steady jobs, together with an unceasing stress upon ever lowered unit cost. Otherwise we shall find ourselves straining to push back, rather than to unleash, the prodigious productive power of modern technology, while government itself degenerates into a savage squabbling between pressure groups, each intent upon enlarging its own slice of the national economic pie, rather than striving to enlarge the size of the pie itself. To produce, and produce and produce again is the sole alternative to the decay of our capitalist system, and the decline of our political democracy.

Hence, *over and above the primary prerequisites of successful collective bargaining, to date, namely the recognition that managements and unions are mutually indispensable and functionally equal, must come this new recognition that to serve themselves best they must serve the common prosperity most.* This is the great imperative of our time. It is no longer a question of lip service to social idealism, but of realistic down-to-brass-tacks appraisal of our economic necessities. Isolationism in the conduct of an interdependent national economy can be as disastrous as isolationism in an interdependent world. To face up to this exigency is less a break with our past attitudes than an explicit appreciation of conditions long implicit within our society, even when seen through a glass darkly.

Widening the Area of Agreements

As steps toward this facing up, *the Committee recommends that managements and unions together explore the advantages arising from a wider application of market-wide collective bargaining.*[6]

6. Both trade-union leaders and representatives of management point out from their practical experience important advantages in regional or industry-wide bargains. It seems to me, however, that the problems of industry-wide bargains need much further analysis before industry-wide bargaining is recommended for large industries such as automobiles, coal, or railroads. The consequences of a breakdown of negotiations in such large industries are different in kind from the consequences of a breakdown in small industries such as glass, pottery, or hosiery. On a number of occasions in recent years the nation has been confronted with either the possibility or the reality of a complete shutdown of the coal industry or railroad transportation. The consequences of such a tie-up to the economic life of the country are obviously far reaching and might easily be disastrous. I am not convinced that the community has learned enough yet about preventing strikes so that it is safe to

To be sure this technique is not without injurious potentialities. It might well encourage excessive and rigid prices. Unless regional and industry-wide collective bargaining fosters lower unit costs, and passes such savings along to the consumer, it could degenerate into a peculiarly vicious kind of protective tariff, safeguarding undue profits and undue wages at the expense of the rest of the community.[7]

Yet already this regional or industry-wide approach, whether in peace or war, has accomplished a great deal to bring stability to coal mining, the needle trades, to shipbuilding and other industries. It provides management with predictables in labor cost. It protects the worker against the capricious wage slash and enterprise in general against the unsettling effects of bidding up wages that accompanies a period of labor shortage with its scampings and pirating. It has often promoted the introduction of laborsaving devices in a sane, "staggered" manner to cushion, or entirely offset, injurious social consequences of mass layoffs, and discharges. Furthermore, since the art of business is being daily transmuted into the science of management, the components of an industry should be enabled to proceed on a more orderly basis.

Today, for example, in the automobile industry, General Motors, Ford, Chrysler, along with Nash, Packard, Willys-Overland, Hud-

---

give several hundreds of thousands of men power to interrupt production in all branches of industry by shutting down all plants in a key industry such as coal, railroads, or automobiles. The report does not come to grips with this problem. A solution of it is a prerequisite to the extension of nation-wide collective bargaining into additional key industries.

There are two sides to the argument that uniformity in wage rates, job classifications, and seniority rules are desirable in all plants in the same industry. "Invidious comparisons" may be a source of dissatisfaction, but they may also be a source of progress. The virtue of uniformity is easily overestimated. The acceptance of the proposition that conditions in various plants must be the same can become a formidable obstacle to new methods of wage payment and new methods of conducting plant operations. Furthermore, the larger the number of parties to the bargain on each side, the more strongly the cards tend to be stacked in favor of the *status quo*. It is not easy, for example, for a large number of employers to agree upon new demands. The lone pioneering employer who wishes to launch an experiment may receive little support even from other employers.—SUMNER H. SLICHTER

7. Unless market-wide collective bargaining is completely democratic in character, it is likely to weaken rather than strengthen the democratic basis of trade unions. The further removed from the individual member is the control of the wage for his service or even of the choice of his negotiating agent, the greater the likelihood of "top controls" of labor unions.—ROBERT J. WATT

son and other independents, all bargain separately with the UAW-CIO.[8] Yet if these manufacturers, acting as a unit, bargained in the bilateral fashion with the union, they could achieve that uniformity in wage rates, job classifications, seniority rules and the like which would obviate comparisons, and retain a satisfied labor force for the whole industry. They could think as an industry for their industry; prepare to level out humps and declivities of seasonal output; even perhaps develop a guaranteed annual wage. They could then concentrate upon the more effective utilization of equipment and man power while preserving their competitiveness in terms of the end product.

Emphasis upon market-wide collective bargaining would inevitably foster the wider use of technical assistants, such as engineers, economists, and sociologists, by managements and unions alike. The Committee recommends that both managements and unions weigh the advantages of invoking this kind of aid in moving toward their collective bargaining purposes. It is apparent that, in view of the delicate interrelatedness of our economy, fact finding and fact interpretation must be the handmaidens of a market analysis more detailed, scientific, and exhaustive than ever before. Both managements and unions need definitive data superior to that which they now usually possess.

Moreover, they must be prepared to disclose all pertinent information at their disposal. The United States community cannot permit collective bargaining to be merely a game of blindman's buff rather than an adult effort to implement illumination. The day is long past when collective bargaining can be adequately carried on in the atmosphere of a David Harum horse trade, or the chaffering of an Oriental bazaar. To the worm's-eye view of management and union, the trained economist, or perhaps a group of economists, to be paid by both employers and employees, within an industry, can add the bird's-eye view of the total situation, with its long-term implications. Certainly the use of such specialized personnel is long overdue.

8. I am not sure that we can say with any authority that the automobile industry would gain by market-wide collective bargaining. It does sound like an apt example, but it might be safer to say that for many industries in which the product and manufacturing process are highly standardized, market-wide or industry-wide collective bargaining looks promising.—FRAZIER D. MacIVER

Better Organization for Bargaining

As another concrete move toward the growth of market-wide collective bargaining, *the Committee recommends that employers within an industry associate themselves into organizations designed to negotiate with unions, not to combat them.* In this respect, the British experience offers an adaptable model. In England, for example, such employer agencies as the Railway Operators devote themselves to collective bargaining with the Transport Union. These employer groups are, in turn, banded into the National Confederation of Employers' Associations (other economic matters are left to the British Federation of Industries), which, unlike our own NAM, or Chamber of Commerce, or trade bodies, concerns itself exclusively with industrial relations. The Confederation's constituent associations of employers in various industries operate on national, regional, plant and local levels. Within each affiliated industry are joint management-union councils. In short, British employers have organizations which, if transposed to this country, would be management equivalents of local unions of the AF of L and CIO. Our own National Association of Manufacturers and Chamber of Commerce have no subdivisions that engage thus directly in collective bargaining.

Because with rare exceptions, we lack any such employer alignment, our bargaining is widely collective, with some notable exceptions, only on the part of one side—labor. It is not collective on the part of both sides.

In the absence of a prototype of the British arrangement for employer bargaining, or pending its establishment, *the Committee therefore recommends the formation of a national management-union council on collective bargaining.* Representation on this council would be drawn from the National Association of Manufacturers, the United States Chamber of Commerce, the American Federation of Labor and the Congress of Industrial Organizations.[9] The council would constantly examine collective bargaining agreements and methods in order to serve as a central clearing house for disseminating practices found especially efficient in

9. It might be in the interest of public policy to have a management-union council also consider the railroad problem.—FRAZIER D. MACIVER

pushing production, making jobs more secure, and promoting a spirit of collaboration between managements and unions.

3. THE POLITICS OF COLLECTIVE BARGAINING

The politics of collective bargaining is an omnibus term used variously to describe (1) the extent of government intervention in industrial relations; (2) political activity by the labor movement to influence the laws and fiats of government; and (3) the distribution and exercise of power within the unions themselves.

The Wagner Act, viewed in the perspective of United States history, is merely the culmination of a long series of laws designed to improve the status of labor. From the 1868 New Hampshire statute to limit the hours of work to ten a day, to the New Freedom's 1915 Clayton Act with its resounding half-truth that "the labor of a human being is not a commodity" up through Section 7(a) of 1933's NIRA, the antecedents of the Wagner Act represent a continuing attempt on the part of the wage earners to get government help when they weren't strong enough to help themselves. The operation of the National Labor Relations Board marks but another effort by government to rectify by the political means imbalance and inequity in the economic sphere. In this respect the NLRB symbolizes that quasi-judicial administrative agency which has its roots in the Interstate Commerce Commission Act of 1887 and which interposes constantly in the production and distribution of goods and services.

Necessarily, with the advent of war, the scope of this government intervention has been immensely enlarged. Many more collective bargaining agreements were in force than ever before. But the functions of collective bargaining—except within narrow limits —were carried on less between managements and unions than by the government. When employers forfeited the right of lockout for the duration, and workers forfeited their most potent economic weapon, the exercise of the right to strike, both sides received in exchange still another quasi-judicial administrative agency—the National War Labor Board. Established in the interests of uninterrupted output of materiel, the Board—with its tripartite composition of employer, public and union members—settled industrial disputes—and more. It was also entrusted with the task of stabilizing wages, root cause of most disputes.

Shall Wartime Controls Be Given Up?

That such controls are mandatory in wartime, none can deny. What is more debatable is the wisdom of continuing them in days of peace. Now, as before, collective bargaining trends will be dominated by the bigger units in business, labor and government.

While 115,000 companies were engaged in war production, 114 of them had 82 per cent of all primary contracts. In many industrial sectors, small and medium-sized enterprises with their secondary contracts were very important, to be sure. But like cuttle fish on a shark they were often only satellites of a Big Ownership that farmed out in bits and pieces work that it could not or preferred not to do.[10] By the same token, while some 23 million workers were engaged in war production, the 12 million organized into the AF of L, CIO and railroad brotherhoods set the pace in determining income and working conditions. It would be a very starry-eyed government, indeed, that refused to expand sufficiently to cope with the concentrations of social power embodied in giant corporations and giant labor organizations; or blinked at the obligation of removing, or reducing, frictions between them.

It is an idle dream to assume that, with the coming of peace, and reconversion to nonmartial pursuits, government intervention in the affairs of managements and unions will now automatically cease. It is easier to imagine a busy street-crossing without policemen or traffic lights. The question is not one of whether or not the government will interpose in collective bargaining, but rather to what degree, and to what purpose war controls will be relaxed or abandoned. The extent of government participation in collective bargaining will wax or wane in direct ratio to the success of voluntary action by managements and unions. That success can be defined by whether or not such self-propulsions promote or detract

10. I do not like the suggestion of the small- and medium-sized enterprises being satellites of Big Ownership. There are too many small- and medium-sized concerns which pretty much stand on their own and do specialized jobs that cannot be done efficiently by Big Ownership.—FRAZIER D. MACIVER

from the public interest—which means the greatest amount of economic opportunity and security for the greatest number.

Stimulating Voluntary Action

But the relationship between management, unions and government also needs to be defined. Certainly government should be prevented from continuing, or taking over, functions that can be more effectively performed by voluntary associations. Even those services of necessity carried on by government should be handled not by administrators alone, but those directly affected must be allowed to share in the formulation of policy. But mere counsel isn't enough. Both managements and unions can at times contribute immeasurably to the success of government action by sharing directly in administration.

The Committee believes that collective bargaining aims are best achieved when government action on the myriad details of the management-union relationship has been reduced to a minimum. The more employers and employees depend upon bargaining by equal parties to achieve a practical compromise on wages, hours and work conditions, the more firmly rooted become the self-disciplines and the obligations to find the solutions among themselves, rather than to ask for solutions ready made.

Hence *the Committee suggests that, now the war is over, voluntary mediation boards, composed equally of management, labor and public representatives be established within every sizable industrial community.*[11] Such boards should adjudicate industrial disputes in their areas, and perhaps even be empowered by the parties at interest to engage in final and binding arbitration rulings.[12] Such boards can be especially useful in the days when the

11. The recommendation for local mediation boards may be useful if market-wide collective bargaining is used only to establish general standards, leaving the details to be worked out locally.—ROBERT J. WATT

12. I think it should be made clear that this is to be made on a voluntary basis. This appears from the statements made later on, but I believe it will be clearer if this fact is emphasized at the outset. It should also be made clear in this discussion that the voluntary local mediation boards are to supplement, not replace, the mediation work of the U. S. Conciliation Service and of state agencies concerned in this field. I would like to see that the Conciliation Service should likewise be strengthened.—EDWIN E. WITTE

no-strike, no-lockout pledges have expired, and when government controls have been relaxed, or abandoned. The very existence of these boards would tend to encourage localized, as against federal, settlement of management-labor controversy; to reverse the centralizing trends of submitting to Washington issues that can be more effectively decided in the local community.

Personnel for these boards can be drawn from chambers of commerce, local unions, state commissions of labor, civic and educational bodies, the panels of the American Arbitration Association, as well as from among those who served on War Labor Board subdivisions throughout the country.

However, *the Committee recommends that, any such voluntary mediation boards foster as much industrial self-government as possible by not trying to impose details, or to deal with questions which should be directly negotiated by management and the union.* Unions and managers are in a position to determine, more efficaciously than outsiders, the fairness of a particular wage scale, the most workable apparatus for adjusting grievances. They are on the scene; they are familiar with conditions. They have the task of living up to the terms of their contract. No third party is equipped to exercise that flexibility of judgment, that knowledge of immediacies which management and union between them possess. They should therefore have an authority in industrial relations to equal their responsibility. Surely no third party has their responsibility for pushing out production. He isn't around when grievances pile up, when the union official has to pacify an angry membership, when the plant manager has to explain to the executive vice president why there is a slump in output.

To further encourage industrial self-government with its accent upon a "settle among ourselves" approach, the Committee suggests that a second type of voluntary mediation board, to be composed of management and labor representatives, be now established within each industry. The personnel for these boards, which would exclude any public representation at all, would be drawn from employer and employee organizations other than those directly involved in a dispute.

Necessarily, before collective bargaining can become a tool for industrial self-government, it must be actively affirmed, rather than merely accepted, by business as well as by labor and government as the keystone in all relations between management and workers. The attitude of some businessmen that collective bargaining is an unwonted interference with the exercise of their prerogatives, is something to be fended off, or outsmarted, or reluctantly tolerated, rather than a technique for harmonizing human relations, and lifting output and morale, remains—in too many cases—a stumbling block to improvement of management-labor affairs. To some extent, this view was neutralized, and even reversed, by the labor management committees sponsored by the War Production Board. Although such committees expressly do not engage in collective bargaining, the very sitting down by labor and management to talk out mutual problems to quicken war output created a climate more favorable to mutual respect and understanding.[13]

Bargaining and Industrial Citizenship

No bargain of any kind can be successful unless the parties to it adequately represent those for whom they act. In collective bargaining, where the bargaining agents speak—at least on the labor side—for thousands and sometimes hundreds of thousands, authentic representation is absolutely crucial. The representatives of the employers must truly speak for management and the stockholders who own the business, and those of labor, for the rank and file who will be affected by the agreement. Usually the employers' agents do in fact represent the employers' interests, but their constituents are far fewer in number than those of labor bargainers and the lines of their responsibility are much more closely drawn. But, even on the employers' side, sound collective bargaining presupposes sufficient control of management by the stockholders of the bargaining firms. It must be emphasized that on labor's side sheer numbers render the situation far more complicated and the chances of inadequate representation become

13. It seems to me that too much is being claimed for the effect of labor-management committees. As far as I know them, many have been more concerned with conservation of materials, war bond drives, etc., under the stimulant of patriotism rather than with the real production problems.—FRAZIER D. MacIVER

correspondingly greater. Back of labor's agents in collective bargaining there must be as genuinely a free and democratic union structure as workability permits.

Furthermore collective bargaining itself is justified not only by protecting the rights of labor but also by extending that diffusion of power which strengthens democracy. Collective bargaining has been, and remains, a brake against the exercise of absolute authority to hire and fire and otherwise determine conditions of employment; this authority is too great to be entrusted, in its entirety, to management alone. Indeed, collective bargaining can introduce into industrial management a number of safeguards that may be likened to our constitutional system of checks and balances. If political government requires constitutional protection against the arbitrary use of power, so too, does industrial government.

In the realm of United States industrial relations free unionism is as indispensable as an independent judiciary. If capricious government is bad government, then capricious management is bad management. If an American has the right to be secure in his home, and in public places, and to speak freely, he has the same essential rights on his job.

Of course, the exercise of arbitrary authority is not confined to management. Within the union, whose *raison d'être* is collective bargaining, the rank-and-file member in some cases has less influence with the leadership than with the employer, less to say about the conduct of union affairs than about affairs in the shop. He can be penalized for denouncing the union administration, or for forming an opposition bloc. The power of top-ranking union officials is sometimes immune to popular control.

Before indicating remedial action to abolish this kind of union rule, a brief analysis of its origins and development may illumine what is perhaps the most obscure, and puzzling, phase in the politics of collective bargaining.

A typical union, as a going concern, is marked by this paradox: it is simultaneously (1) a business service organization and (2) a humanitarian enterprise. This dual nature engenders many conflicts in purpose and function. In its role as a business organization, the union must have competent bureaucratic personnel, very like an insurance company for example. The average union member resembles a client who pays for a certain service, but doesn't intervene in administrative questions since these are the province of trained people chosen for such duties. But as a reformist movement for bettering the lot of the common man, the union is a vehicle for altruism.

This hybrid character of the union evokes corresponding contradictions and cleavages in the leader. He is called on to be a smart businessman on the one hand and on the other the champion of the underdog's cause. He is supposed to live up to both; and while his own adherents may admire him for business acumen, he is elsewhere under attack for not being a selfless crusader. The fact is, of course, that he is more the "idealist" in the first struggling days when the union is being built and trying to achieve recognition; he is more the pragmatist when the union gets entrenched and the realistic and practical business aspects supersede the altruistic ones.

Dangers of Concentrated Power

As the union achieves status, and expands, power tends to concentrate at the top. In the beginning the union is run like any other embodiment of primitive democracy, like a town meeting, say, in which every taxpayer participates. But as the union keeps growing, and its affairs become more complex, and its functions multiply, a whole group of full-time, paid officials, usually the original sponsors of the union, come to the fore. They cope with the countless issues, large and small, that make up the union's existence. Into their hands gravitates more and more responsibility until the membership meeting, even the executive board recedes, as the group of paid officials, commonly called "the office," assume increasing control. The day-by-day decisions are theirs; and since such decisions shape policy, they acquire the fundamental policy-making authority.

Within this framework, which is rarely a violent usurpation of power, but rather something that flows from the growth of organization itself, individual ambition and the desire to command readily flourish. The "office" may become a cohesive clique of top officialdom who, to retain their prerogatives, build political machines and distribute favors and patronage. So long as they "deliver" in terms of lifting wages and otherwise improving conditions, the average unionist is satisfied. He takes the view that this is what the officials are paid to do, and why should he waste his time at union meetings as long as they give him his money's worth —service in exchange for his dues. He is usually no more concerned with the principle of democratic self-rule in his union than in the Republican or Democratic parties. He is willing, even eager, to delegate responsibility, in accord with the great American tradition of "Let George do it." Only when the going gets rough does he turn to the union, attend its sessions, and generally become "active." Sometimes, too, his interest may be aroused by a factional fight among the leaders. Otherwise, he goes fishing.

Along with the tendency of power to gravitate to the top, and the indifference of the rank and file as long as things are going well, is a third factor, often overlooked. Far more than most men in comparable vocations, the union official depends on his job for his livelihood as well as for the psychic rewards of leadership. Hence to the deep-seated human drive toward self-expression and self-assertion is added the urgency of economic self-preservation. The official, almost by reflex action, perpetuates himself in office by maintaining his reputation for performance and by keeping effective power in his own hands and those of his colleagues.[14]

Bureaucracy and Efficiency[15]

In some unions the president, with the consent of an executive board, which is often a rubber stamp, appoints such key function-

14. This seems to me an overstatement. While there are some instances of union officers who have been able to hold their jobs for decades, there are more cases where union officials who have put their all into the union have been left high and dry through defeat in a union election. I doubt whether the average length of service of the international union officers is anywhere nearly as long as the average length of service of corporation executives; and but few unions ever take care of the old officers whom they scrap. In local union offices, changes are even more frequent.—EDWIN E. WITTE

15. This part of the report is overstated in my opinion and gives a completely wrong impression. Although there may be union executive groups who constitute

aries as organizers who are liaison between local affiliates and the national office. He has a hand in the editorial policy of all publications. He furthermore names all committees (including the crucial credentials committee) for national conventions. The selection of delegates to these sessions, which form the legislative arm of unionism, in turn mirrors the same kind of machine control on the part of the local union officials as that used by the national leadership.

However, in all fairness, it should be pointed out that long tenure in union office, everywhere duplicated in the industrial and government worlds, derives as much from complete membership approval as from rigging the gear and tackle of a political machine. Usually, it is a blend of both. But since democracy depends upon diffusion of power, even as an autocracy depends upon the density of power, unions too closely resemble the kind of constitutional monarchy where the monarchial outweighs the constitutional. On the other hand, no modern enterprise of any appreciable size can be run efficiently and systematically without somebody authorized to make quick final decisions. To refer all decisions back to the membership is the road to anarchy. And to be free to make decisions, even the most high-minded leadership is compelled to resort to the inescapable methods of power politics: manipulation, and the imposition of the leader's will and judgment, as against a course of action arrived at by considering the different choices put forward by all members of the union. Hence the dilemma of enough delegated power to direct the show well, but not too much power lest the very plot ring down the curtain on dictatorship, is not alone the dilemma of Big Unionism. It is equally the dilemma of Big Ownership and Big Government.

By its very nature the bigness of union structure encourages the kind of bureaucracy that freezes into a ruling caste while the membership (read also stockholder or voter) tends to degenerate into a plebiscitary body. Surely this is the dominant trend as union locals over the past decade have grown from 30 members to 300

---

a rubber stamp for the president, they are the exception. As a matter of fact, American trade unions are far ahead of any other element in American life in the operation of democracy.—ROBERT J. WATT

to 3,000 or more. Even in the many unions where leadership is eager to develop rank-and-file participation, the membership meeting itself is more often a medium for endorsing, rather than forming, policy. Under such circumstances, the demogogic, the unscrupulous, even the terrorist, personality can gain a foothold. But it must be remembered that such exploit an underlying institutional condition. They are jackals feasting on the corpse of democratic participation. The question of how to rid unions of their few but sensational shakedown artists, and other symptoms of moral leprosy, merely highlights the more fundamental question of how to curtail abuses resulting from undue centralization of power in unions conducted by able and honorable leadership. If the second problem is solved, the first ceases to exist; for racketeers have never made headway in a union genuinely controlled by its own members.

Guarantees of Democratic Unionism

Before outlining corrective measures, a clear distinction must be drawn between two types of disciplinary action. The first type consists of what the United States courts have declared to be the just and proper exercise of official union authority: a member can be fined, suspended or expelled for failure to pay dues, acting as a strikebreaker, or agent provocateur, or as spokesman for a rival union, or refusing to comply the terms of a collective bargaining agreement with an employer.

The second type violates the civil rights of the union member. The courts have declared that no unionist can be fined, suspended or expelled for adverse criticism of the administration; for setting up an opposing faction, for protests against the handling of union affairs. Disciplinary action in unions is sometimes marked by the high-handed and imperious.

There is still a third, if hybrid, type of disciplinary action which can be directed against a combination of civil and economic rights. This is favoritism in job placement under a closed shop where the union acts as labor-supply or hiring agent for the employers. When a tight little clique of officials controls job assignments, dissidents can be penalized by being kept at the bottom of the list when employment opportunity opens up; in a time of work scarcity this deprives them of their means of livelihood.[16]

To ensure that labor's agents in collective bargaining represent their constituents and to protect the individual union member in his civil and economic rights within the union, the Committee recommends the establishment of federal and state tribunals to enforce fair union practices and to be known perhaps as fair labor practice boards.[17] They should be quasi-judicial, administrative bodies empowered to hear and subpoena witnesses and otherwise take testimony in cases where accusations of unjust disciplinary action are made. They should restore rights and prerogatives to those unjustly punished by union officialdom. They should levy heavy fines upon the guilty, or deprive them of office for a probationary period. The decisions of such boards should be final and

16. Though it would be possible to leave to the gradual building up of court decisions the complete definition of what kinds of disciplinary action belong to the first type and to the second type, and what the courts might do about the hybrid third type, yet it would be better to take now, by affirmative action, some steps which would lead more quickly to the elimination of these seeds of discord. The problems are highly specialized. They do involve human rights which have brought about appeals to the courts, but they are not matters with which the courts have frequently to deal. Under such circumstances, an administrative treatment of the problem is indicated and points to the establishment of special tribunals.—WILLIAM H. DAVIS

17. I object to this proposal on the ground that: (1) it fails to describe with any assurance of safeguards how these boards will be fairly constituted; and (2) it goes too far in granting these boards original jurisdiction over internal union disputes thereby setting aside union tribunals, instead of following the sounder practice of the courts which limit their review of the decisions of union tribunals to a correction only of arbitrary or unfair action and then only after a member has exhausted reasonably available union remedies.—CLINTON S. GOLDEN

This recommendation would put the government into labor unions and might result in *government labor unions*. If government tribunals were to determine labor-union personnel practices, it would be necessary to police corporations and other voluntary associations. At least in the case of labor unions their actions are public while in many other cases the job is done in a silent, but nonetheless effective way. I prefer the statement under "Bargainers Must Represent Their Constituents," which states, "The Committee well recognizes that no fiats, no courts, no laws, no external compulsions can be a substitute for genuine up-and-down membership participation, which is a change that must come within unionism itself." I prefer to allow democracy of wage earners to set up its own rules and learn wisdom by experience with the minimum of government interference.—ROBERT J. WATT

I doubt whether this should be done. It is vastly preferable that all unions themselves establish machinery and principles to accomplish the purposes set forth in this paragraph, as quite a few unions have done. I regard it as certain, however, that unless all unions do so voluntarily, government intervention will occur sooner or later.—EDWIN E. WITTE

binding, and revoked only by the superior state and federal courts.

To contend that no "outsiders" should be permitted to interfere with the internal affairs of unionism is to dodge the reality of what unionism means today. The unions cannot claim public protection under the Wagner Act, and similar legislation, and in the same breath deny that the public has no legitimate concern with the way they are run. Unions are no longer strictly private, voluntary associations which a worker may or may not join. They have become semipublic, sometimes compulsory bodies. Their operations in the civil and economic spheres is unequivocally "affected with a public interest," quite as much as the sale of stocks and bonds now regulated by the Securities and Exchange Commission.

Along with such guarantees of civil and economic rights, *the Committee recommends that all union finances be under law opened to public scrutiny, as many are, and that full reports of receipts and expenditures be prepared, certified and regularly published.*[18] On the other hand, *the Committee is firmly of the opinion that incorporation of unions is an adventure in futility since incorporation is a device to limit, not to increase, liability.*

Bargainers Must Represent Their Constituents[19]

The Committee well recognizes that no fiats, no courts, no laws, no external compulsions can be a substitute for genuine up-and-down membership participation, which is a change that must come within unionism itself. The Committee is aware that such

18. I object to this proposal on the ground that (1) it fails to distinguish between the different problems of local and national bodies; (2) it does not allow exceptions from the necessity of financial disclosure where secrecy is essential, as in the face of employer hostility to a newly organized union; and (3) its proposed opening to scrutiny of *"all* union finances" is dangerous, unnecessary, loose wording. Financial regulation of business does not throw open *all* its finances to public scrutiny; it only requires certain specified reports.—CLINTON S. GOLDEN

19. I object to this entire section on the following grounds: (1) it proposes to solve the problems of union government by establishing a government within the government but it fails to tell how this novel inner government is to be set up and what is to happen to the present governmental structure of unions; (2) its statement that the problem of member participation is to be solved by having "nearly every member" in a council illustrates the triumph of a fanciful theory over troublesome facts; (3) its statement that job distribution will be settled by "simple" seniority, i.e., the oldest union member having first claim to a job, illustrates its inaccuracy and oversimplification of difficult questions; and (4) the problems of democratic union government cannot be settled by such speculative schemes; there is no substitute for plain hard work on them, day in and day out.—CLINTON S. GOLDEN

experiments in union reform as limts on tenure of office, statutory meetings, constitutional revisions, the use of the referendum and recall, all snip at the top leaves but fail to get at the roots of the basic issue: meaningful self-government.

Since the majority of faults and excesses stem from the impersonal structure of unionism itself, *the Committee recommends that United States labor leadership enlarge and intensify all present programs designed to decentralize power and function and to make rank-and-file members partners in a common venture. Delegate councils, drawn from the grass roots should ascend, stratum by stratum, up through the local and regional to the general headquarters.*[20] The aim here is to enlist from each local union a group of active participants who, by their very existence, will—up to a point, at least—overcome the apathy and indifference toward policy questions all too common. Each council, or subgroup, should be entrusted with its own particular task such as seeing to it that delegates to the national convention are nominated at an open meeting, and elected by secret ballot. It should be possible to have nearly every union member active in some council.

Such local groups, and not the national and local officials, should make sure that: (1) jobs are assigned on the basis of simple seniority—i.e., the oldest union member has first claim to a job, or arrange the share-the-work system when times are hard, (2) special assessments are levied only after majority sanction, and that no member be assessed for a political or "educational" purpose of which he does not approve, (3) appropriations from union funds for any public cause, from community chest to Red Cross, be made only with membership approval, (4) all changes in the constitution be undertaken only after full debate and prior notification, (5) all minutes, records, by-laws are available to any

20. It is my belief that some unions suffer from too great diffusion of responsibility and too many elections. A workable democracy within unions, as in government, can be attained, not through diffusion of power but through making the officials who exercise power truly responsible to the membership. I doubt the wisdom of creating machinery duplicating the regular union organization. Vastly preferable, it seems to me, is the inclusion in the union constitution and by-laws and within the regular structure of the union of the safeguards which it is suggested are to be exercised through the rank-and-file delegate councils. The first function suggested, that relating to the observance of seniority principles, clearly is a matter for collective bargaining between the employer and the union and must be so dealt with rather than as an internal union problem.—EDWIN E. WITTE

member, (6) copies of all collective bargaining contracts be placed in the hands of every member affected, (7) decisions of the president, executive board and other official groups be printed in the union paper, or otherwise publicized, (8) members charged with offense against the union receive a fair, open trial before a special council composed of others than those who brought the charges, (9) business agents be nominated by the local union membership, (10) a network of councils choose the committees for national conventions, and (11) that elections be supervised in a manner to guarantee honest expression of opinion.[21]

The councils might also study and report on such issues as the Little Steel formula, arbitration, upgrading, and the like. Labor leaders have often assured employers that the way to make unions more responsible is to let them have more responsibility. This same precept has substantial merit when applied to the conduct of internal union affairs. In the days ahead, union leadership— even of the loftiest sort—will be only as effective and useful as an alert, informed, interested rank and file allows it, or inspires it, to be.

New Spirit Called For

More fundamentally, the Committee realizes that new forms are meaningless unless animated by a new spirit. The top-flight leadership of labor could no nothing better than to start to revalue some of its existing values in the search for a new conscientiousness that would not be entirely divorced from overtones of a new conscience.

But the need for that search is hardly confined to unionism's officialdom. Leaders of industry and government have a like concern. That concern should become the keystone in the psychology

21. I think the suggestion for "delegate councils" is too dogmatically stated, and with some of its suggestions, I would not be able to agree even if they were less dogmatically stated. This decentralizing of power and function, and making rank-and-file members partners in a common venture, could hardly be achieved unless it begins at the very grass roots—in the locals—and is consistently carried through the regional offices to the general headquarters. Only in that way, by a consistent and thoroughgoing adherence to a basic idea, would it be possible to enlist from each local union a group of active participants who would at once represent and assure the elimination of that apathy and indifference toward policy questions which too often prevails at the local level.—WILLIAM H. DAVIS

of collective bargaining and its appendages. The spokesmen at the collective bargaining conference, as well as those who carry out the terms of any such agreement, must authentically represent their constituencies. This is a moral obligation of the first importance. Since "all power corrupts and absolute power corrupts absolutely," the persons who exercise power for either side must be on their guard against the too-easy assumption that their judgment —because it is backed by a certain economic potency—is therefore immunized against error, against prejudice and against ignorance. It should be kept in mind that workers want to count, to belong, to be recognized for their contribution, to feel more significant than merely a badge number. More than a financial stake is involved during a collective bargaining negotiation. The decisions made affect not only the attitudes of employees in a particular plant but also countless other invisible participants.

In the light of this approach, collective bargaining should no longer be the arena in which an executive indulges in ego expansion, or a union spokesman thumps the table to swing his weight around. The employer might particularly remind himself that paternalism is a remnant of feudal days and has nothing to do with democracy. The government official might well remind himself that self-rule, even when its results seem a blunder, is infinitely preferable to any foray into the most "enlightened" statism. Unless spokesmen for Big Ownership, Big Unionism and Big Government acquire a sharper awareness of their separate and joint obligations to society all three will become like the dinosaurs which grew too big and stupid to survive. The representatives of each, sitting around the collective bargaining table, must become—more consciously than ever before—trustees of other people's money, skills, and aspirations. *It is the Committee's earnest belief that this change in the moral and psychological climate of collective bargaining is vital, necessary, and long overdue.*

WILLIAM H. DAVIS, *Chairman*
WILLIAM L. CHENERY
HOWARD COONLEY
CLINTON S. GOLDEN

FRAZIER D. MacIVER
SUMNER H. SLICHTER
ROBERT J. WATT
EDWIN E. WITTE

INDEX

ADAMSON ACT, 83

Admission fees, *see* Union membership

Agreements, 4, 49-60; administration, 116-129, 224f; arbitration, 54; coverage and term, 10, 51f; grievance machinery, 117ff; legal aspects, 58ff; municipalities, 156; negotiation of, 52ff; policing the contract, 119; purpose and forms, 50f; tests for success of provisions, 54; *see also* Psychology of labor relations

Allis-Chalmers dispute, 162

American Federation of Labor, 5, 12, 18, 20, 31, 40, 80, 82, 132, 165, 167

"American Plan," 41

Antiunion activity, 22

Apprenticeship, 94f; Act (1937), 95

Arbitration: forms of, 124ff; and government, 128; lack of machinery in government collective bargaining, 148ff; municipalities, 156; place of, 54f; World War II, 162, 163

Automobile, Aircraft and Agricultural Implement Workers of America, International Union of United, 13

Automobile industry, 11, 67, 87, 88, 89, 91, 98, 101, 105, 118, 122, 123, 220f, 233f

Automobile Workers, United, 69, 111, 163

BALTIMORE and Ohio Railroad, 133, 134f

Bargaining for members only, 38, 40, 42

Beyer, Otto S., 135, 136

Big steel case, 183, 185

British experience, 24, 42, 49

Building and construction industry, 11, 14, 16, 85, 86f, 108, 118, 119

Building Trades Department (AF of L), 14f

CAPTIVE mines, 164

Chamber of Commerce of the U.S., 24, 165, 167

Checkoff, 39, 42n

Clayton Act, 236

Closed shop, 36, 39, 40, 45; advantages and disadvantages, 43, 44; defined, 35; development, 40f; in Europe, 42f; job security, 93; outlook, 47f; World War II, 164, 165, 176

Closed union, 35, 95f

Clothing Workers of America, Amalgamated, 15, 65, 75, 133, 139f

Coal mining, 11, 85, 119, 129

Collective bargaining: defined, 1-9; 222f;

economics of, 225ff; effects on wages, 62; employers' attitude toward, 7, 22ff, 47; history, 4ff, 215ff; legislation, 236; market-wide, 232ff; New Deal, 217; politics of, 236ff; postwar, 186f; psychological attitudes, 188ff; role of, 215ff; versus individual bargaining, 218ff; World War I, 6, 8; World War II, 8, 162ff, 217

Committee for Industrial Organization, *see* Congress of Industrial Organizations

Commonwealth Edison Co., 206

Company unions, 6, 7, 24, 30ff

Conciliation, 124; commissioners, 55; lack of machinery in government, 148ff

Congress of Industrial Organizations, 12, 18, 20f, 32, 107, 165, 167

Construction trades unions, *see* Building and construction industry

Contracts, *see* Agreements

Cooperation, *see* Psychology of labor relations

Coordination allowances, 99

Craft unions, 12, 93f, 109

DAVIS, William H., 164, 166, 176, 246n, 249n

Discharge, 56, 97, 98f, 185, 202f

ELECTRICAL, Radio and Machine Workers of America, United, 125

Electrical manufacturing, 122, 132

Electrical Workers, Brotherhood of, 206

Employee representation plans, 132

Employer associations, 22-33; *Committee recommendation,* 235

Erectors' Association, National, 25, 41

Exclusive bargaining shop, 37, 39f

FAIR labor practice boards, *Committee recommendation,* 246

Fair Labor Standards (Wages and Hours) Act, 63, 68, 80, 83, 84, 89

Federal Employees, National Federation of, 143, 147

Federal Shipbuilding and Drydock Co., 163, 177f

Federal Workers of America, United, 143, 147

Fire Fighters, International Association of, 143; and strikes, 146f

Firestone Tire Co., 124, 129

Flat glass union, 53, 123

Ford Motor Co., 69, 82, 97n, 111

Full-fashioned hosiery industry, 103, 127

GARMENT trades, 86, 89, 99, 118, 123, 139f
General Electric Co., 125, 184
General Motors Corporation, 128
German experience, 42, 43, 49
Glass Bottle Blowers' Association, 112
Glass union, 111, 112, 122, 131, 216
Golden, Clinton S., 246n, 247n
Gompers, Samuel, 63
Goodrich, B. F., Co., 124
Goodyear Industrial Assembly, 32
Government: agencies for arbitration, 128; attitude toward closed and union shops, 46f; and postwar collective bargaining, 238; regulations and policies, 6, 8. Federal, state, local and collective bargaining, 11, 142-161; conciliation and arbitration machinery, 148ff; employees, 11; parallels with private enterprise, 144f; strike limitations, 145ff; unions, 143; wages, 151
Government Employees, American Federation of, 143, 147
Green, William, 107
Grievances, 117ff, 121f

HART, Schaffner & Marx, 140
Harvill Aircraft case, 178
Hawthorne plant (Western Electric Co.), 196f
Henderson, L. J., 194
Hosiery industry, 98, 131, 132
Hours, 8, 79-91; municipalities, 156; overtime, 88ff; seniority, 85f; shorter hours issues, 80ff; standardized by law, 82f; standards for, 83ff; union versus nonunion, 82; vacations, 87f; work day and week, 79ff, 90; work sharing, 85ff

IMPARTIAL chairman, 127
Incentive bonus and wage plans, see Wages
Independent unions, 12, 30n
Individual bargaining versus collective bargaining, 218ff
Industrial unions, 12
Industry-Labor Conference (1941), 164ff
Industry-wide collective bargaining, see Market-wide collective bargaining
Initiation fees, see Union membership
Institute of Municipal Law Officers, 152
International Ladies' Garment Workers' Union, 18, 26, 56n, 57n, 131
Interstate Commerce Commission, 113, 236

JOB classification, 181ff
Job control rules, 92
Job security, 92-103

Jurisdictional disputes, 15, 16f, 19, 22, 44, 114f

KNIGHTS of Labor, 5

LABOR Committee Report and Recommendations, 215-250; administration of contracts, 224f; bureaucracy in unions, 243f; collective versus individual bargaining, 218ff; economics of collective bargaining, 225ff; politics of collective bargaining, 236ff; postwar controls, 237ff; price-wage equation, 231; role of collective bargaining, 215ff; union power, 242f. Recommendations: employer associations, 235; fair labor practice boards, 246; management-union council, 235; market-wide collective bargaining, 232ff; membership representation in unions, 247f; morale and psychological changes in collective bargaining, 250; pricing process, 230f; union finances, 247; union incorporation, 247; voluntary mediation boards, 238ff
Labor-management production committees, see Union-management cooperation
Labor relations executives, 28ff
Laborsaving devices, see Technological change
Layoffs, 85f, 87, 100
Leadership, see Psychology of labor relations
Le Play, Frédéric, 189ff
Letter Carriers, National Association of, demands, 144f
Lewis, John L., 164
Little Steel formula, 180
Lockout, 56f, 58, 165
Longshoremen, 85, 118

MACHINISTS, International Association of, 13, 19, 49, 57n, 71n
MacIver, Frazier D., 218n, 227n, 234n, 235n, 237n, 240n
Maintenance-of-membership shop, 36, 39, 44n, 47, 163, 177ff
Make-work rules, 108
Management security, see Psychology of labor relations
Management-union council, Committee recommendation, 235
Marine and Shipbuilding Workers, 163, 177f
Maritime Union of America, National, 13
"Market" agreements, 26
Market-wide collective bargaining, Committee recommendation, 232ff

Mediation, 163; voluntary boards, *Committee recommendation*, 238ff
Men's clothing workers, 14, 16, 101
Merit increase plan, 183ff
Metal Trades Association, National, 26, 41
Mine Workers of America, United, 12, 15, 21, 39, 44n, 164
Molders' union, 40
Morale, *see* Psychology of labor relations
Murray, Philip, 32, 107

NATIONAL Association of Manufacturers, 24, 41, 165, 167
National Defense Advisory Commission, 162
National Defense Mediation Board, 47, 162ff
National Industrial Recovery Act, 7, 20, 83
National Labor Relations (Wagner) Act, 7, 22, 37, 38, 39, 46, 80, 141, 149, 154, 158, 171, 174, 175, 216, 217, 236
National Labor Relations Board, 7, 38, 46, 149, 157, 171ff, 174f, 236
National Railroad Adjustment Board, 126
National War Labor Board, *see* War Labor Board
Naumkeag Steam Cotton Mills, 133, 137f
Needle trades, 123
Nelson, Donald, 133, 134
Newark Public Works Dept., 149ff
New Deal policies, 217
Newspaper Guild, 12n, 72, 99
Newspaper Publishers Association, American, 24f
New York City Board of Transportation, 154
New York City cloak and suit trade strike, 37
New York State Labor Relations Act, 154
New York State Mediation Board, 128
New York Title and Guaranty Co. case, 150
Norris-LaGuardia Anti-Injunction Act, 7

OFFICE of Production Management, 162
Ohio Public Service case, 174, 175
Open shop, 39, 41
Open union, 36
Overtime, 8, 83, 84, 85, 88ff, 156

PAYROLLS, and national income, 62
Percentage shop, 36
Picketing, 57
Piecework, *see* Wages, systems of payment
Plant elections, 7
Postal service, unions, 143
Pottery industry, 118n, 131

Preferential shop, 37, 39
Price-wage equation, 231
Pricing process, 228; *Committee recommendation*, 230f
Printing trades, 14, 16, 40, 66, 85, 86, 89, 94, 97, 100, 112f, 118, 122, 128, 139
Psychology of labor relations, 188-211; administration of agreements, 207ff; changes necessary, *Committee recommendation*, 250; cooperative capacity, 195; leadership, 195f, 210f; management security, 202f; mechanization and morale, 190ff; morale experiments, 196f; seniority, 208ff; stages in union recognition, 197ff
Public employees, 142ff

RADIO, overtime, 89
Railroads, 11, 12, 40, 49, 82, 84f, 86, 89, 99, 100, 102, 113f, 122, 130f
Railway Executives, Association of, 25
Railway Labor Act, 6, 7, 46, 157
Railway Labor Executives' Association, 25
Retail trades, 11, 85
Retirement plans, municipalities, 156
Roethlisberger, F. J., 193f
Roosevelt, Franklin D., 46, 153, 165
Rubber workers, 15, 16, 67, 85, 86, 88, 90, 97, 104, 118, 122, 123, 129
Rubber Workers of America, United, 16
Ryan Aeronautical case, 178

SAN Francisco Employers' Council, 27f
Security, *see* Job security
Seniority, 99ff; grievances, 122; hours of work, 85f; municipalities, 156; veterans and war workers, 156; *see also* Psychology of labor relations
Separation pay, *see* Discharge
Shop committeemen, and seniority, 101
Shop stewards, 101, 123
Sick leave, municipalities, 156
Sit-down strike, 57
Slichter, Sumner H., 45n, 54n, 63n, 218n, 228n, 230n, 232n
Slowdown, 110
Soft coal, 121, 122
Speed-up, 109f
State, County and Municipal Employees, American Federation of, 143, 147
State, County and Municipal Workers of America, 143, 147, 149ff, 159
Steel industry, 15, 86, 88, 103, 104, 118, 121, 123, 125, 136f, 216f
Steelworkers of America, United, 12n, 15f, 133, 216
Steel Workers Organizing Committee, 15f, 38n, 136f, 216

Stove Founders' National Defense Association, 26
Stove industry, 40
Street and Railway Employees, Amalgamated Association of, and NLRB, 172f
Strikes, 4, 56; compact provisions, 57; hours of work, 79, 80n, 82; limitations among government employees, 145ff; over union shop, 46n; penalties, 57f; printing trades, 14; sympathetic, 57; World War II, 163, 164, 165, 176
Swedish experience, 24, 42

TAFT-Walsh War Labor Board, 185
Taylor, George W., 203
Teachers, American Federation of, 143
Technological change, 80, 82, 104-115
Tennessee Valley Authority, 157, 158; production committees, 133
Textile Workers Union, 13
Thomas, Elbert D., 164, 166
Time-and-a-half payment, 83, 84
Time wages, see Wages, systems of payment
Trade associations, 24
Transit Workers, New York City, 154
Transport Workers Union, 154
Typographical Union, 87, 128, 132; see also Printing trades

UNION-management cooperation, 130-141; joint research, 133, 137f; outlook, 140f; planning committees, 136f; production committees, 133, 134ff; union production advisers, 133, 139f
Union membership, 6, 7, 10, 16; admission fees, 95f; AF of L, 18; CIO, 21; coverage, 11; fees and dues, 96; initiation fees, 96; public employees, 142, 143; responsibilities of, 43; working permits, 96
Union recognition, 34-48, 197ff
Union security, 164
Union shop, 36, 39, 40, 41, 43, 44, 45, 47f, 155
Unions, 10-21; bureaucracy and efficiency, 243ff; concentrated power dangers, 242f; dissension, 17f; finances, Committee recommendation, 247; history, 4ff; incorporation, Committee recommendation, 247; make-work rules, 108; membership representation, Committee recommendation, 247f; shorter hours fight, 79f; slowdown, 110; speed-up, 109f; stewards and committeemen training, 123f; structure, 12ff; technological change, 104ff; varieties of status, 34ff; work rules,

104ff; see also Government and other headings under Union
United States Conciliation Service, 149, 162, 175
United States Steel Corp., 41, 164, 181
Unorganized workers, 10, 11, 218

VACATIONS, 87f; municipalities, 156
Veterans, and seniority, 156
Virginia Electric and Power Co. case, 172f

WAGES, 61-78, 225ff; coverage of agreements, 62; differentials, 64ff; dismissal, 98f, 185; incentive bonus, 76ff; incentive pay, 72f, 76; level, 226; Little Steel formula, 180; merit increase plan, 183ff; municipalities, 156, rate fixing, 74f; rates, 8; scales, 221; stabilization, 180f; straight pay versus piecework, 73f; structure, 70ff; systems of payment, 70ff; time, 71f, 76; union versus nonunion shops, 64, 70; World War II, 183
Wages and Hours Act, see Fair Labor Standards Act
Wage Stabilization Division (WLB), 167
Wagner National Labor Relations Act, see National Labor Relations Act
Walkouts, 57
Walsh-Healey Act, 83
War Labor Board, 149ff, 236; and collective bargaining, 175f; decentralized, 167ff; dismissal pay, 185; establishment, 47, 165, 166ff; functions, 166f; job classification, 181ff; jurisdiction, 169ff; maintenance of membership, 36, 177ff; merit increase plan, 183ff; versus NLRB, 171ff; panels, 168f, 181; regional boards, 168; wages, 167, 180f, 183
War Labor Disputes Act, 171
War Production Board, 137, 141, 240
War workers, and seniority, 156
Watt, Robert J., 233n, 238n, 243n, 246n
Western Electric Co., experiments in morale at Hawthorne plant, 196f
Window Glass Workers Union, National, 108
Witte, Edwin E., 58n, 238n, 243n, 246n, 248n
Woods, S. A., Co. case, 178
Working permits, see Union membership
Work rules, 104-115
Work sharing, 85ff
World War I, 6, 8, 47, 185
World War II, 8, 36, 162-187, 217, 236; see also War Labor Board

ZISKIND, David, 145

HD6483 .T94   c.1
Twentieth century   100106 000
Trends in collective bargainin

3 9310 00013043 3
GOSHEN COLLEGE-GOOD LIBRARY